Policy Scenarios for Eliminating Plastic Pollution by 2040

OECD

BETTER POLICIES FOR BETTER LIVES

This document has been produced with the financial assistance of the United Kingdom and the European Union.

Please cite this publication as:
OECD (2024), *Policy Scenarios for Eliminating Plastic Pollution by 2040*, OECD Publishing, Paris, https://doi.org/10.1787/76400890-en.

ISBN 978-92-64-34733-5 (print)
ISBN 978-92-64-90385-2 (PDF)
ISBN 978-92-64-63785-6 (HTML)
ISBN 978-92-64-70708-5 (epub)

Photo credits: Cover © FOTOKITA/Shutterstock.com.

Corrigenda to OECD publications may be found at: https://www.oecd.org/en/publications/support/corrigenda.html.

Preface

The flexibility and versatility of plastics is difficult to match. However, escalating levels of plastics production and use, particularly in short-lived applications, have led to increasing waste levels and pollution of this all-pervasive material in recent decades. Plastic pollution can be found in the water we drink, the air we breathe and the food we eat, posing an increasing threat to the environment and human health, with consequences for sustainable economic growth and human well-being. Without more ambitious policies, the proliferation of plastic production, use and waste will further expand by 70% by 2040.

The ongoing negotiations to develop an international legally-binding instrument on plastic pollution provide a unique opportunity for governments to create a powerful global response to this environmental issue. Building on the modelling framework of the OECD's flagship Global Plastics Outlook publications, this new report, *Policy Scenarios for Eliminating Plastic Pollution by 2040*, intends to assist these negotiations by presenting a viable path towards ending plastic leakage to the environment by 2040.

Since 2000, we have seen plastics production, use and waste more than double with significant amounts of plastic leaking into the environment each year. Business as usual is unsustainable while plastic flows and their environmental impacts continue to rapidly increase. As governments around the globe come together to tackle this issue, our analysis shines a light on the environmental benefits and economic costs of alternative policy scenarios with varying levels of ambition. Covering a set of ten policy instruments, the scenarios encompass various stages of the plastics lifecycle but differ in terms of policy ambition and geographical coverage.

Achieving the goal to eliminate plastic pollution requires ambitious action by all countries, with policy measures implemented at all stages of the plastics lifecycle. Strong international co-operation and resource mobilisation will be essential to overcome technical, economic and governance challenges.

It is my hope that the findings presented in this report will serve as a reference for negotiators and policymakers as they develop the treaty and contemplate new policies for ending plastic pollution. The OECD is committed to assisting governments in designing, developing and implementing the ambitious and co-ordinated policies needed to meet the challenge.

Jo Tyndall

Director, OECD Environment Directorate

Foreword

Plastics provide multiple benefits to society, but their lifecycle - from feedstock extraction and polymer production to use and disposal - contributes heavily to pollution, climate change and biodiversity loss. Current policies are inadequate to meaningfully alter trends in plastic flows and related pollution, but negotiations are underway to develop an international, legally-binding instrument on plastic pollution to drive more ambitious and co-ordinated policy action.

In light of the ongoing negotiations, this new report intends to offer insights on the potential effectiveness of alternative versions of an international treaty in terms of reducing and ending plastic pollution, as well as on the related implementation costs. This is a follow-up report to earlier publications "Global Plastics Outlook: Economic Drivers, Environmental Impacts and Policy Options" and "Global Plastics Outlook: Policy Scenarios to 2060", both released in 2022. This new report focuses on policy scenarios characterised by more rapid reductions in plastic flows and plastic pollution, with a 2040 horizon.

The methodology employed in this report builds on the foundational methodological framework employed in the previous Global Plastics Outlook publications, to quantify the main mechanisms driving plastics production and use, waste and pollution. Using state-of-the-art environment-economy modelling, this report provides detailed sectoral and regional projections of the plastics lifecycle, including different polymers and applications, waste generation and treatment, as well as related leakage to aquatic and terrestrial environments.

Based on this, the report then presents and contrasts alternative policy scenarios with varying levels of policy ambition. In addition to a Baseline scenario, the report develops five policy scenarios that differ according to three dimensions: geographical coverage (global or Advanced economies only), lifecycle scope (broad coverage of policies along the lifecycle or downstream policies only), and policy stringency (high stringency, low stringency or current policy stringency). All scenarios contain ten policy instruments, grouped into four policy pillars: i) curb plastics production and demand; ii) design for circularity; iii) enhance recycling; and iv) close leakage pathways.

This document was approved by OECD's Environmental Policy Committee on 2 August 2024 and prepared for publication by the OECD Secretariat.

Acknowledgements

This report was prepared by Rob Dellink and Elena Buzzi (OECD Environment Directorate), under the overall supervision and guidance of Shardul Agrawala, Head of Division of the Environment and Economy Integration Division in the Environment Directorate of the OECD. Peter Börkey (OECD Environment Directorate) provided expert input and feedback throughout the preparation of the report. Ruben Bibas (OECD Environment Directorate) contributed to the development and refinement of the modelling framework and provided useful comments on earlier drafts. Bum Cheul Park (previously, OECD Environment Directorate) co-authored Chapter 2 and contributed to other parts of the report. Emma DeRoy, Kate Hassett, Yuko Ishibashi, Kumi Kitamori, Elisa Lanzi and Toon Vandyck (all OECD Environment Directorate) provided valuable feedback on earlier drafts. Laurent Lebreton (The Ocean Cleanup) contributed with the modelling of plastic leakage to aquatic environments.

Illias Mousse Iye (OECD Environment Directorate) provided administrative support. Emma DeRoy, Sarbjit Gill, Sebastián Higuera and Bum Cheul Park (OECD Environment Directorate) provided valuable contributions to preparing all graphs. Elizabeth Del Bourgo and Emma DeRoy (OECD Environment Directorate), as well as Catherine Bremer (OECD Directorate for Communications) provided assistance with communications and outreach aspects of the report. The report was prepared for publication by Meral Gedik (independent consultant).

The authors are thankful to delegates of the Working Party on Resource Productivity and Waste and the Working Party on Integrating Environmental and Economic Policies, who reviewed earlier drafts. Financial contributions by the United Kingdom and the European Commission are gratefully acknowledged.

Table of contents

FIGURES

INFOGRAPHICS

TABLES

BOXES

Abbreviations and acronyms

ABS	Acrylonitrile butadiene styrene
ASA	Acrylonitrile styrene acrylate
Bln	Billion
CO_2	Carbon dioxide
CO_{2e}	Carbon dioxide equivalent
EPR	Extended producer responsibility
EU	European Union
EUR	Euro
GDP	Gross domestic product
GHG	Greenhouse gas
Gt	Gigatonnes (billion tonnes)
HDPE	High-density polyethylene
LCA	Lifecycle assessment
LDPE	Low-density polyethylene
LLDPE	Linear low-density polyethylene
Mln	Million
Mt	Million tonnes
ODA	Official development assistance
OECD	Organisation for Economic Co-operation and Development
PBT	Polybutylene terephthalate
PET	Polyethylene terephthalate
PP	Polypropylene
PS	Polystyrene
PUR	Polyurethane
PVC	Polyvinyl chloride
R&D	Research and Development
SAN	Styrene acrylonitrile
UNEA	United Nations Environment Assembly
UNEP	United Nations Environment Programme
USD	United States Dollar

Executive summary

This report investigates the potential benefits and consequences of varying levels of international policy ambition to tackle plastic pollution. It delivers the following key messages:

1. **Business as usual is unsustainable as plastic flows and their environmental impacts will continue to grow rapidly.**
    a. Annual plastics production and use is projected to rise from 435 million tonnes (Mt) in 2020 to 736 Mt in 2040 in the *Baseline* scenario. The share of recycled plastics would remain unchanged at 6% of total plastics use (41 Mt in 2040).
    b. While waste management is expected to improve, advances will not keep pace with the growth of plastic waste (617 Mt in 2040, up from 360 Mt in 2020), resulting in 119 Mt of mismanaged waste in 2040 (increasing from 81 Mt in 2020).
    c. Leakage of plastics to the environment will continue (30 Mt in 2040, up from 20 Mt in 2020), amplifying adverse environmental and health impacts. The stock of plastics in rivers and oceans will almost double from 152 Mt in 2020 to 300 Mt by 2040.
    d. The plastics lifecycle will emit 2.8 gigatonnes of carbon dioxide equivalent ($GtCO_2e$) of greenhouse gas (GHG) emissions annually by 2040 (5% of global emissions), up from 1.8 $GtCO_2e$ in 2020, primarily driven by the production and conversion of plastics.
2. **Partial measures, such as policy responses focused on enhancing waste management alone or global action with broad policy coverage but with low policy stringency, are likely to fall short of ending plastic pollution, as are policy responses with ambitious action along the lifecycle implemented only in advanced economies.**
    a. Enhancing waste management globally can reduce the share of mismanaged waste to 9% by 2040 (compared to 23% in 2020). However, 54 Mt of plastic waste would still be mismanaged in 2040.
    b. Stringent policy action in advanced economies only is unlikely to reduce mismanaged plastic waste below 2020 levels. Similarly, global action with broad policy coverage, but low policy stringency, is unlikely to significantly alter *Baseline* trends.
    c. These partial ambition strategies cannot reduce primary plastics production and use below 2020 levels. Mismanaged plastic waste will not be eliminated without highly-stringent measures to curb production and demand implemented globally.
3. **The implementation of stringent policies along the plastics lifecycle in all countries can prevent growth in primary plastics production from 2020 levels and nearly end plastic leakage to the environment by 2040.**
    a. Stringent policies to curb production and demand (limiting total plastics use to 508 Mt in 2040), combined with policies to enhance recycling rates (quadrupling to 42%), can ensure that all growth in plastics use is met through recycled plastics rather than through primary production.
    b. This policy package can nearly eliminate mismanaged waste by 2040 (97% below *Baseline* levels) and prevent 74 Mt of plastics from entering rivers and oceans relative to the *Baseline* scenario.
    c. Stringent policy action can reduce plastics-related GHG emissions to 1.7 GtCO2e by 2040, well below the projected *Baseline* level of 2.8 GtCO2e in 2040.
4. **Global ambition has modest macroeconomic costs overall, however these costs are unevenly distributed across regions.**
    a. The implementation of stringent global policy action along the lifecycle is projected to incur a 0.5% global GDP loss in 2040 compared to the *Baseline* scenario but result in vastly improved environmental outcomes. A slower pace of policy action may have some short-term economic benefits but leads to significantly higher pollution levels.

   b. Non-OECD countries will face higher costs than OECD countries on average (0.6% vs. 0.4% GDP loss compared to the *Baseline*, respectively, in 2040), as the strongest policy efforts are needed in countries with less advanced waste management systems, particularly in Sub-Saharan Africa (1.5% GDP loss).

5. **Implementation of an ambitious whole of lifecycle approach globally requires overcoming significant technical, economic and governance barriers.**
   a. Enhancing waste collection systems, especially in many low- and middle-income countries, is essential to reduce mismanaged waste, but requires robust policy frameworks and adequate and stable sources of finance.
   b. Ending plastic leakage by 2040 relies on significant improvements in waste sorting and recycling yields and quality in all regions (to reach a global recycling rate of 42% in 2040, up from 9.5% in 2020). Robust markets for scrap and secondary plastics are required to ensure a viable business case for plastics recycling.
   c. Internationally harmonised standards and co-ordinated research efforts are needed to establish eco-design criteria for phasing out problematic or unnecessary plastics and hazardous chemicals, as well as for facilitating waste sorting and recycling.
6. **Ending plastic leakage warrants mobilising significant financial resources and strengthening international co-operation.**
   a. Under current policies, global investment needs for plastic waste management are projected to amount to USD 2.1 trillion between 2020 and 2040. Waste reduction policies, alongside redirecting investment flows towards waste sorting and recycling, could limit additional investment needs required to end plastic leakage to only USD 50 billion by 2040.
   b. Successful policy implementation will require leveraging diverse sources of public and private finance and directing capital flows towards interventions along the plastics lifecycle, including to scale up reuse systems and promote eco-design.
   c. Developing countries, often the most vulnerable to plastic pollution, are expected to undertake major policy efforts. This underscores a need for enhanced international co-operation and financing. Development finance can play a catalytic role to leverage other sources of finance.
   d. Strengthened technical co-operation, capacity building and technology transfer are essential to establish robust policy frameworks, ensure reliable revenue streams for domestic financing of waste collection and treatment (e.g. Extended Producer Responsibility), and target problematic applications.
7. **Eliminating plastic leakage is critical, but other plastic pollution aspects require additional interventions.**
   a. Despite the large benefits of globally ambitious action, the policies modelled are insufficient to mitigate all aspects of plastic pollution, beyond leakage to the environment. Additional, targeted interventions will be needed to reduce risks associated with microplastic pollution and chemicals of concern.
   b. Even with global ambition, stocks of plastics in the environment will continue to grow, with 226 Mt of plastics in rivers and oceans by 2040 (up from 151 Mt in 2020). Cost-effective remedial interventions are needed to mitigate environmental and health risks, especially in pollution hotspots.
   c. Further reducing plastics-related GHG emissions to align with the ambitions of the Paris Agreement requires dedicated climate mitigation policies, potentially including reforms of government support for primary polymer production and conversion.

1 Towards the elimination of plastic pollution: Mapping alternative pathways

This chapter presents the main insights from the report and puts them into the wider policy context. It also provides an overview of the modelling framework and describes the policy scenarios developed in the report.

1.1. Context and objectives

The large and growing role played by plastics in the economy, combined with increased public, scientific and policy attention to the fate of plastics in the environment, has led to unprecedented scrutiny of the health, environmental and socio-economic consequences associated with the plastics lifecycle. On the one hand, plastics bring innumerable benefits to society, as exemplified by the widespread use of plastics in consumer products such as beverage containers, as protective medical equipment, or as cheap lightweight material in cars. On the other hand, the production, use and disposal of plastics comes with severe negative consequences for the environment, human health and our economies and livelihoods (OECD, 2022[1]; OECD, 2022[2]).

In March 2022, all 193 UN Member States united in a landmark decision to develop an international legally binding instrument on plastic pollution, including in the marine environment, based on a comprehensive approach that addresses the full lifecycle of plastics (UNEA Resolution 5/14 entitled "End Plastic Pollution: Towards an International Legally Binding Instrument"). Despite a growing sense of urgency to mitigate and prevent the multitude of adverse consequences of plastic pollution, current policies have fallen short of significantly altering trends in plastic flows and pollution. The future legal instrument presents a unique opportunity to scale up policy efforts and catalyse a much-needed, immediate and global response to plastic pollution. The International Negotiating Committee (INC) to develop the instrument began its work during the second half of 2022, with the ambition to complete the negotiations by the end of 2024 (UNEP, 2024[3]) and adopt a treaty in early 2025.

As international negotiations unfold, policymakers and negotiators are discussing the strategies, targets and actions that could achieve the ambitious goal set by UNEA Resolution 5/14. In this context, there is growing political momentum for implementing comprehensive policy approaches that address the full lifecycle of plastics, towards a common international target to 2040 to eliminate plastic pollution. Beyond submissions by some member states to the INC, the following international initiatives aim to bolster the ambition to end plastic pollution by 2040:

- Signatories of the High Ambition Coalition to End Plastic Pollution[1] (2024[4]) have called for the establishment of an international legally binding treaty, based on "a comprehensive and holistic approach able to end plastic pollution by 2040, including by committing to take immediate actions at all levels and across the full life cycle of plastics", in order to protect human health and the environment from plastic pollution while contributing to the restoration of biodiversity and curbing climate change.
- In April 2024, the G7 Ministers of Climate, Energy and the Environment (2024[5]) renewed their commitment to ending plastic pollution, announcing the ambition "to reduce additional plastic pollution to zero by 2040", and to take "ambitious actions throughout the full life cycle of plastics to end plastic pollution and call on the global community to do the same, with the aspiration to reduce and, as appropriate, restrain the global production and consumption of primary plastic polymers".

At the same time, countries and regions around the world have diverse preferences regarding the types and stringency of potential policy instruments to achieve these objectives. Accordingly, different jurisdictions have taken different positions on the intended scope of the future treaty and its elements, including regarding the balance between actions to reduce primary plastics production and demand versus actions to improve waste collection and treatment. Furthermore, countries may face significant challenges in ramping up policy action and investments. Ending open dumping and open air burning and setting up waste collection and management systems are notable challenges faced in many low-income countries. The absence of sufficiently strong support for policy implementation could lead to barriers to effective actions to reduce, let alone eliminate, leakage of plastics to the environment.

Without prejudice to their outcome, this report intends to inform ongoing negotiations by providing insights regarding the potential benefits and consequences of varying levels of international ambition towards the elimination of plastic pollution. To do so, the report develops and contrasts alternative policy scenarios that simulate varying degrees of policy stringency, lifecycle scope and geographical coverage.

The report aims to provide insights on the following main questions:

- What package of policies could achieve a sustainable plastics economy and set countries on the path towards eliminating (specific aspects of) plastic pollution by 2040? What opportunities, barriers and priorities lie ahead for policymakers in order to meet this goal?
- What are the trade-offs, in terms of environmental consequences (including waste mismanagement, leakage to the environment, including in in rivers and oceans, greenhouse gas emissions) and economic implications (including GDP impacts and waste management costs) of limiting policy ambitions?
    - Limited lifecycle scope, with a policy mix focused on enhanced waste collection and treatment, but limited or absent interventions to reduce the flows of (primary) plastics into and through the economy.
    - Limited geographical coverage, with high ambition limited to a group of advanced economies that implement ambitious policy mixes covering the entire lifecycle to aim for a 2040 target for the elimination of plastic pollution.[2]
    - Broad action in terms of geographical coverage and lifecycle scope, but with limited policy stringency, such as lower tax rates and less ambitious recycling targets.

This report is structured as follows. The current chapter provides an overview of the methodology, as well as a high-level summary of the main insights stemming from the analysis. Chapter 2 presents projections and findings for a *Baseline* scenario to 2040. Chapter 3 details the modelling framework and introduces the policy scenarios used in the analysis. Chapter 4 discusses the impacts of scenarios with partial ambition. Chapter 5 then highlights the benefits of more integrated and ambitious scenarios that combine broad policy action across geographical coverage and lifecycle scope. Chapter 6 compares the macroeconomic and waste management costs across the various scenarios. Finally, Chapter 7 puts the results into context by highlighting the challenges that must be overcome to reap the environmental benefits in a cost-effective manner.

1.2. Overview of the methodological framework

The policy scenario analysis builds on the previous two OECD Global Plastics Outlook publications and exploits the same modelling framework to quantify the main mechanisms driving plastics production and use, waste and pollution (OECD, 2022[1]; OECD, 2022[2]).[3] The modelling framework is summarised in Infographic 1.1.

The OECD's in-house dynamic computable general equilibrium model ENV-Linkages is used to estimate the economic activities that drive plastics use. ENV-Linkages is a dynamic multi-sectoral, multi-regional model that links economic activities to energy and environmental issues and provides annual projections of economic activity and environmental pressures between 2020 and 2060.[4] ENV-Linkages has been enhanced to include data on plastics use, waste and end-of-life treatment (see OECD (2022[6]) for more details). The modelling framework links plastics use directly to specific inputs in production processes and the consumption of goods, enabling detailed sectoral and regional projections of the plastics lifecycle by polymer and application. A wide range of policy instruments can be modelled in this framework, including upstream and midstream policies to influence production and consumption, as well as downstream policies to enhance recycling and reduce mismanaged waste.

Infographic 1.1. Overview of the modelling framework employed in this report

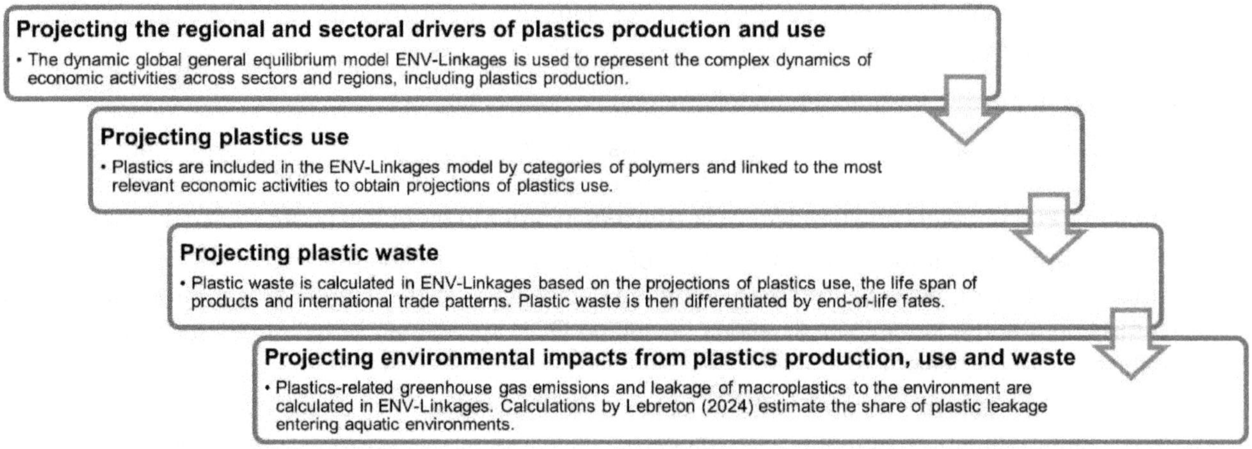

Infographic 1.2. Policy pillars and the ten policy instruments considered in the analysis

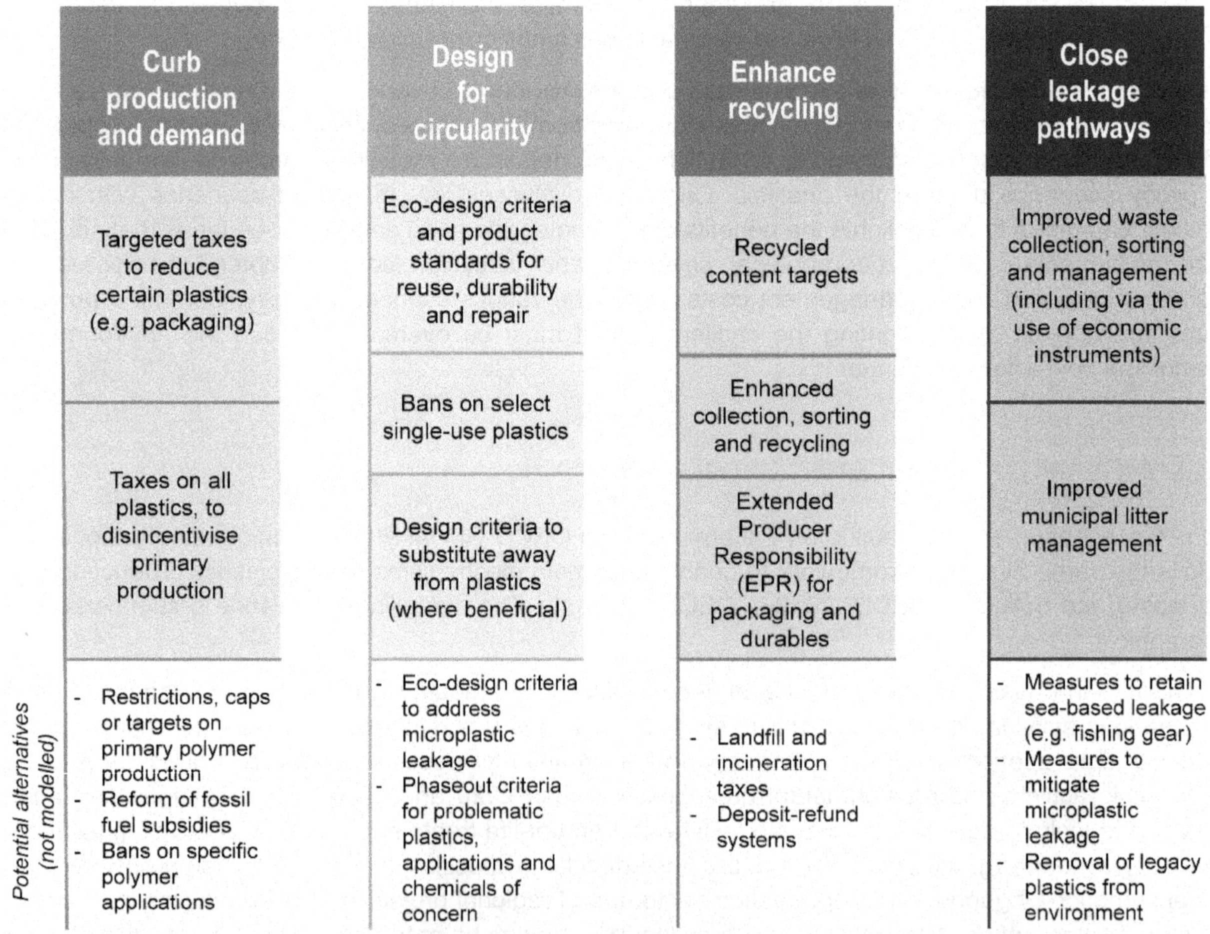

Source: Authors' own elaboration.

In this report, policy scenarios model alternative policy packages. All scenarios contain (a subset of) the same ten policy instruments covering multiple stages of the plastics lifecycle, but differ in terms of policy ambition. In addition to a *Baseline* scenario, the report develops five policy scenarios that differ along three dimensions: geographical coverage (global or Advanced economies only), lifecycle scope (broad lifecycle policies or downstream policies only), and policy stringency (high stringency, low stringency or current policies). Three hypothetical partial ambition scenarios simulate stylised directions for the international treaty currently being negotiated, including:

- high policy stringency focusing exclusively on enhancing downstream waste collection and treatment (policy pillars 3 and 4) with global scope (*Global Downstream High stringency* policy scenario)
- high policy stringency throughout the plastics lifecycle, but limited to a selected set of economies (*Advanced economies Lifecycle High stringency* policy scenario) and
- common global targets and measures across the plastics lifecycle, with relatively low policy stringency (*Global Lifecycle Low stringency* policy scenario).

Two hypothetical integrated, high ambition scenarios are also investigated, including:

- global alignment on the lifecycle scope of policies, with mixed policy stringency (*Global Lifecycle Mixed stringency* policy scenario) and
- high policy stringency and full global alignment on the need for stringent interventions for all four policy pillars (*Global Lifecycle High stringency* [*Global Ambition*] policy scenario).

Table 1.1 describes the policy scenarios and presents a visualisation of the policy packages modelled in each. Chapter 3 goes into more details on the set-up of policy scenarios and the policy instruments modelled. The full details of the numerical implementation of the policy scenarios in the modelling framework are presented in Annex B.

Table 1.1. Overview of policy scenarios developed in this report

Full name	Description	Visualisation[1]
Baseline	The *Baseline* scenario reflects the impacts of current policies and projects trends in the socioeconomic drivers of plastics production and use, as well as technology developments.	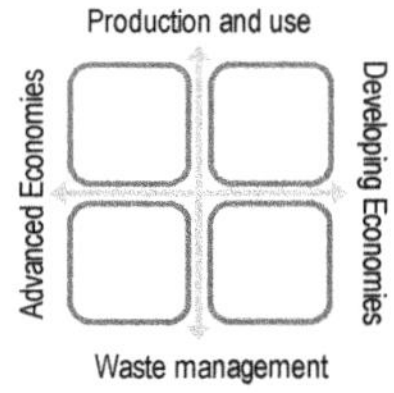
	Partial ambition policy scenarios	
Global Downstream High Stringency	The *Global Downstream High stringency* policy scenario reflects an outcome of treaty negotiations focused on targets and policies for waste management (pillars 3 and 4 of the policy package), without additional policies to curb production and demand or improve eco-design. The scenario models a landscape of high policy stringency globally to improve plastic waste collection, management and recycling, as well as municipal litter collection. For measures influencing plastics production and demand and those aimed to design for circularity, current policies continue to apply.	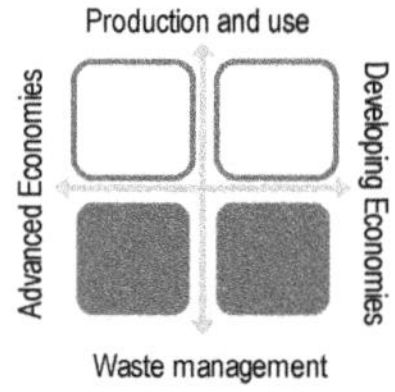
Advanced economies Lifecycle High stringency	The *Advanced economies Lifecycle High stringency policy scenario*reflects a scenario where, in the absence of globally agreed, legally binding targets with high policy stringency, only select countries enhance policy stringency along the plastics lifecycle. Advanced economies (approximated as OECD and non-OECD EU countries) implement a high level of policy stringency, while others do not go beyond improvements already expected in the *Baseline* scenario.	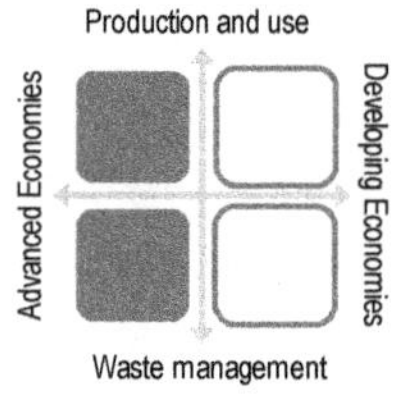
Global Lifecycle Low stringency	The *Global Lifecycle Low stringency* policy scenario reflects an outcome characterised by the absence of internationally-agreed, legally binding targets with high policy stringency. The scenario implies additional and incremental policy action in all countries for measures across all four pillars, but with relatively low policy stringency.	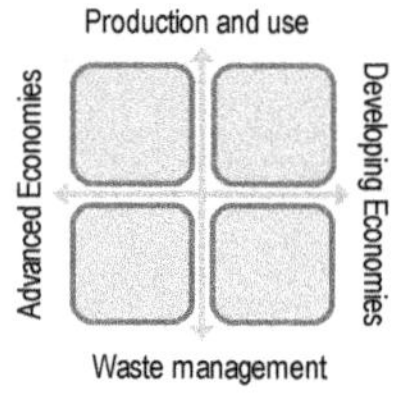
	Integrated, high ambition policy scenarios	
Global Lifecycle Mixed stringency[2]	The *Global Lifecycle Mixed stringency* policy scenario reflects an outcome of mixed policy stringency and moderate global alignment on the lifecycle scope of policies: • Advanced economies implement policies with high stringency along the plastics lifecycle (aligned with the *Advanced economies Lifecycle High stringency* policy scenario). • Other countries implement high stringency for downstream policies (aligned with the *Global Downstream High stringency* policy scenario) and low stringency on upstream and midstream policies (aligned with the *Global Lifecycle Low stringency* policy scenario).	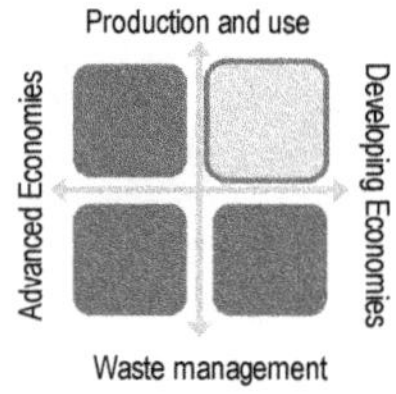
Global Lifecycle High stringency [Global Ambition]	The *Global Lifecycle High stringency [Global Ambition]* policy scenario models a comprehensive and co-ordinated approach that entails a global ramp up of high stringency policy action across the plastics lifecycle, in line with the common ambition to end plastic pollution by 2040. This policy scenario reflects a common target with a more restricted scope: to end macroplastic leakage by 2040. This scenario provides the basis for a discussion on the opportunities, barriers and priorities for policymakers to chart a pathway to a 2040 target.[3]	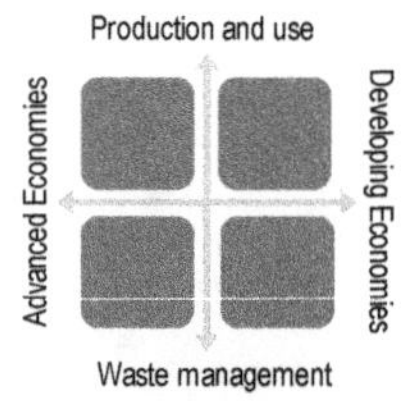

1. White boxes reflect the *Baseline* scenario, i.e. current policies and accompanying assumptions; light shaded boxes reflect low policy stringency and dark shaded boxes reflect high policy stringency.
2. The *Global Lifecycle Mixed stringency* policy scenario could be more precisely described as the Global Downstream High stringency, Advanced economies Upstream/Midstream High stringency, and Emerging and Developing Economies Upstream/Midstream Low stringency.
3. Chapter 6 explores a variant of the *Global Lifecycle High stringency* [*Global Ambition*] policy scenario called *Global Lifecycle Delayed stringency* policy scenario where the targets are met by 2060 rather than 2040.
Source: Authors' own elaboration.

Box 1.1. Clarifications on the scope of the present report and limitations of the analysis

Projections are not predictions or forecasts; rather, they are stylised representations of how specific assumptions, e.g. regarding policy changes, will affect the evolution of key variables. Models represent a stylised version of reality that omits numerous factors that can influence economic and environmental outcomes. Projections over long time horizons are inevitably subject to uncertainties, since it is not possible to foresee socio-economic changes in the coming decades with a high degree of accuracy. Nevertheless, policy scenarios remain valuable insofar as they can highlight the possible long-term consequences of current policy choices and the costs and benefits of ambitious policy action.

By comparing the alternative hypothetical scenarios presented in this report, policymakers can gain insights into the environmental and economic consequences of different choices in the development of an international legally binding instrument on plastic pollution. The policy scenarios presented in this report are not intended to precisely represent ongoing treaty negotiations, nor to describe specific country positions. However, their design is informed by cross-cutting issues currently under discussion in the context of treaty negotiations, such as the balance between measures to curb plastics production and demand, and measures to enhance waste management.

This report recognises that plastic pollution encompasses all emissions and risks resulting from the plastics lifecycle (OECD, 2022[2]). However, for the purpose of the analytical modelling carried out in this report, policy scenarios are constructed with a focus on the leakage of macroplastics to the environment (including by singling out the share entering to rivers and oceans). This focus is driven by issues of limited data and information on other aspects, for instance on:

- microplastic leakage or the effectiveness of policies to mitigate microplastic pollution. However, quantifications for microplastic leakage are presented in previous reports that contain similar modelling efforts (OECD, 2022[1]).
- greenhouse gas (GHG) emissions. This report can only quantify GHG emissions from certain stages of the plastics lifecycle, specifically from production and conversion, and from recycling and incineration at the end-of-life stage. Analysis of climate change mitigation policies specifically aimed at reducing GHG emissions is beyond the scope of this report. However, (OECD, 2022[1]) investigates the interactions of plastics policies with mitigation policies.
- a variety of other impacts resulting from the plastics lifecycle, including resource scarcity, land use, ground-level ozone formation and human toxicity, are also beyond the scope of this report. However, (OECD, 2022[1]) details a (global) lifecycle analysis (LCA) for the production and disposal of seven commonly used polymers, showing impacts on land use, ozone formation, eutrophication, ecotoxicity, toxicity and acidification, with projections until 2060.

The modelling employs mostly economic instruments to represent interventions at specific steps in the lifecycle of plastics, such as taxes on plastics consumption by downstream industries and households. These instruments constitute a cost-effective benchmark against which countries can evaluate alternative instruments. Due to a lack of a detailed modelling of plastics production at the regional level, the report does not model measures that would directly aim to control or otherwise restrain the production of primary or total plastics. However, in the economic model, behaviour is driven by the wedge between producer prices and consumer prices such that a tax on consumption has an equivalent effect to a tax on production with partial feedthrough to consumers. The analysis does not consider options for the reform of subsidies to primary plastics production, including for instance subsidies on the use of fossil fuels as feedstock, due to a lack of data.

Some of the policy scenarios presented in this report build on the earlier analysis presented in (OECD, 2022[1]). Box 1.2 clarifies the scope of the current analysis with respect to such earlier work.

Box 1.2. How does this analysis link to the OECD Global Plastics Outlook?

This report employs the methodology developed in the OECD Global Plastics Outlook reports (OECD, 2022[2]; OECD, 2022[1]), notably the ENV-Linkages model, which calculates macroplastic leakage. Macroplastic leakage to the aquatic environment is derived from the ENV-Linkages projections using a spatially explicit model (Lebreton, 2024[7]) that assesses the probability that plastic waste ends up in aquatic environments (OECD, 2022[1]). Plastics-related GHG emissions are also quantified in the ENV-Linkages model. The quantification of other adverse environmental and health impacts related to plastics is beyond the scope of this analysis, although some of these aspects are qualitatively assessed to provide additional context.

Some of the policy scenarios presented in this report have already been explored in the Global Plastics Outlook (OECD, 2022[1]). An earlier version of the *Global Lifecycle Low stringency* policy scenario was labelled in the earlier report as "Regional Action" and an earlier version of the *Global Lifecycle Delayed stringency* policy scenario was labelled "Global Ambition". These scenarios have been recalculated using updated economic baseline projections (OECD, 2021[8]), as well as with minor adaptions to the policy packages. The numbers presented here are therefore an update from those presented in the Global Plastics Outlook. The projections herein exhibit minor differences in numerical projections compared to the Global Plastics Outlook scenarios due to differences in the underlying Baseline economic trends, however the overall trends in plastic flows remain very similar.

1.3. Main insights from the analysis

The report explores the environmental and economic consequences of policy scenarios reflecting different levels of policy ambition. As described in Section 1.2 and illustrated in Figure 1.1, all policy scenarios implement (a subset of) the same ten policy instruments, but with different levels of ambition along three dimensions:

- **policy stringency**, i.e. the envisioned targets for each policy measure modelled
- **lifecycle scope**, i.e. either a focus on policy measures that aim at improving waste collection and treatment or the implementation of measures throughout the plastics lifecycle
- **geographical coverage**, i.e. only a selected set of countries taking more ambitious policy action versus the same level of ambition spread out across all world regions.

Figure 1.1. Visualisation of policy scenarios modelled in the report

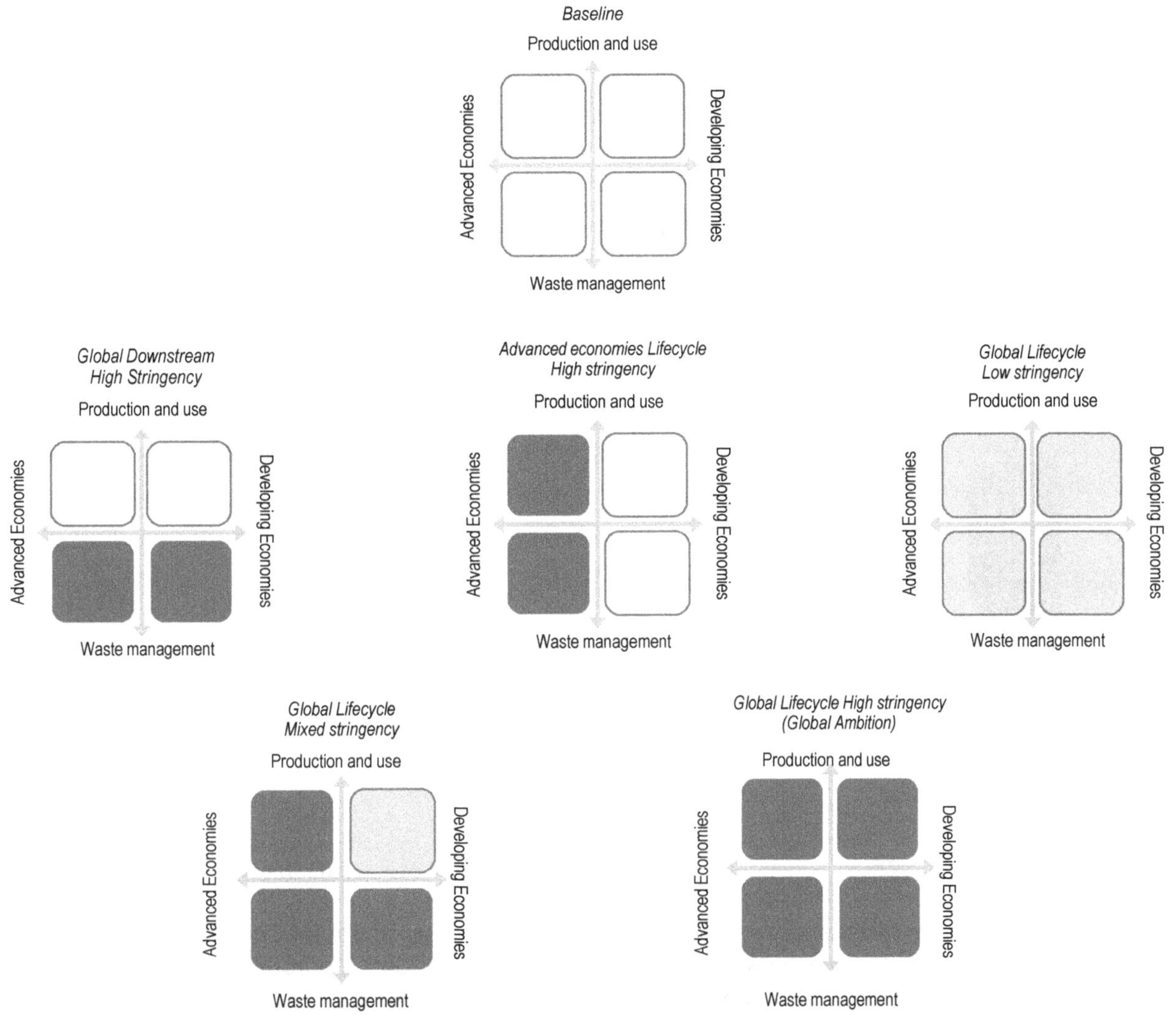

Note: White boxes reflect *Baseline*, i.e. current policy assumptions; light shaded boxes low stringency of policy action and dark shaded high stringency.
Source: Authors' own elaboration.

The environmental benefits of the policy scenarios modelled depend on four policy pillars: i) reducing the production and use of primary plastics, ii) reducing the plastics intensity of the economy, iii) increasing recycling rates, iv) eliminating plastic leakage to the environment.[5]

1.3.1. Under business as usual, plastic pollution is projected to increase further

The *Baseline* scenario projects population growth (though not in all regions), income growth in all regions, as well as technological developments that lead to efficiency improvements in production and structural change (including towards a higher share of services) in all regions. These drivers interact and, in combination, lead to a 70% global increase in annual plastics production, use and waste generation in 2040 compared to 2020 (Figure 1.2). Total plastics use would rise from 435 million tonnes (Mt) in 2020 to 736 Mt in 2040, with primary plastics constituting a roughly constant 94% of the total over this period.

Increases in plastics use comes from all applications and involves all polymers. The fastest growth rates in plastics use are expected in emerging and developing economies such as India and Sub-Saharan Africa.

Figure 1.2. Packaging, textiles and transportation will drive growth in plastics production and use

Global plastics production and use in million tonnes (Mt) by application (left-hand panel), and by polymer (right-hand panel), in 2020 and 2040

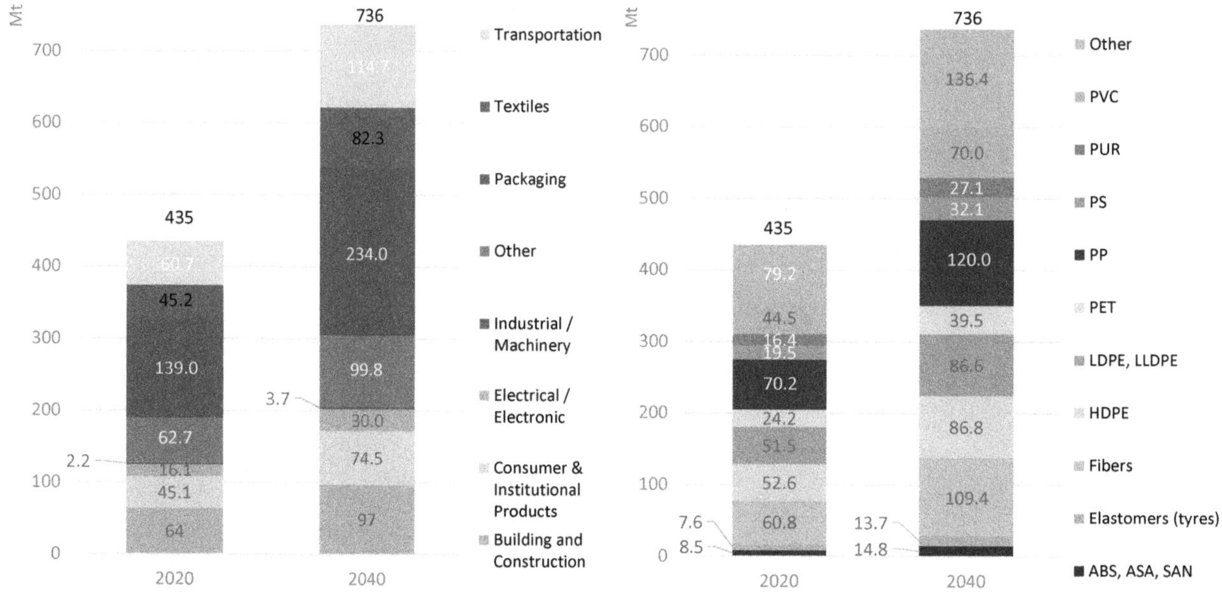

Source: OECD ENV-Linkages model.

StatLink https://stat.link/5dwu9g

Despite expected improvements in waste collection, sorting and treatment that are projected to emerge under current policies, higher plastic waste generation (617 Mt in 2040, up from 360 Mt in 2020) would lead to an increase in the absolute volumes of mismanaged waste (i.e. waste that is not disposed of in an environmentally sound manner) from 81 Mt in 2020 to 119 Mt in 2040 (Figure 1.3; left-hand panel) in the Baseline scenario. Similarly, while recycling output is set to continue to increase, higher plastic waste generation would lead to the continued prominent role of landfilling and incineration in the end-of-life treatment of plastic waste.

In the absence of more stringent policies, burgeoning plastics production, use and waste would continue to amplify the associated environmental risks. As a result of the increase in mismanaged plastic waste, leakage of macroplastics to the environment are projected to continue to grow, amounting to 30 Mt annually by 2040 (compared to an estimated 20 Mt in 2020). The majority of plastic leakage (by weight) is to terrestrial environments, but a significant share of leaked plastics end up in aquatic environments (9.3 Mt by 2040; right panel of Figure 1.3). The model projections suggest that, by 2040, accumulated plastics in the environment would amount to 300 Mt in rivers and oceans alone (up from the estimated 152 Mt in 2020). In other words, unless plastic pollution policies are amplified, in a mere 20 years the total amount of plastics accumulating in aquatic environments (148 Mt of accumulated aquatic stocks) would be about as large as all historically accumulated leakage in aquatic environments before 2020 (152 Mt).

Figure 1.3. Adverse impacts of plastics are set to increase substantially without more ambitious policies

Plastic end-of-life fates (left-hand panel), and plastics leakage to environmental media in million tonnes (right-hand panel) in million tonnes (Mt), *Baseline* scenario

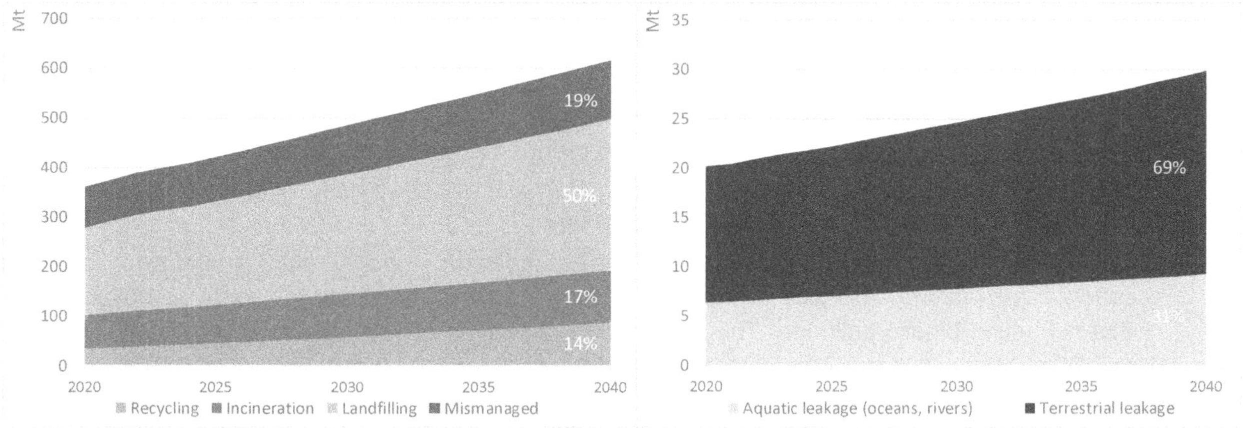

Note: In both panels, shares in total in 2040 are also indicated in data labels.
Source: OECD ENV-Linkages model.

StatLink https://stat.link/o9h1r2

Beyond plastic leakage, other types of pollution associated with the production and lifecycle of plastics are also projected to grow significantly. Not all sources of pollution related to the production, use and end-of-life treatment of plastics can be quantified in this study. The broad environmental impact assessment presented in (OECD, 2022[1]) shows significant increases in a wide range of environmental and human health issues in the coming decades due to plastics-related pollution. Specifically for the *Baseline* projection, emissions of greenhouse gases (GHG) are projected to increase in line with increased volumes of production, conversion and waste management. Despite current climate mitigation policies, GHG emissions from plastics are projected to account for 5% of global GHG emissions in 2040 (2.8 of in gigatonnes of carbon dioxide equivalent [$GtCO_2e$]), which is not in line with the Paris Agreement.[6] In the *Baseline*, the production and conversion stage of plastic manufacturing accounts for almost 90% of quantified plastics-related emissions.[7] As a result, other negative impacts on ecosystems, human well-being and coastal economies continue to be amplified in the *Baseline* scenario, risking potentially irreversible damage.

1.3.2. Policy action with partial ambition would at best slow down plastic leakage

The scenarios characterised by limited policy ambition in terms of lifecycle scope, geographical coverage or stringency (*Global Downstream High stringency, Advanced economies Lifecycle High stringency,* and *Global Lifecycle Low stringency*) would all fall short of significantly altering trends in plastic pollution, with limited outcomes in all four policy pillars and the associated environmental benefits (Figure 1.4):

- None of these scenarios can **stabilise primary plastics production and use at or below 2020 levels**, which is essential to i) reduce GHG emissions and other adverse impacts associated with extraction and production, and ii) slow down the use of plastics in the economy and reduce the amount of waste to be managed. The more stringent policies to curb production and demand and to improve eco-design, implemented in *Advanced economies Lifecycle High stringency,* reduce primary plastics use only in the selected economies.
- **Reducing the plastics intensity of the global economy** would allow for a decoupling of economic growth from plastics production and use, thereby facilitating economic development while mitigating plastic pollution. The *Advanced economies Lifecycle High stringency* scenario is partially effective, but the improvements are largely limited to the countries undertaking policy action, i.e. the OECD and non-OECD European Union, with very small effects on other countries and overall marginal impacts on global plastic flows. The *Global Downstream High stringency* scenario has virtually no effect on the plastics intensity of the global economy, as its policies focus on the downstream stages of the plastics lifecycle. With limited policy stringency, the *Global Lifecycle Low stringency* scenario would only partially reduce plastics use and plastics intensity.
- **Increasing recycling rates to make recycling the main waste management option** is a prerequisite for transitioning to a circular economy and crucial for creating the scrap needed to produce secondary plastics that could displace primary plastics. Increasing recycling rates also contributes to avoiding mismanaged waste. All scenarios that include downstream policies with high stringency (*Global Downstream High stringency* and *Advanced economies Lifecycle High stringency*) would lead to large improvements in recycling. Assuming that existing barriers to further scaling up mechanical recycling are overcome, the *Global Downstream High stringency* scenario achieves a quadrupling of the global recycling rate. Thus, by 2040 42% of plastic waste is collected for recycling, processed, and used for the production of secondary plastics. The *Global Lifecycle Low stringency* scenario is less effective in enhancing recycling, and improvements in recycling are limited to a subset of countries in the *Advanced economies Lifecycle High stringency* scenario.
- In terms of **plastic leakage to the environment**, which is a core aspect of reducing plastic pollution, the *Global Downstream High stringency* scenario achieves a considerable reduction (-55% compared to Baseline), showing that stringent downstream policies are important for reducing waste mismanagement and plastic leakage. At the same time, the *Global Downstream High stringency* scenario cannot close all leakage pathways in the absence of action to reduce plastics use and related plastic waste generation to more manageable levels.

Figure 1.4. All partial ambition scenarios fail to eliminate plastic leakage

Key indicators across partial ambition scenarios in 2040, compared 2020 levels and the *Baseline* scenario

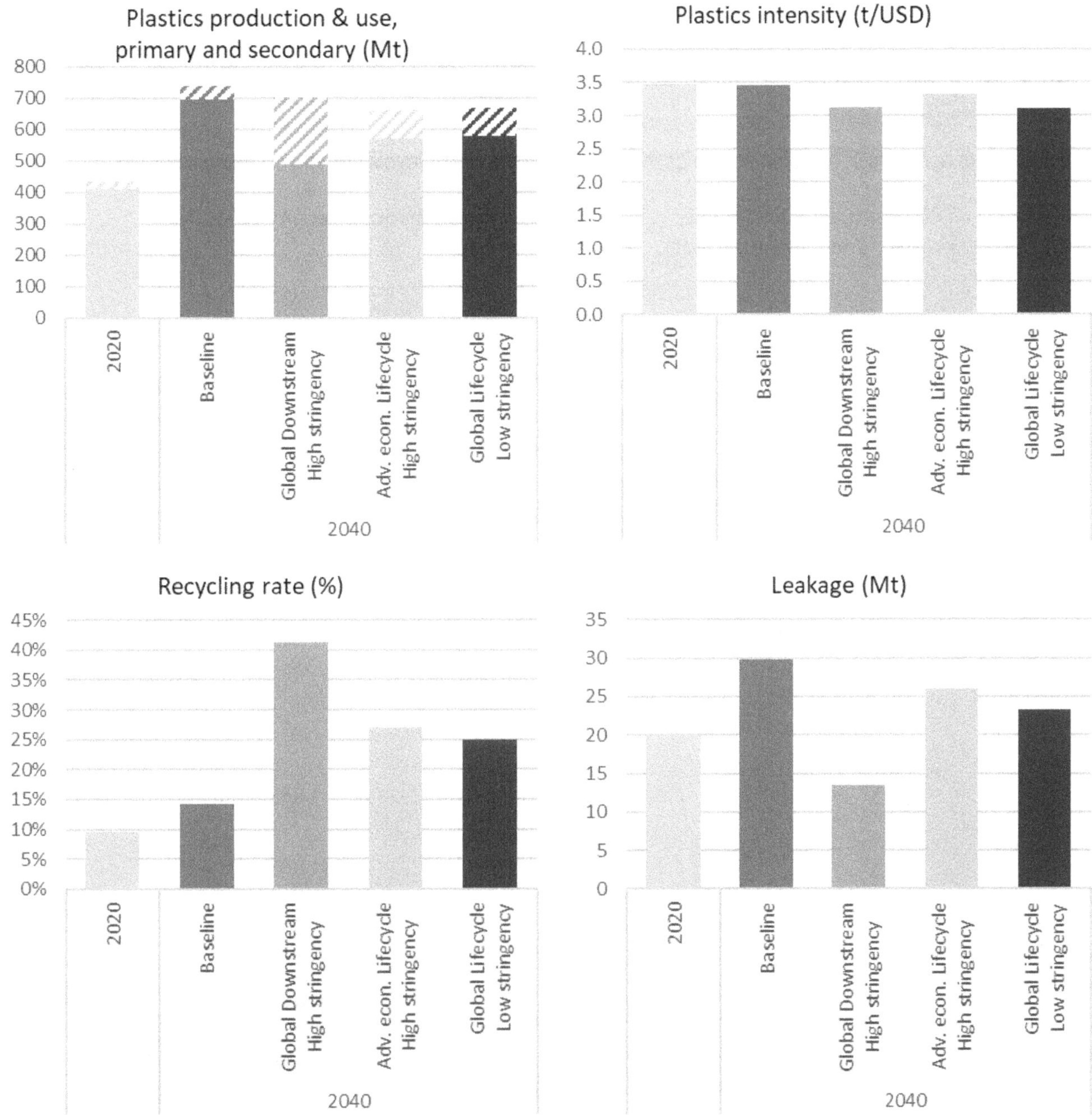

Note: The striped portion of the bars for plastics use indicate secondary plastics.
Source: OECD ENV-Linkages model.

StatLink https://stat.link/praol3

The combined effect of policies along the lifecycle (to curb production and demand, to improve eco-design and to improve waste collection and management), as simulated in the *Global Lifecycle Mixed stringency* scenario, would generate sufficient incentives to alter plastic flows at the global level, reducing both plastics production and use, as well as leakage to the environment below 2020 levels (Figure 1.5). By combining reductions in total plastics demand with improved recycling, this scenario ensures that all growth in plastics use is met through secondary plastics. However, the *Global Lifecycle Mixed stringency* scenario leads only to marginal improvements in terms of overall (primary and secondary) plastics production and use and in terms of reductions in plastics intensity. Moreover, the *Global Lifecycle Mixed stringency* scenario does not completely eliminate plastic leakage to the environment, as it lacks ambitious upstream and midstream action (to curb production and demand and to promote eco-design) in the less advanced economies.

Figure 1.5. *Global Ambition* can achieve major improvements on all key indicators compared to partial ambition scenarios

Key indicators across high ambition scenarios in 2040, compared 2020 levels and the *Baseline* scenario

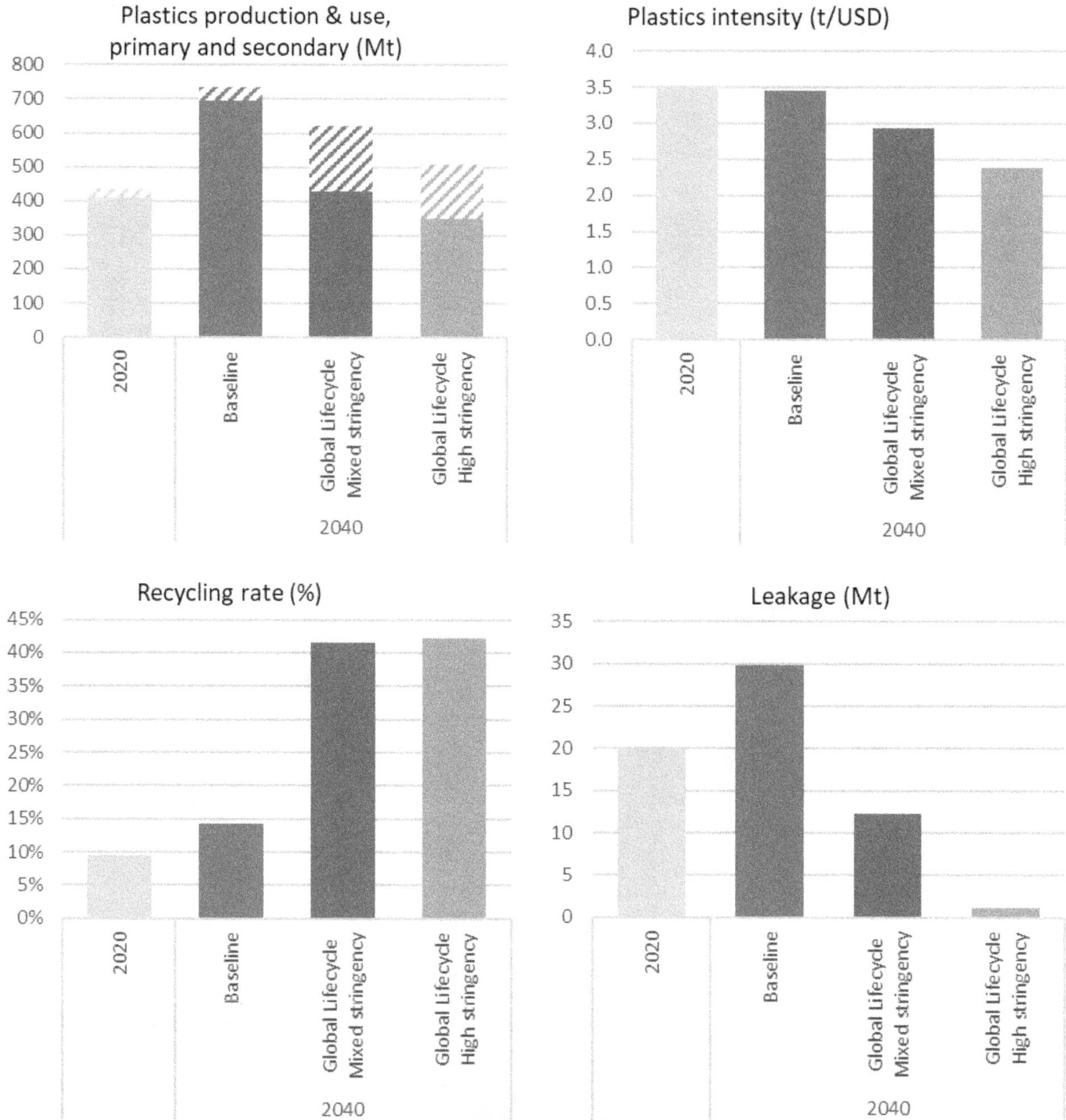

Note: The striped portion of the bars for plastics use indicate secondary plastics.
Source: OECD ENV-Linkages model.

StatLink https://stat.link/h40jwe

By contrast, implementing a high stringency policy package in all world regions and covering all four policy pillars (*Global Lifecycle High stringency* [*Global Ambition*]), would outperform the other scenarios across multiple aspects, as shown in Figure 1.5. Only the *Global Lifecycle High stringency* [*Global Ambition*] scenario can eliminate plastic waste mismanagement and plastic leakage, as this requires both limiting the amounts of total waste generated, as well as enhancing waste management systems.

1.3.3. Global Ambition with high stringency and broad lifecycle scope can chart a viable path to eliminating plastic leakage by 2040

The *Global Lifecycle High stringency* [*Global Ambition*] scenario would achieve an almost total elimination of mismanaged waste and macroplastic leakage by 2040. In this scenario only 4 Mt and 1.2 Mt of mismanaged waste and macroplastic leakage remain in 2040, respectively (Figure 1.6; 3rd and 4th panel).[8] In countries with advanced waste management systems, macroplastic leakage already steadily falls in the *Baseline* scenario, but in other regions this policy package is able to overcome otherwise significant *Baseline* growth in annual amounts of plastic leakage.

The projections indicate that an ambitious scale-up of interventions downstream in the plastics lifecycle will be needed in order to reduce plastic leakage. In particular, enabling all countries to have adequate waste management systems in place by 2040 will be crucial to ending macroplastic leakage. While most developed countries already have widespread municipal waste collection and treatment, this is not the case in a large share of developing countries, especially in non-urban areas. An urgent expansion of waste collection systems is a crucial prerequisite for ending plastic pollution, as waste that is not collected is mostly mismanaged and may end up in natural environments or be burned informally, leading to serious adverse consequences for human health and ecosystems. At the same time, a scale-up of waste treatment infrastructure is also required, including in both OECD and non-OECD countries, to support improved recycling.

Figure 1.6. Comprehensive policies throughout the lifecycle contribute to eliminating plastic leakage

Percentage change compared to the *Baseline, Global Lifecycle High stringency* [*Global Ambition*] scenario

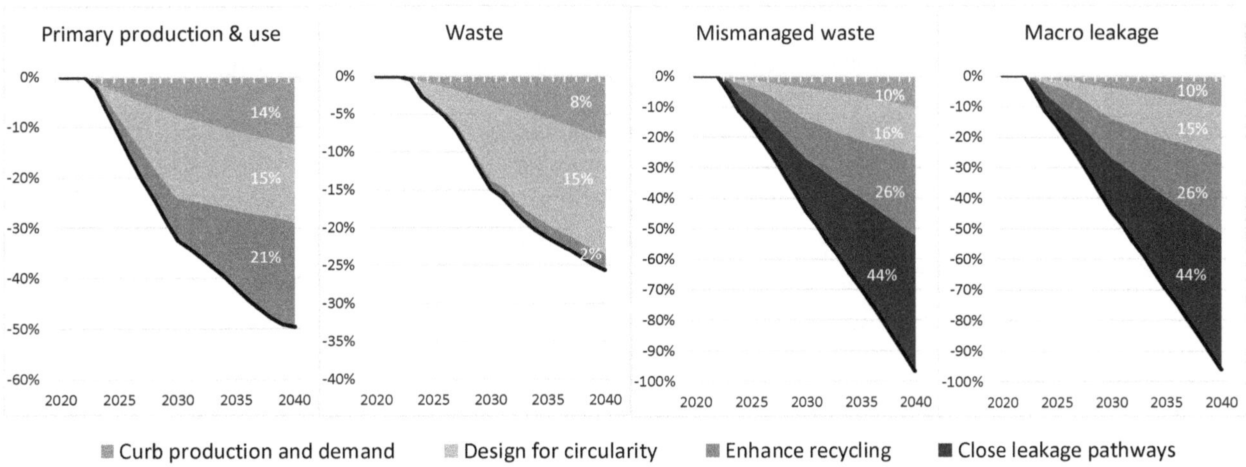

Source: OECD ENV-Linkages model.

StatLink https://stat.link/jgur1h

Interventions that curb primary plastics production and demand and incentivise the eco-design of plastic products and packaging are pivotal to reduce plastic waste volumes to be collected and treated, as well as to mitigate adverse environmental and health impacts along the plastics lifecycle. Policy measures in the *Global Lifecycle High stringency* [*Global Ambition*] scenario would reduce primary plastics use by one-half (both for packaging and non-packaging applications) compared to the *Baseline* scenario (Figure 1.6; 1st panel). This impact is primarily driven by policy measures to curb production and demand and to improve eco-design for circularity. Overall plastics use would be reduced by one-third (not shown in the chart). As growth in plastics use is mitigated, the resulting plastic waste is reduced by one-fourth compared to *Baseline* level (Figure 1.6; 2nd panel). The prevention of approximately 158 Mt of waste generation by 2040 (compared to the *Baseline* level) would help to relieve the burden on waste management systems around the globe. Importantly, projected waste generation in non-OECD countries would fall from a projected doubling in the *Baseline* scenario between 2020 and 2040, to a 40% increase over the same time frame in the *Global Lifecycle High stringency* [*Global Ambition*] policy scenario.[9]

The policy pillars to curb production and demand and to design for circularity also contribute to reducing mismanaged plastic waste and leakage to the environment. By scaling down the total amounts of waste generated, significant improvements can be made on these downstream outcomes even in absence of improved waste management systems. To comprehensively eliminate plastic leakage, however, efforts to enhance recycling and improve waste collection, sorting and treatment are also essential, contributing to 26% and 44% of total reduction in leakage, respectively. The comprehensive policy package in the *Global Lifecycle High stringency* [*Global Ambition*] scenario also facilitates the transition to more circular plastics use, as secondary plastics production rises in parallel to the increased availability of scrap from downstream recycling efforts. As a result, demand for primary plastics would be lower than in 2020.

The comprehensive mix of upstream, midstream and downstream policies envisioned in the *Global Lifecycle High stringency* [*Global Ambition*] scenario promises to deliver ample global benefits for ecosystems and human health. The combination of waste prevention measures and improvements in waste collection and management leads to an almost immediate fall in the leakage of macroplastics to the environment and a near elimination of leakage by 2040. This scenario is also likely to deliver considerable benefits for human health, in particular by mitigating adverse impacts on human health associated with unsafe waste disposal practices, such as air pollution from open pit burning.

Importantly, the plastics lifecycle is closely linked to climate change, due to the fossil-based origins of most plastics and the domination of fossil-based primary plastics in current production and use. As discussed in (OECD, 2022[1]), a reduction in plastics-related GHG emissions is essential for achieving ambitious climate scenarios, including net-zero emissions scenarios. Implementing the *Global Lifecycle High stringency* [*Global Ambition*] scenario could achieve a 41% reduction in plastics-related GHG emission levels compared to levels expected in 2040 under a business-as-usual policy course (1.7 $GtCO_2e$ in 2040 versus 2.8 $GtCO_2e$ in *Baseline*). This scenario would also prevent significant increases compared to 2020 levels but would not be compatible with the ambitions of the Paris Agreement.

The *Global Lifecycle High stringency* [*Global Ambition*] scenario achieves very significant reductions of the accumulated stock of plastics in aquatic environments compared to *Baseline* levels, preventing up to 64 Mt in rivers and up to 11 Mt in oceans from being added to existing stocks. Although projections of all major flows of plastics in aquatic environments are significantly lower in the policy scenario compared to the *Baseline* scenario, stocks are nevertheless projected to grow under the policy scenario, reaching 226 Mt of total accumulated plastics in 2040. As even a full elimination of plastic leakage by 2040 cannot prevent an increase in the stocks of plastics in oceans and rivers over this period, cost-effective remediation measures will be required to mitigate the risks of terrestrial and aquatic plastic pollution.

Despite the large benefits expected from the *Global Lifecycle High stringency* [*Global Ambition*] scenario, the ten policies modelled to eliminate plastic waste mismanagement and macroplastic leakage would not be sufficient to fully address all aspects of plastic pollution. Chemicals of concern also need to be phased out to reduce risks for human health and the environment and enable safe reuse and higher recycling rates. It is also essential to advance policies to mitigate the leakage of microplastics, such as losses of plastic pellets as well as unintentional releases from vehicle tyres, textiles or paints (see also Section 1.3.4).

1.3.4. A range of policy interventions are nevertheless required to overcome significant technical and economic barriers to Global Ambition

As the *Global Lifecycle High stringency* [*Global Ambition*] scenario significantly increases the level of policy stringency on the ten policies included in the policy package, significant technical and economic barriers will need to be overcome in order to enable its implementation.

Curb production and demand, including via improved eco-design and a scale-up of reuse systems. To curb plastics demand and decouple it from economic growth, it is essential to promote the eco-design of products and packaging that is aligned with safe reuse and recycling, such as the development of product standards at the international level. Reuse models could play a critical role in reducing demand for short-lived applications and keeping plastic materials in use for longer before they are disposed, but stronger public incentives and harmonised reuse standards are required to facilitate investments in infrastructure and the scale-up of reuse models. Advancing research on the environmental impacts of on alternative materials in different applications will be needed in order to better inform product design and avoid the risk of unanticipated impacts associated with substitute materials. Furthermore, even if the *Global Lifecycle High stringency* [*Global Ambition*] scenario could achieve a 41% reduction in plastics-related GHG emission levels, 1.7 $GtCO_2e$ of GHG emissions from plastics production would persist in 2040.

Enhance waste collection, sorting and treatment, especially in developing countries. Improvements in waste collection are essential to reduce mismanaged waste, especially in developing and emerging economies. Many low- and middle-income countries tend to have lower use and waste generation rates, compared to advanced economies. However, these countries lack well-functioning waste collection and management services, often resorting to informal waste picking and practices such as open dumping and burning that exacerbate environmental and human health concerns. Governance challenges and limited financial resources currently hinder the rapid establishment of effective waste management infrastructure in these contexts. Solutions that ensure the integration of the informal sector in waste management systems would allow for the participation of waste pickers in improving reuse systems and increasing collection rates, while also mitigating human health concerns for workers. At the same time, curbing expected growth in demand can play an important role in managing the costs of waste collection and treatment.

Encourage improvements in sorting and recycling as well as technological innovation. The *Global Lifecycle High stringency* [*Global Ambition*] scenario also assumes very significant improvements in recycling in all regions, with an increase in the average global recycling rate from 9.5% in 2020 to 42% in 2040. This includes also large increases in mechanical recycling for polymers and applications for which recycling is currently minimal. Achieving this ambition would require significant improvements in recycling yields and quality, as well as reductions in recycling losses to ensure sufficient availability of scrap material. Scaled investments in recycling technologies, combined with improved design for recycling, are required to expand the sources of viable feedstock for mechanical recycling. Scaling up well-functioning markets for scrap and secondary plastics is essential to providing a business case for plastics recycling. Should the expected technical breakthroughs fail to materialise, meeting the ambitions of the policy package will require heightened ambition in other parts of the policy package, for instance via reductions in the use of hard-to-recycle polymers or via more significant reductions in demand.

Enhance municipal litter management. Even the implementation of the ambitious policy package envisioned in the *Global Lifecycle High stringency* [*Global Ambition*] scenario would not eliminate plastic pollution completely. By 2040, about 4 Mt of plastics would still be mismanaged in this scenario, largely due to littered waste that is difficult to collect via municipal litter collection. Large increases in municipal litter management are expected especially in Africa and India (from 65% in 2020 to 75% in 2040 in the policy scenario).

Encourage research to support the implementation of cost-effective policy measures targeting microplastic leakage. The leakage of microplastics remain largely unaddressed in all the scenarios. While reducing the plastics intensity of the economy may help to reduce microplastic leakage, targeted solutions are also required. These may include interventions to prevent pellet losses (e.g. best handling practices, mandatory certifications), improved eco-design of products (e.g. tyres, vehicles, roads, paints and textiles) to minimise emissions, uptake of best practices during use, and end-of-pipe capture solutions at hotspots (e.g. improved treatment of road runoff and stormwater).

Consider the relevance of remedial interventions. Legacy plastic pollution and additional contributions that are still expected between 2020 and 2040 would lead to continued increases in plastic pollution. Stocks of macroplastics accumulating in rivers and oceans, often used as an indicator of global pollution, would still rise from 152 Mt in 2020 to 226 Mt in 2040 in the *Global Lifecycle High stringency* [*Global Ambition*] scenario (74 Mt less than in the *Baseline* scenario). In addition to the policy interventions envisioned in the policy scenario, remedial interventions would have an important role to play in mitigating environmental risks, especially in developing countries most affected by plastic pollution. Clean-up interventions, such as citizen clean-ups and interventions targeted at hotspots, may also help to gather data on environmental pollution and inform policy efforts. At the same time, specific attention should be paid to the potential environmental impacts of clean-up interventions, especially with respect to technologies that may be associated with risks of ecosystem damage and low cost-efficiency.

Enable quantification of the broader environmental impacts associated with plastics. The Global Plastics Outlook (OECD, 2022[1]) contains a lifecycle environmental impact assessment of the plastics lifecycle at the global level, rather than at regional levels. Furthermore, the reductions in pollution from mismanaged waste from closing leakage pathways could not be quantified beyond plastic leakage to the (aquatic) environment. A better understanding of the environmental impacts of plastics at regional levels is essential for effective management and identifying the most appropriate policy measures for ending plastic pollution.

1.3.5. Intervening across the plastics lifecycle is more effective and less costly than focussing solely on downstream action

Unbalanced policy packages that ignore upstream action increase costs

The *Global Lifecycle High stringency* [*Global Ambition*] scenario can achieve the largest benefits and limit the overall costs of the transition, compared to less ambitious and less balanced scenarios (Figure 1.7). Stringent supply-side and demand-side interventions are the most effective way to slow plastics production and consumption and reduce environmental impacts. At the same time, stringent waste management policies are critical to ensure the safe disposal of waste and reduce risks to the environment and human health. Improved waste sorting and recycling infrastructure is also critical to improving recycling rates and transitioning from primary to secondary plastics.

Implementing the ten policy instruments modelled in the *Global Lifecycle High stringency* [*Global Ambition*] scenario would cost 0.5% of global GDP in 2040. Overall, implementation costs are substantially higher in non-OECD countries than in OECD countries (0.62% vs. 0.37% of GDP in 2040, respectively, in the *Baseline* scenario). These costs exclude the avoided costs of inaction and should be considered in the context of vastly improved environmental outcomes. Substantial economic benefits would result from reduced pressures on the environment, climate and human health along the plastics lifecycle. Even if such benefits have not been included within the scope of the projections in this analysis, it is expected that they would largely offset the quantified costs (OECD, 2022[1]).

Significant differences in the macroeconomic impacts of the *Global Lifecycle High stringency* [*Global Ambition*] scenario exist across policy pillars (see Chapter 6). Policies to enhance recycling are the largest drivers of macroeconomic costs. Policies to design for circularity, in contrast, are characterised by lower costs. These include some policies that can bring both economic and environmental benefits, as they focus more on improving the economic efficiency of plastics use (i.e. reducing the plastics intensity of the economy). Such measures are not profitable in the *Baseline* scenario, where plastics remain cheap, but they become cost-effective when combined with policies that increase the costs of primary plastics use (e.g. plastic taxes contained in the curb production and demand pillar). Policies to close leakage pathways can be relatively cheap from a macroeconomic perspective, but only if total waste volumes are not too high.

Figure 1.7. It is more costly and less effective to focus solely on downstream policies

Percentage change in GDP (left axis) and in plastic leakage (right axis) compared to *Baseline* in 2040

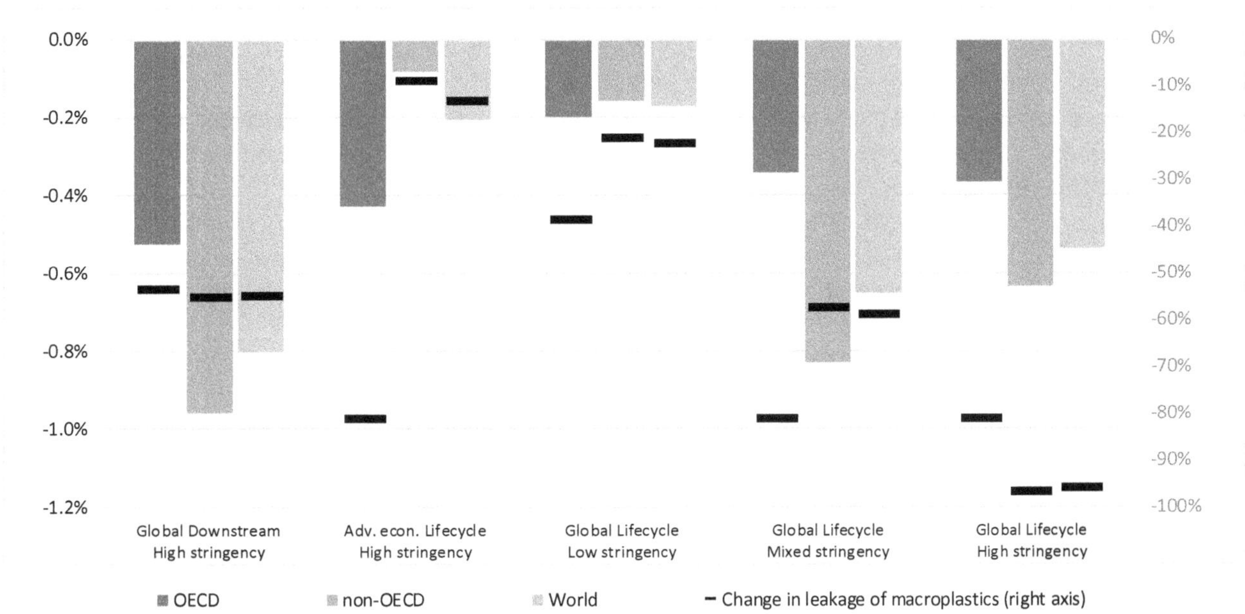

Note: The lower reduction in leakage in OECD countries compared to non-OECD countries in the *Global Lifecycle Mixed stringency* and *Global Lifecycle High stringency* [*Global Ambition*] scenarios reflects the lower share of mismanaged waste in these scenarios, rather than a lower level of ambition.
Source: OECD ENV-Linkages model.

StatLink https://stat.link/c69p7y

Ambitious action would require major redirections in investment flows to support the implementation of stringent policies along the lifecycle across countries, including significant improvements in plastic waste management – i.e. enhancing waste collection, sorting and treatment – expected in the *Global Lifecycle High stringency* [*Global Ambition*] scenario. Baseline investment needs for plastic waste collection, sorting and treatment are projected to amount to more than USD 1 trillion between 2020 and 2040 for non-OECD countries combined. The *Global Lifecycle High stringency* [*Global Ambition*] scenario would have two distinct effects on these investment needs: i) on the one hand, the upstream and midstream measures (of the first and second policy pillars) can reduce total plastic waste volumes, thereby reducing the costs of collection, sorting and treatment; ii) on the other hand, the downstream measures imply larger shares of waste (and litter) are collected, and more expensive waste management options are used, such as for recycling. On balance, an additional USD 50 billion in investment is required in this policy scenario relative to levels projected in the *Baseline* scenario.

In contrast, policy packages that focus purely on downstream measures, i.e. the *Global Downstream High stringency* scenario, reduce plastic leakage without reducing total plastic waste. As a consequence, the total waste management costs increase significantly, making the effort needed to eliminate leakage much more difficult and likely impossible (Figure 1.8). This is particularly an issue for developing countries with less developed waste management systems, including in Sub-Saharan Africa and Asia, which would face very significant increases in waste generation and waste management costs. Beyond considerations of cost-effectiveness, uncertainty exists regarding the viability of a downstream-oriented strategy in low- and middle- income countries, as this scenario assumes that nations that currently lack robust waste management collection and treatment systems can swiftly implement the necessary measures to improve these systems. Technological constraints, e.g. the time needed to establish sanitary landfills or recycling facilities, as well as governance challenges may impede a rapid development of waste management systems and inflate the economic costs of this development. Overall, as the modelling in this report shows, upstream and midstream solutions that reduce the amount of plastic materials in the economy are critical to an efficient policy mix that can make waste management solutions less costly and easier to implement.

Directing policy ambitions to OECD and non-OECD European Union countries only, as in the *Advanced economies Lifecycle High stringency* scenario, will have very limited effects on waste management costs, as most advanced economies have very high waste collection rates and adequate treatment facilities, as reflected in the *Baseline* scenario. Correspondingly, the reduction in global plastic leakage in this scenario remains small.

The *Global Lifecycle Low stringency* scenario, which balances upstream and downstream measures with partial ambition levels, suggests that additional and incremental improvements to current policies would fall far short of eliminating plastic pollution in the absence of common, ambitious targets and policies.

Bringing the three partial ambition scenarios together, in the *Global Lifecycle Mixed stringency* scenario, helps to avoid the largest costs of the *Downstream* scenario by incorporating ambitious upstream and midstream policies in advanced economies (as in the *Advanced economies Lifecycle High stringency* scenario), although these remain limited in emerging and developing economies (with the same level of stringency as in the *Global Lifecycle Low stringency* scenario). However, this integrated, high ambition policy scenario does not eliminate all plastic leakage and still overly relies on downstream policies and associated excessive costs.

The *Global Lifecycle High stringency* [*Global Ambition*] scenario can improve on the *Global Lifecycle Mixed stringency* scenario by further aligning upstream policies over all countries, eliminating plastic leakage and simultaneously reducing total global waste management costs.

Figure 1.8. A balanced policy package is significantly more cost-effective than a package that relies mostly on downstream measures

Percentage change in plastic leakage compared to *Baseline* in 2040, versus cumulative waste management costs for 2020-2040 (in USD billion)

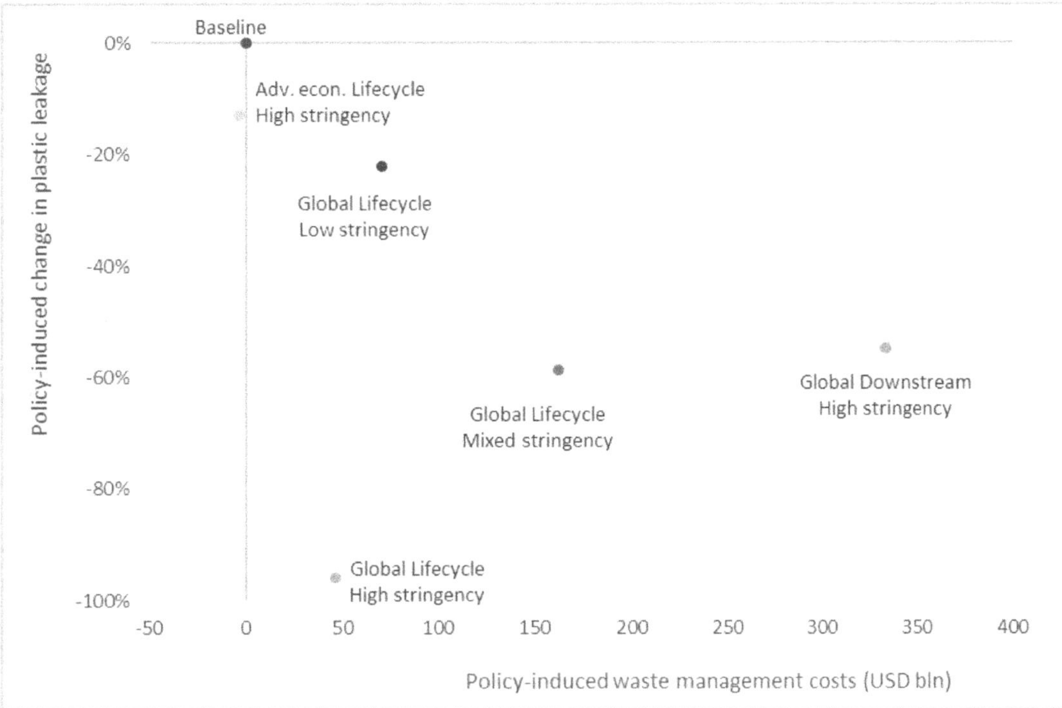

Source: OECD ENV-Linkages model.

StatLink https://stat.link/2897lo

Balanced whole-of-lifecycle approaches are the most cost-effective strategy to work towards ending plastic pollution, but their implementation requires strong international co-ordination on shared targets and approaches. Upstream in the plastics lifecycle, in particular, the absence of strong co-ordination across countries could limit the potential of interventions required to alter plastic flows significantly and achieve a safe and circular economy for plastics. International co-ordination is beneficial for the introduction of harmonised eco-design criteria, the development of common standards on reuse, as well action on chemicals of concern and problematic plastics and polymers.

Limited international co-ordination or failures to overcome the technical, political and financial barriers to the implementation of the *Global Lifecycle High stringency* [*Global Ambition*] scenario could result in slower global action, with large environmental and health repercussions for future generations (see Section 6.5 in Chapter 6). Delayed action (*Global Lifecycle Delayed stringency*, with a 2060 target for the elimination of macroplastic leakage) could reduce macroeconomic costs until 2040, while costs to 2060 would be of similar magnitude to *Global Lifecycle High stringency* [*Global Ambition*]. However, short-term economic savings would come at the expense of substantially lower environmental and climate benefits, with repercussions in the long term.

Large financial needs and an uneven geographical distribution of costs imply a need for international co-operation

Although there is no perfect correlation between the increase in waste management costs and the impacts of the policy scenarios on GDP, the largest costs both in terms of policy-induced waste management costs and the change in GDP resulting from ambitious global action are projected for fast-growing countries with less advanced waste management systems, especially in Sub-Saharan Africa (Figure 1.9). In the *Baseline* scenario, waste management costs are relatively low in Sub-Saharan Africa, and the increase in collection and transition towards recycling comes with significant additional costs. Reduced waste management costs associated with measures that slow plastics production, use and waste generation cannot fully compensate for the increase related to higher collection and recycling rates.

Figure 1.9. Costs to eliminate leakage are unevenly distributed across world regions

Distribution of economic costs (change in GDP) of implementing the policy scenario and policy-induced cumulative waste management costs by region, both in percentage changes compared to the *Baseline* in 2040, *Global Lifecycle High stringency* [*Global Ambition*] scenario

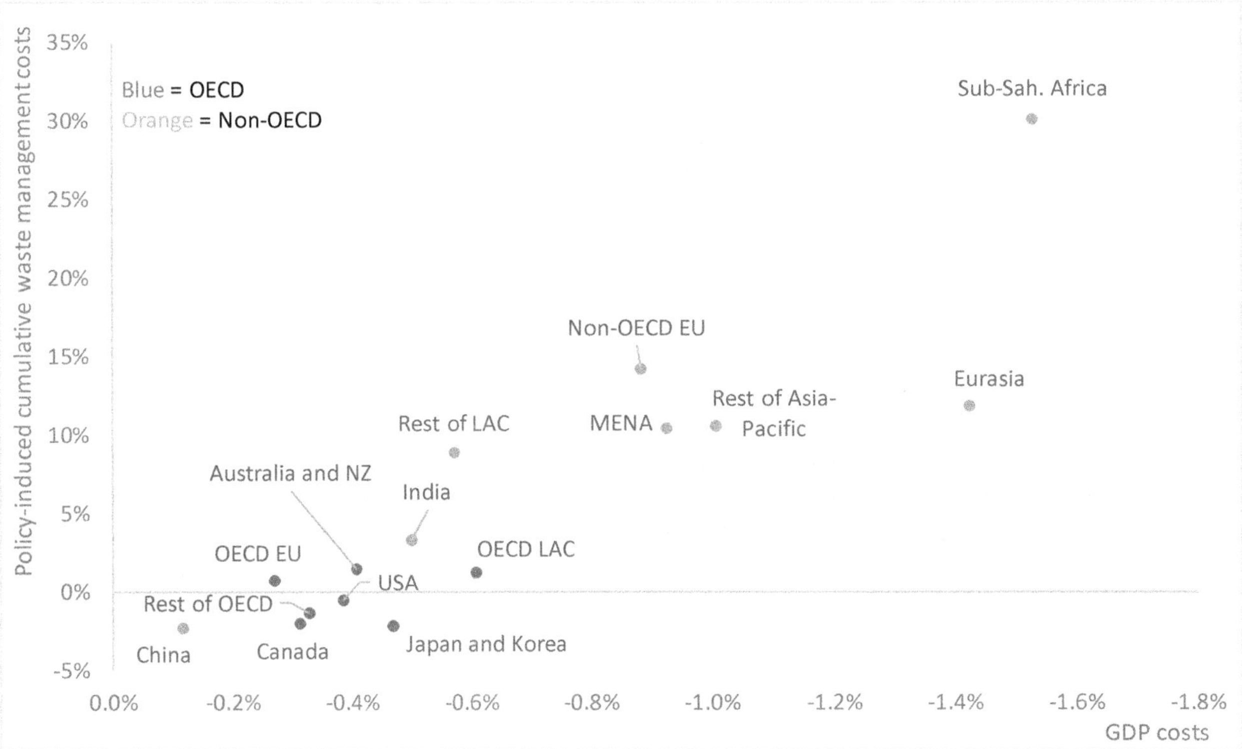

Source: OECD ENV-Linkages model.

StatLink https://stat.link/mxr0v7

The People's Republic of China (hereafter China) and OECD countries generally have advanced waste management systems in place, and recycling rates are already higher than the global average in the *Baseline* scenario. As such, the *Global Lifecycle High Stringency* [*Global Ambition*] scenario entails limited additional costs associated with downstream policies, while the cost savings from upstream and midstream policies are significant. Furthermore, stable, diversified economies can absorb the shocks of the upstream plastics policies more easily, and thus limit macroeconomic impacts (on GDP).

While progress towards the goal of ending plastic pollution is likely to benefit all countries, the larger cost burden in developing countries suggests a strong need for enhanced international co-operation to achieve these benefits. Developing countries, including small island developing states, generally face greater challenges to reducing plastic pollution. On the one hand, they are often the most affected by such pollution, along with accompanying negative impacts on human well-being and economic sectors such as tourism or fisheries. On the other hand, these states would need to make the greatest efforts to close leakage pathways, as they do not yet have the waste collection and treatment systems in place to manage the increases in waste generation that are expected in the coming years (even in the presence of policies to curb production and demand).

The large financial needs and uneven distribution of costs across countries imply a need for international co-operation in the form of strengthened technical, technological and financial support. The investment needs for waste management systems in non-OECD countries would amount to more than USD 1 trillion over a 20-year period in the *Global Lifecycle High stringency* [*Global Ambition*] scenario. Investments would also be required to support the implementation of ambitious upstream and midstream policies such as restrictions on problematic or unnecessary plastics, reuse systems, eco-design and the promotion of material substitutes.

Given the critical role of developing countries in ending plastic pollution, achieving this target requires adequate development finance, including the re-orientation and scale-up of Official Development Assistance (ODA). Flows of ODA to support actions to curb plastic pollution have been increasing in recent years, amounting to USD 269 million for plastics specifically and USD 1 191 million for solid waste management more generally in 2022. While ODA alone will not suffice to cover all investment needs required in future years, there are ample opportunities to increase its impact via better targeting, especially to ensure that it reaches regions where the majority of leakage is expected to occur in future years. Also, a catalytic role of ODA can help to leverage other sources of financing, including private finance.

Strengthened technical support is required to progress with the implementation of robust policy frameworks that would support the goal to end plastic pollution and generate an enabling environment for investments. This includes setting up reliable revenue streams for domestic financing of waste collection and treatment (e.g. Extended Producer Responsibility) or targeted bans or fees on problematic plastic applications. As discussed above, the inclusion of measures to reduce plastic flows in the economy is likely to increase the cost-effectiveness as well as the technical viability of the transition.

A redirection of financial flows will be required all over the world. In OECD countries, where mismanaged waste levels are already largely eliminated in the *Baseline* scenario, additional costs are concentrated in recycling activities, amounting to more than USD 120 billion over the 2020-2040 period in the *Global Lifecycle High stringency* [*Global Ambition*] scenario. Beyond scaling up recycling and enabling the substitution of primary plastics with secondary plastics, redirecting investments will be required to support the implementation of solutions upstream and midstream in the plastics value chain, including to implement reuse systems for packaging and products. Aligning financial flows from both public and private sources with the objectives of the legally binding instrument currently being negotiated is critical to enabling a comprehensive transition across the entire lifecycle of plastics.

References

Château, J., R. Dellink and E. Lanzi (2014), "An Overview of the OECD ENV-Linkages Model: Version 3", *OECD Environment Working Papers*, No. 65, OECD Publishing, Paris, https://doi.org/10.1787/5jz2qck2b2vd-en. [10]

G7 Ministers of Climate, Energy and the Environment (2024), *Climate, Energy and Environment Ministers' Meeting Communiqué (Torino, April 29-30, 2024)*, https://www.g7italy.it/wp-content/uploads/G7-Climate-Energy-Environment-Ministerial-Communique_Final.pdf (accessed on 5 June 2024). [5]

High Ambition Coalition to End Plastic Pollution (2024), *High Ambition Coalition Ministerial Joint Statement INC-4*, https://hactoendplasticpollution.org/hac-member-states-ministerial-joint-statement-for-inc-4/ (accessed on 11 June 2024). [4]

Karali, N., N. Khanna and N. Shah (2024), *Climate Impact of Primary Plastic Production*, https://escholarship.org/uc/item/12s624vf. [9]

Lebreton, L. (2024), *Quantitative analysis of aquatic leakage for multiple scenarios based on ENV-Linkages*, unpublished. [7]

OECD (2022), *Global Plastics Outlook: Economic Drivers, Environmental Impacts and Policy Options*, OECD Publishing, Paris, https://doi.org/10.1787/de747aef-en. [2]

OECD (2022), *Global Plastics Outlook: Policy Scenarios to 2060*, OECD Publishing, Paris, https://doi.org/10.1787/aa1edf33-en. [1]

OECD (2022), *Modelling plastics in ENV-Linkages: A novel approach to projecting future plastics use and waste*, https://www.oecd.org/environment/plastics/Technical-Report-Modelling-plastics-in-ENV-Linkages.pdf. [6]

OECD (2021), "Long-term baseline projections, No. 109 (Edition 2021)", *OECD Economic Outlook: Statistics and Projections* (database), https://doi.org/10.1787/cbdb49e6-en (accessed on 18 March 2024). [8]

UNEP (2024), *Intergovernmental Negotiating Committee on Plastic Pollution*, https://www.unep.org/inc-plastic-pollution. [3]

Notes

[1] The High Ambition Coalition to End Plastic Pollution (HAC) is a group of 64 like-minded countries committed to developing an ambitious legally binding international instrument to end plastic pollution by 2040. As of March 2024, 28 OECD countries are members of the HAC.

[2] The group of advanced economies is taken as a proxy for countries that have communicated the ambition to implement ambitious policy mixes covering the entire lifecycle and to aim to eliminate plastic pollution by 2040. For the purposes of the modelling, "advanced economies" includes OECD countries as well as non-OECD EU countries.

[3] The terminology in this report uses "primary production" to refer to "production of primary polymers", "leakage" to refer to "emissions and releases to the environment", and "mismanaged" to describe all waste categories that are not recycling, incineration or sanitary landfilling. This terminology is meant to be widely understandable and consistent with related OECD reports, including the Global Plastics Outlook.

[4] See Chateau, Dellink and Lanzi (2014[10]) for a comprehensive model description.

[5] This is a subset of outcomes with possible environmental benefits, as further improvements can be reached through e.g. targeting specific polymers, problematic applications or harmful chemicals, and implementing policies to deal with microplastics. An assessment of these outcomes is beyond the scope of the current analysis.

[6] If the decarbonisation of other sectors continues or accelerates, this share may grow even more rapidly. More ambitious climate policies could incentivise emission reductions in plastics production, use and waste management.

[7] This finding points to the important contribution of the extraction and production stages to plastics-related GHG emissions and is aligned with the Global Plastics Outlook (OECD, 2022[1]). Karali et al (2024[9]) found that 75% of production-related GHG emissions are generated in steps before polymerisation.

[8] A full reduction of 100% is not feasible as some waste streams will continue to evade the modelled waste management systems, including microplastics and uncollected litter.

[9] See Chapter 5; result not shown in Figure 1.6.

2 Business-as-usual is unsustainable

This chapter outlines the business-as-usual trends as projected in the *Baseline* scenario. The *Baseline* scenario models current plastic flows in the economy and generates projections to 2040, including for plastics production and use, waste and end-of-life fates, mismanaged plastics, leakage to the environment and greenhouse gas emissions. *Baseline* projections for plastic flows are derived from country-specific socio-economic trends expected over the next decades.

2.1. Production of and demand for primary plastics would continue to grow

As detailed in the Global Plastics Outlook (OECD, 2022[1]), the industrial production and use of plastics started gathering pace in the post-war period and has since grown more rapidly than any other commodity, highlighting an increased reliance of our economies on plastics. Global production and demand for plastics, including fibres and additives, reached 435 million tonnes (Mt) in 2020. While plastics bring many benefits to society, current flows of plastics in the global economy are not sustainable nor circular. The *Baseline* scenario as projected with the ENV-Linkages model (see Chapter 3 and Annex A) would see current trends of population growth and higher incomes lead to a 70% increase in annual plastics production and use in 2040, from 435 Mt in 2020 to 736 Mt in 2040 (Figure 2.1).[1] Overall, relentless growth in plastics production and use raises concerns for the amplification of adverse consequences on human health, the environment and livelihoods.

Plastics use is projected to increase in all regions, but the regional composition of global plastics use is projected to continue to change as a consequence of rapidly growing demand in emerging economies in Asia, Africa and Latin America. As global population rises and living standards continue to improve, emerging and developing economies gradually catch up with higher income countries in terms of plastics use. Together with efficiency improvements in production and structural change, especially towards services, this has implications for materials demand, including plastics. Global growth in plastics production and use is projected to outpace population growth. Plastics use is expected to grow fastest in India and Sub-Saharan Africa, while China is expected to remain the region with the highest share of global plastics use (22%). Although the share of global plastics use in OECD countries is expected to decline, plastics use is still projected to grow in OECD countries, as well as in non-OECD Latin American and Eurasian countries.

Figure 2.1. Plastics use is projected to grow by more than two-thirds worldwide

Global plastics use in million tonnes (Mt) (left-hand panel), and by regions (right-hand panels)

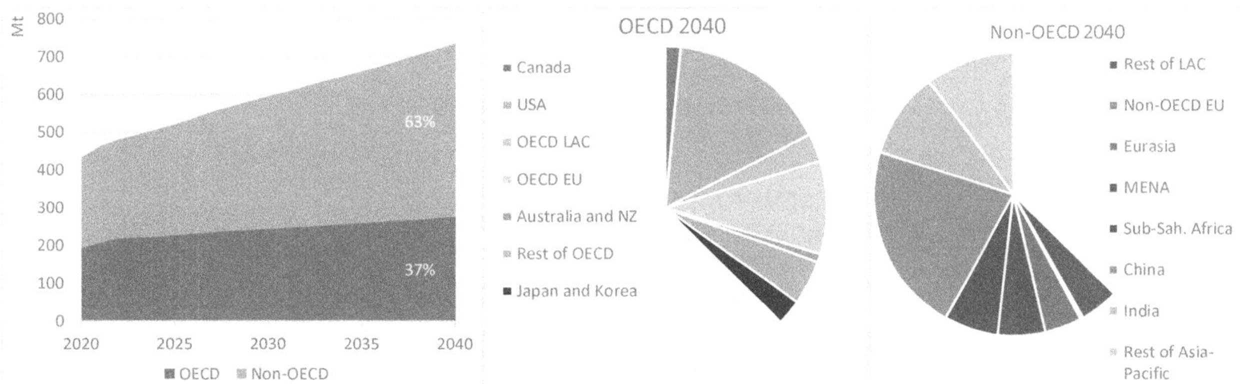

Notes:
1. In the left-hand panels, regional shares in total in 2040 are indicated in data labels.
2. The rapid growth in 2021 and (to a lesser extent) 2022 reflects the recovery from the COVID-19 crisis.
Source: OECD ENV-Linkages model.

StatLink https://stat.link/ytzbcm

At the global level, the expected increase in plastics use between 2020 and 2040 is somewhat lower than the expected increase in GDP. Thus, the plastics intensity of the economy, measured as plastics use in tonnes divided by GDP in million USD, gradually declines, albeit by a small amount and not in all regions (Figure 2.2). Reductions in intensity result from a combination of technological progress that allows faster growth of value added than of the material inputs in production (OECD, 2022[1]). Shifts in economic specialisation also play a role. For example, shifts towards services, which have a below-average plastics intensity, cause a decline in average plastics intensity, whereas industrialisation generally leads to increasing plastics intensity.

The *Baseline* scenario assumes no new policies are implemented to incentivise a shift away from primary plastics. This leads to an increase in the production of secondary plastics due to expected growth in recycling that keeps pace with growth in demand (increasing 70% between 2020 and 2040) and primary production. As a result, the share of secondary plastics in total production remains fairly stable at a global average of 6%.

Figure 2.2. Convergence of plastics use per unit of GDP across regions is very limited

(Primary and secondary) plastics intensity of the economy, in tonnes per unit of GDP (t/USD), in 2020 and 2040, *Baseline* scenario

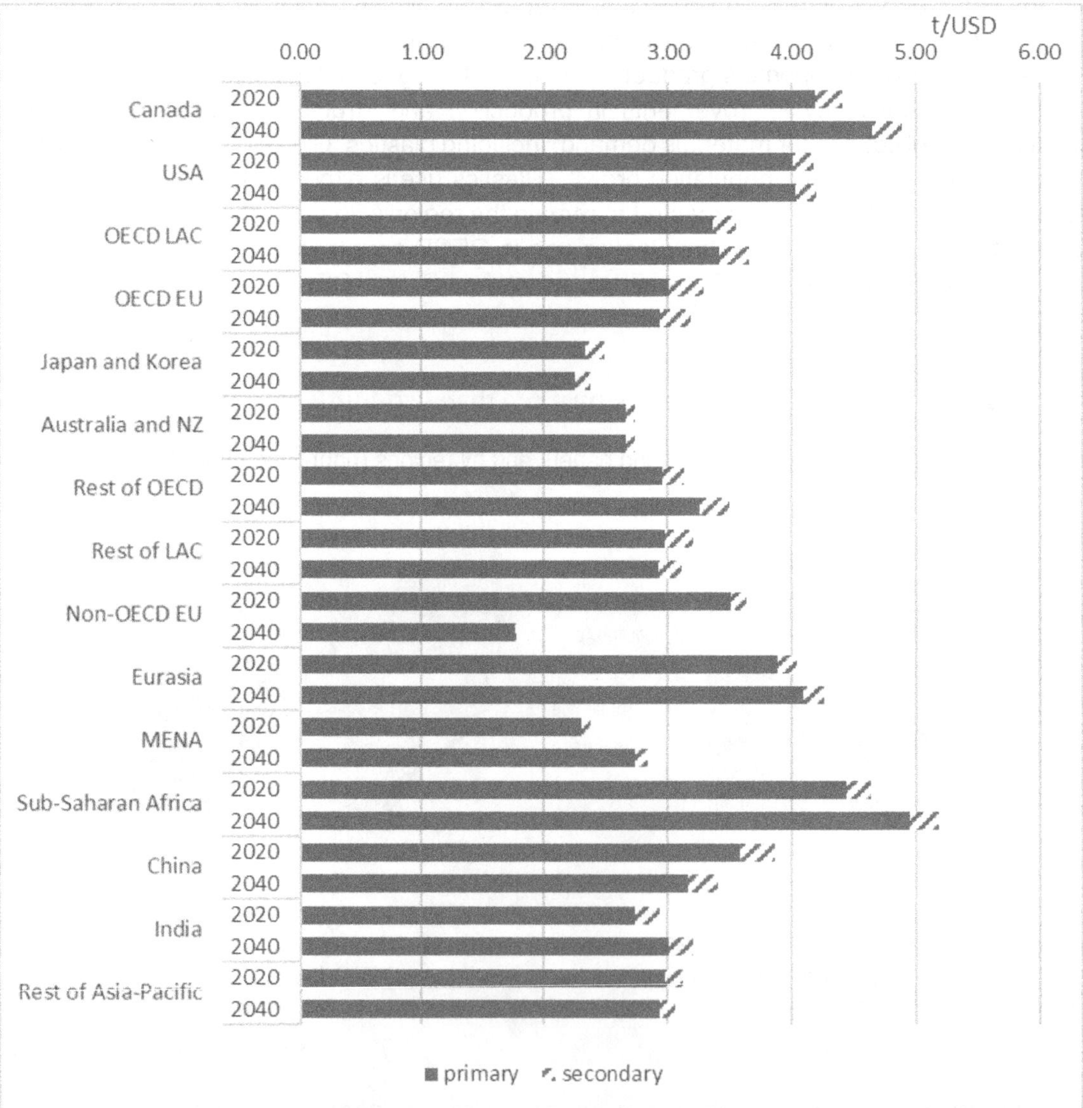

Note: LAC = Latin America and the Caribbean; EU = European Union, NZ = New Zealand, MENA = Middle East and North Africa. See Table A A.2 in Annex A for a more detailed description of the countries covered in each region.
Source: OECD ENV-Linkages model.

StatLink https://stat.link/m32hn7

While plastics are produced and consumed everywhere, regional variations exist regarding total plastics demand. Two-thirds of current use is concentrated in OECD countries and China. As with all materials used as inputs in production processes, there is a strong link between plastics use and socio-economic development. In line with changing economic dynamics of regions and countries, the relative importance of OECD countries in global plastics consumption has been steadily decreasing, while economic growth in emerging economies is now driving growth in global plastics use, as discussed in (OECD, 2022[2]).

To help understand changes in use by application and the related demand for plastic polymers, the ENV-Linkages model maps plastics use by polymer and application to the model sectors (see also Annex A). The links between different polymers and applications is complex, as the same polymers can be used in different ways in various applications, and some polymers represent a wide range of different plastics that are grouped in single category because they share certain characteristics. For instance, PP (polypropylene) is used for packaging, amongst other applications, and is implicated in several sectors, including food products and business services.

The *Baseline* scenario suggests that applications Electrical/Electronic and Transport will see the fastest growth in plastics use between 2020 and 2040 (Figure 2.3). The Electrical/Electronic application is relatively small compared to some other applications, but linked to many polymers and projected to grow from 9 Mt in 2020 to 21 Mt in 2040 in non-OECD countries, reflecting strong industrial growth. Growth in plastics use for this application is limited in OECD countries, increasing from 7 Mt in 2020 to 9 Mt in 2040. Growth in plastics use for transport is also strong, in this case because use is more concentrated in fast-growing emerging economies and developing countries than for other applications: less than 30% of plastics use for transportation in 2040 is projected to take place in OECD countries.

Plastics use for packaging, the single largest application, is projected to grow by almost 70% between 2020 and 2040, making it the application with the largest absolute growth (+95 Mt between 2020 and 2040). This substantial increase includes increases in low-density polyethylene (LDPE and linear LDPE), polypropylene (PP), high density polyethylene (HDPE) and polyethylene terephthalate (PET).[2] This shows that policies currently in place are not sufficient to offset the increase in plastics use by key sectors that rely on packaging, including business services, food products and trade.

Polyvinyl chloride (PVC), mainly used in construction, is the slowest-growing polymer with an increase of less than 60% between 2020 and 2040. Nevertheless, it is a sizeable category with an absolute increase of 15 Mt between 2020 and 2040 in construction alone (right-hand side of Figure 2.3). In contrast, fibres, which are used for textiles, and elastomers for tyres, are projected to increase by around 80%, from 61 Mt to 109 Mt. These differences in trends across polymers and applications are the result of differences in regional sectoral economic growth and highlight the importance of a detailed approach where plastics use is linked to specific economic activities in specific sectors and countries.

Figure 2.3. Packaging is projected to remain most significant application for plastic polymers, followed by the transportation and textile sectors

Polymer types linked to the relative applications in million tonnes (Mt), in 2040

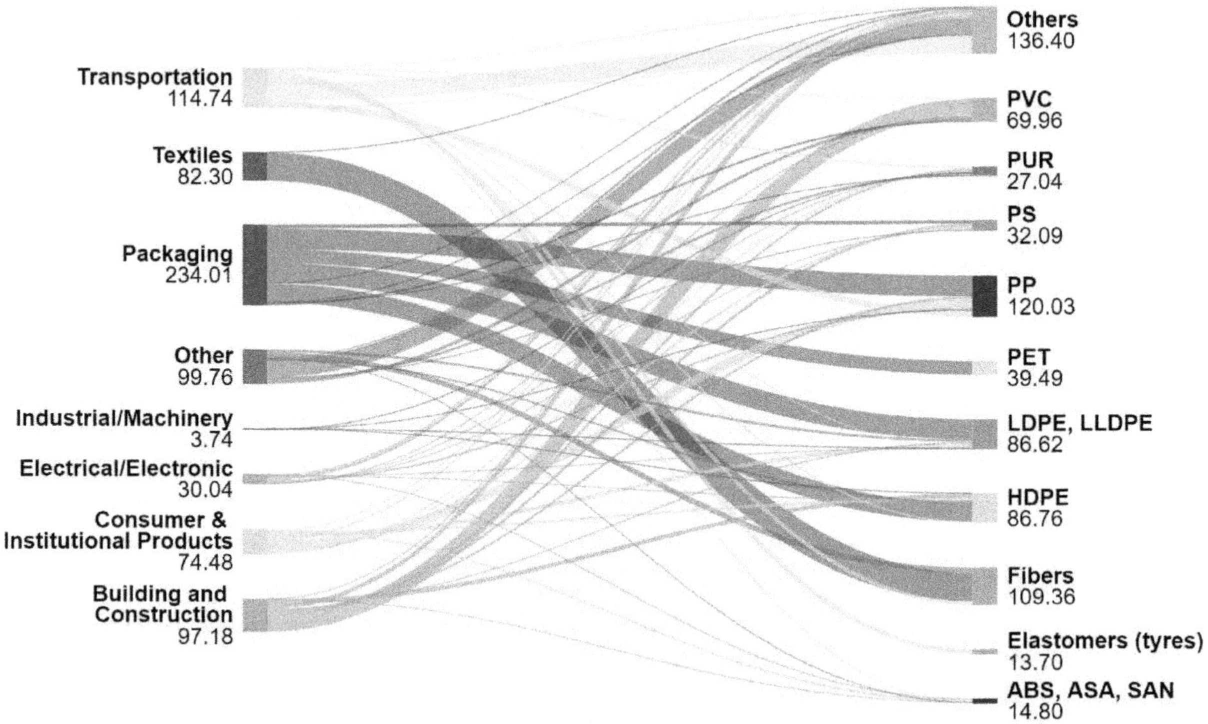

Note: HDPE = high-density polyethylene; LDPE = low-density polyethylene; LLDPE = linear low-density polyethylene; PET = polyethylene terephthalate; PP = polypropylene; PS = polystyrene; PUR = polyurethane; PVC = polyvinyl chloride; ABS = acrylonitrile butadiene styrene; ASA = acrylonitrile styrene acrylate; SAN = styrene acrylonitrile.
Source: OECD ENV-Linkages model.

StatLink https://stat.link/yhzegp

Box 2.1. Alternatives to fossil fuel-based plastics? Biobased, compostable and biodegradable plastics and challenges with material substitution

Biobased plastics are plastics that are fully or partially made from biological resources, rather than fossil fuels. In the *Baseline* scenario, biobased plastics production is projected to increase, although at a slower rate than total plastics production. Overall, its share as a fraction of total plastics production remains marginal (0.5% in 2040). The environmental impacts of growth in bioplastics use are not straightforward to calculate. On the one hand, biobased plastics may offer benefits insofar as their production is less carbon-intensive than fossil-based plastics. On the other hand, concerns exist regarding implications for land use, as increased demand for biobased plastics could increase the area of cropland needed, potentially driving forest conversion and consequent increases in greenhouse gas emission.

One specific case is that of **compostable plastics**, a subset of biodegradable plastics that decompose in industrial composting facilities. Compostable plastics may be biobased or produced from fossil fuels. If sourced responsibly, compostable plastics may play an important role in reducing the environmental impacts of plastics and the associated reliance on fossil fuels. The existence of well-functioning collection systems, with separate collection for organic waste, is essential to ensure that these materials are well-managed at the end-of-life. The European Union recommends that compostable plastics are reserved only for specific applications. For instance, the use of compostable plastics in applications such as fruit stickers and bags for compostable food waste could help to prevent contamination of the organic waste stream (European Commission, DG for Research and Innovation, 2021[3]). On the other hand, compostable (and biodegradable) plastics should be avoided in contexts characterised by a high risk of leakage to the environment, as biodegradation in natural environments is limited or not possible. In no case should compostable or biodegradable plastics be considered a solution for littering or inappropriate waste management. Furthermore, the separate collection and management of compostable plastics requires specific infrastructure that is not yet available in the majority of countries.

Besides the substitution across different types of plastics, plastics can also be replaced by **other materials**, depending on the sector and product. For instance, paper and wood are increasingly used to produce single-use products such as plastic plates, or to turn single-use products into reusable products, as has been done for instance for reusable water bottles made of metal. Alternatives to plastics are less available for other applications, such as in the production of electronics. Options for material substitution should be evaluated on a case-by-case basis to assess net environmental and socio-economic consequences. Due to a lack of data and information, as well as the overall complexity and context-dependency of environmental impacts resulting from substitution, it is not possible to generate projections for these types of alternatives within the current modelling exercise. However, the ENV-Linkages modelling framework takes into account how various materials grow in response to changes in product prices and demand and includes substitution effects from plastics to paper, metals, non-metallic minerals and wood products as part of the considered policy packages.

2.2. Plastic waste would continue to grow, mainly driven by short-lived applications and growth in emerging economies

The current use of plastics generates high amounts of waste, including industrial and municipal solid waste. In the *Baseline* scenario, plastic waste generation would increase by 70% between 2020 and 2040, from 360 Mt to 617 Mt, leading to significantly larger burdens related to plastic waste collection and treatment. Single-use and other short-lived applications are in the main sources of plastic waste (Figure 2.4). At the global level, the share of packaging in waste remains roughly constant over time, while the share of plastics from Buildings and construction increases from 14% in 2020 to 22% in 2040 (Figure 2.5). Plastic waste generation will increase most in Sub-Saharan Africa, India and the Rest of Asia region.

Figure 2.4. Short-lived applications are the major contributor to plastic waste generation

Shares of various applications in total plastic waste (and relative average lifespans), in 2040

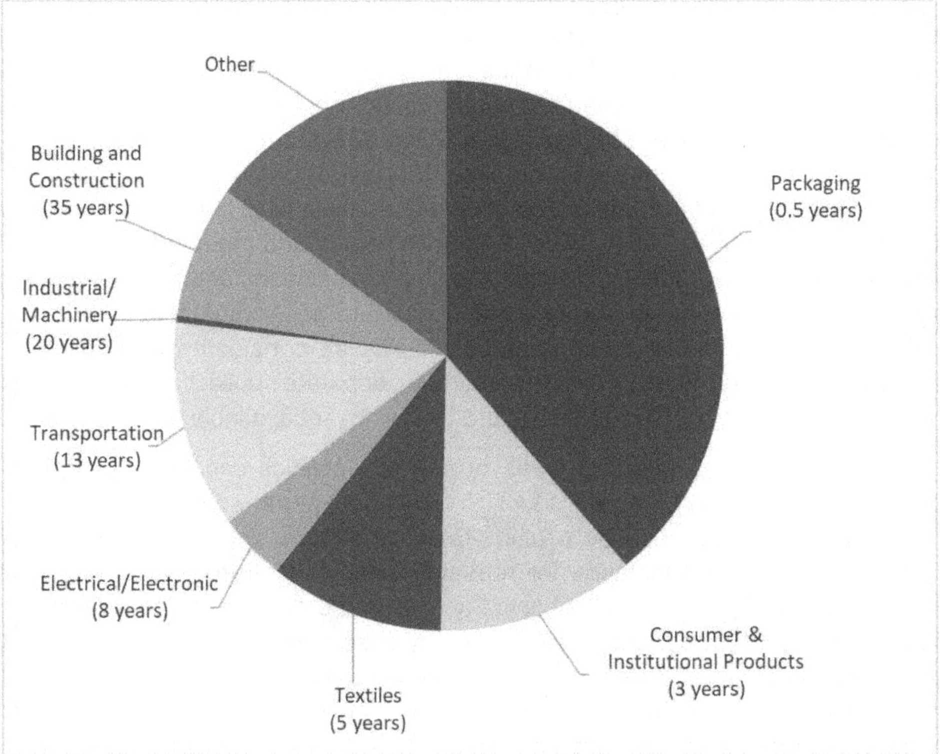

Source: OECD ENV-Linkages model.

StatLink https://stat.link/p9ukx7

Figure 2.5. Without additional policies, plastic waste from all applications would continue to grow

Evolution of plastic waste in million tonnes (Mt) by plastic application

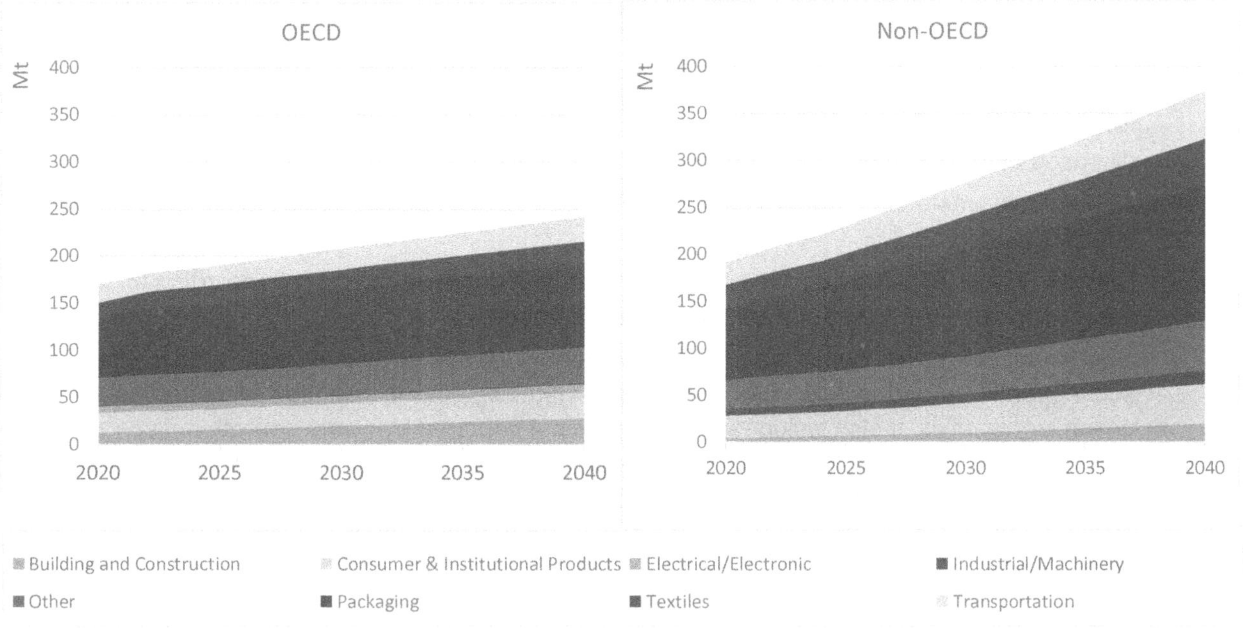

Source: OECD ENV-Linkages model.

StatLink https://stat.link/qbu4r7

2.3. In 2040, more than a hundred million tonnes of plastic waste would still be mismanaged

Out of the 360 Mt of plastic waste generated in 2020, 34 Mt were recycled, 245 Mt were incinerated for energy recovery or landfilled, while 81 Mt were mismanaged, i.e. they were not disposed of in an environmentally sound manner. Within the mismanaged category, 20 Mt leaked to terrestrial or aquatic environments, while the rest mostly ended up in dumpsites or was openly burned.

As discussed in OECD (2022[1]), ENV-Linkages projects waste generation and the future end-of-life fates to 2040. Average lifespans for various applications are used to project when products will become waste. The projections on end-of-life fates rely on a set of assumptions, including that the share of plastic waste collected for recycling continues to grow at the same average rate as over the last 40 years, and that countries with growing incomes invest in better waste collection and treatment and litter clean-up. The end-of-life fates of plastics vary by region, depending on waste management capacity and regulations. Not all plastic that is collected for recycling is actually recycled; in 2020, an estimated 57 Mt were collected, but only 34 Mt actually recycled.[3] There are multiple reasons for this discrepancy, including a lack of recycling capacity and the poor quality of some waste that is collected for recycling.

Box 2.2. Definitions of end-of-life fates for plastics

The ENV-Linkages model distinguishes between four different categories for the end-of-life fate of plastics:

- Recycling: waste that is collected for recycling, processed, and used for the production of secondary plastics. This waste stream excludes the residues from recycling processes that are disposed of using the other waste management categories.
- Incineration: waste that is incinerated in a state-of-the art industrial facility, either with or without energy recovery.
- Landfilling: waste that is disposed of on the land, in a controlled way and according to state-of-the art sanitary, environmental and safety requirements.
- Mismanagement: all other waste. This category includes waste that is collected and subsequently burned in open pits, dumped in water bodies or disposed of in dumpsites and unsanitary landfills. It also includes waste that is not captured by waste collection, such as road markings. This category also includes uncollected litter, i.e. waste that results from littering by individuals or from fly-tipping, and that is not collected via street sweepings or other clean-up actions. It does not include collected litter that is ultimately disposed of through one of the other categories.

Source: (OECD, 2022[1]).

In the *Baseline* scenario, it is expected that countries continue to make improvements in waste collection, sorting and treatment, to progress towards environmentally sound management of all waste and enhance recycling. As a result, it is expected that the world would be able to safely manage an additional 219 Mt of waste in 2040, compared to 2020. Improvements in waste sorting and recycling infrastructure would lead to 14% of waste that is recycled in 2040 (compared to 9.5% in 2020; Figure 2.6). However, higher plastic waste generation would lead to a continued prominent role for landfilling (remaining stable as an end-of-life fate for half of total waste from 178 Mt in 2020 to 305 Mt in 2040), while incineration would slightly decrease in percentage terms (from 19% in 2020 to 17% in 2040).

Similarly, despite expected improvements in waste collection, sorting and treatment, higher plastic waste generation would lead to an increase in the absolute amounts of mismanaged waste (i.e. waste that is not disposed of in an environmentally sound manner) compared to 2020 levels. Projected mismanaged waste in emerging economies in Asia and Africa would contribute to the vast majority of the growth in mismanaged waste volumes.

Figure 2.6. Half of plastic waste will still be landfilled and almost one-fifth mismanaged in 2040

Global end-of-life fates for plastic waste, in million tonnes (Mt), in 2020-2040 (left-hand panel), and by region, as a share of total waste (top right-hand panel) and in Mt (bottom right-hand panel) in 2040

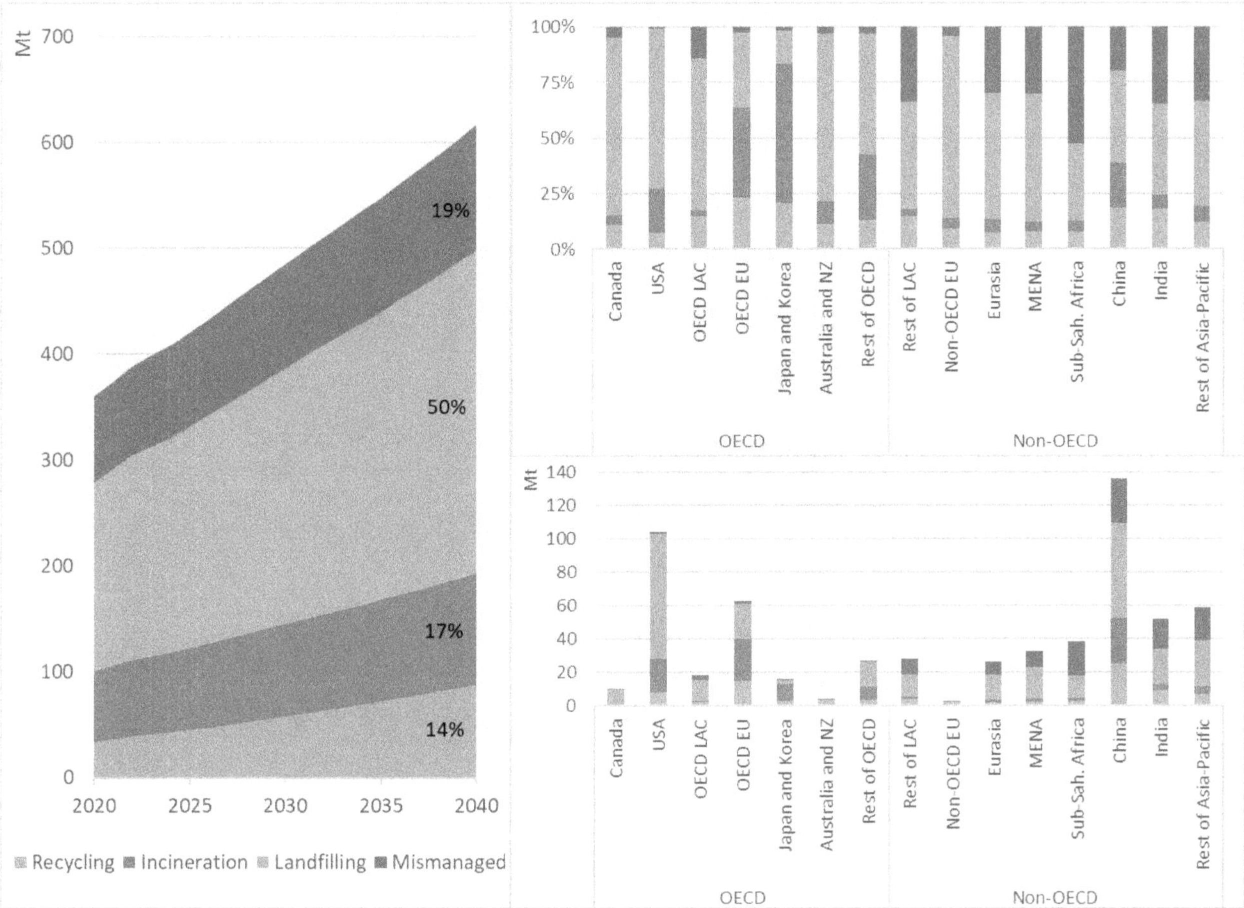

Note: In the left-hand chart, shares of total are indicated in data labels.
Source: OECD ENV-Linkages model.

StatLink https://stat.link/7t84z3

2.4. Growing levels of plastics use and waste would amplify adverse consequences for ecosystems, climate mitigation efforts and human health

As a consequence of projected trends in plastics production and use, plastic leakage to both terrestrial and aquatic environments is set to accelerate, leading to further adverse consequences for the environment. Annual leakage of macroplastics alone would increase by 50% between 2020 and 2040 to 30 Mt (Figure 2.7). All regions would contribute to increased plastic leakage. Leakage volumes tend to be rather small in OECD and non-OECD EU countries (and declining with 30% in aggregate from 2.3 Mt in 2020 to 1.7 Mt in 2040), while the largest growth rates are expected in India (doubling to 4.1 Mt), other developing and emerging economies in Asia (Rest of Asia; +60% to 5.0 Mt), and Sub-Saharan Africa (doubling to 6.5 Mt). It is expected that the leakage of microplastics, for instance from the wear of plastic materials such as vehicle tyres and synthetic textiles, the use and loss of paints, as well as spills of plastic pellets, would also continue to grow in all regions, in line with higher plastics intensity.

Figure 2.7. Plastic leakage to the environment will increase by half to reach 30 Mt in 2040

Plastic leakage to the environment in million tonnes (Mt), by region, *Baseline* scenario

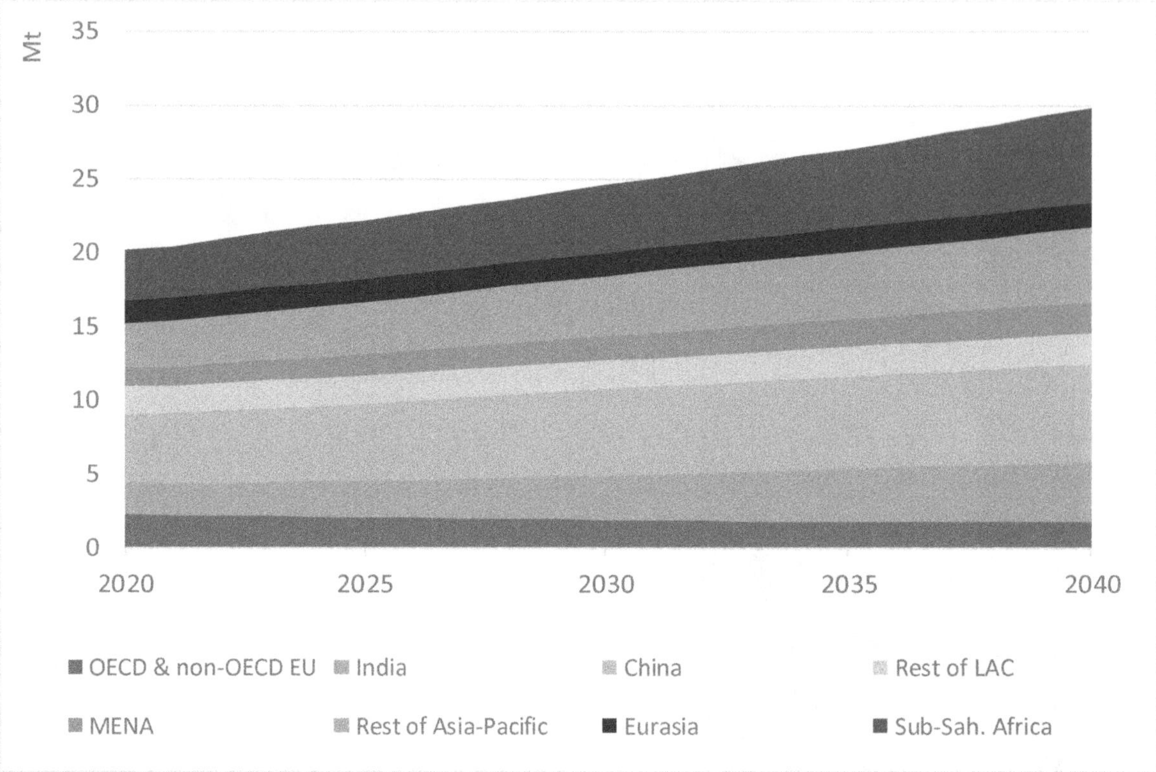

Source: OECD ENV-Linkages model.

StatLink https://stat.link/xc0ng2

Importantly, the accumulation of plastics in aquatic environments will continue to increase. Leakage to rivers and oceans would amount to 9 Mt per year in 2040. Continued leakage to the environment would lead to a doubling in the cumulative stocks of plastics in rivers and oceans, to reach 300 Mt by 2040 (from an estimated 152 Mt in 2020; Figure 2.8), amplifying negative impacts for ecosystems, human well-being, coastal economies as well as risks of potentially irreversible damage.

Figure 2.8. Stocks of plastics in rivers and oceans will double between 2020 and 2040

Stocks of plastics accumulated in aquatic environments in million tonnes (Mt), *Baseline* scenario

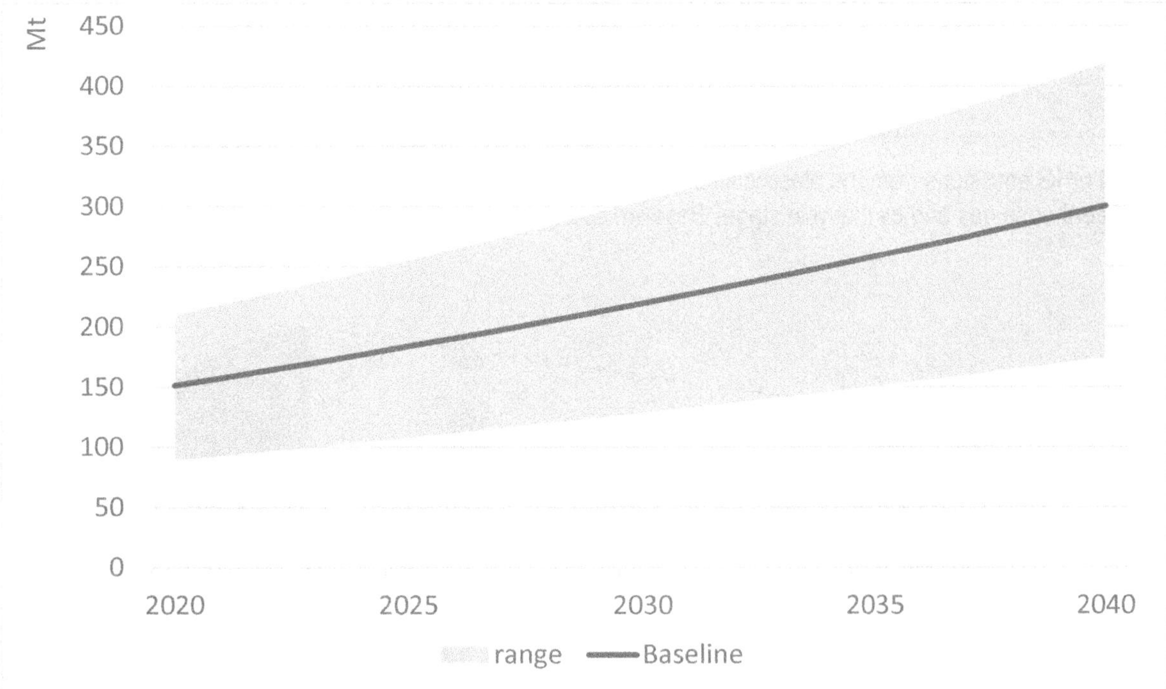

Note: The range reflects the uncertainty associated with the projections related to flows of plastics in aquatic systems, with the edges representing low and high estimates.
Source: (Lebreton, 2024[4]), based on OECD ENV-Linkages model projections.

StatLink https://stat.link/y851cd

The plastics lifecycle is expected to be a growing source of greenhouse gas (GHG) emissions in the coming decades. In the *Baseline* scenario, GHG emissions from the plastics lifecycle would increase by 60% in 2040 compared to 2020 levels (1.8 $GtCO_2e$). This is despite the effect of current policies in place as of 2021 that would already limit the growth of GHG emissions. Emissions from the plastics lifecycle accounted for 3.6% of total global emissions in 2020, and the share is projected to rise to 5.0% by 2040; an outcome that is not in line with the Paris Agreement. The increasing share reflects a combination of the continued pace of growth in emissions related to plastics and a slower pace growth in overall emissions due to climate policy commitments.

The entire plastics lifecycle contributes to climate change. Approximately 90% of plastics-related emissions are attributed to the production and conversion stage in plastic manufacturing (Figure 2.9) and are relatively hard to abate. Karali et al (2024[5]) attribute GHG emissions from plastics production to its different stages, finding that 75% of production-related GHG emissions are generated in the steps before polymerisation (20% from the extraction of fossil fuels needed for feedstock and energy, 29% from the refining of hydrocarbons and the production of other non-hydrocarbon chemicals, and 26% from monomer production), while 8% is generated in polymerisation and 17% in product construction.

Significant GHG emissions also come from the end-of-life stage. The mismanagement of plastic waste can contribute to climate change in ways that are difficult to quantify. Plastic waste that is burned informally contributes to emissions of GHG as well as air pollutants, while plastics and microplastics in marine environments may interfere with the oceans capacity to absorb and sequester carbon dioxide.

Efforts to mitigate climate change and to eliminate plastic pollution mitigation are intrinsically linked. Approximately 99% of plastics come from feedstock of fossil fuels, which are the main driver of GHG emissions. The global petrochemical industry is growing at unprecedented speed, mainly driven by expansion in China's petrochemical sector (IEA, 2023[6]). As global demand for oil from combustible fossil fuels (excluding biofuels, petrochemical feedstock and other non-energy uses) is expected to peak by 2028, petrochemicals are driving additional investments and will likely be the main driver of global oil demand in the next decades (IEA, 2023[7]).

Figure 2.9. Annual greenhouse gas emissions from plastics are projected to increase by more than half

Quantified GHG emissions from the plastics lifecycle in gigatonnes of carbon dioxide equivalent (GtCO2e), split by type of greenhouse gas and by lifecycle stage, *Baseline* scenario

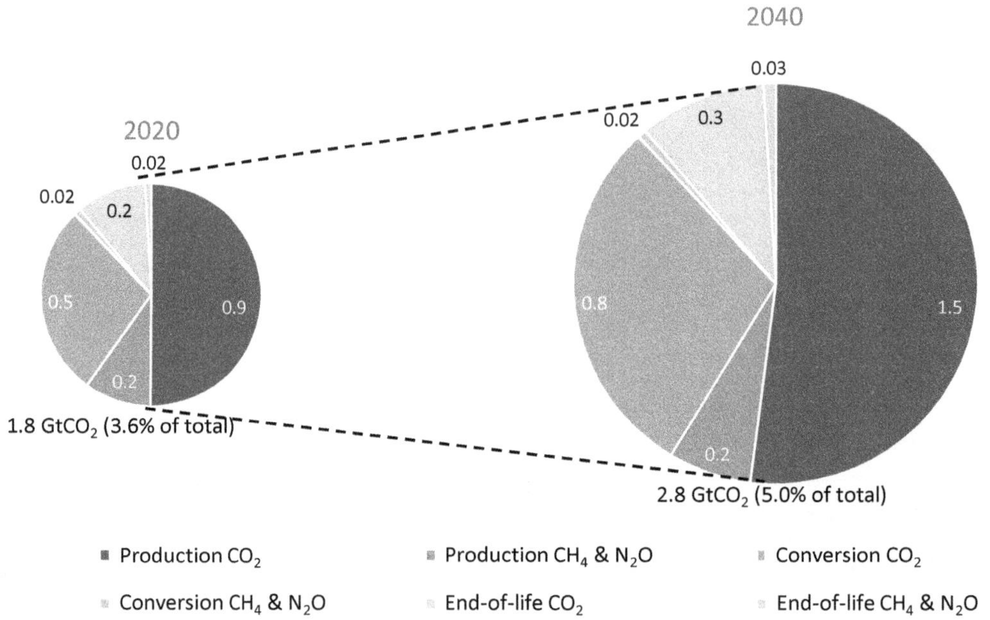

Notes: CH_4=methane; CO_2= carbon dioxide; N_2O=nitrous oxide. Shares of total plastics-related GHG emissions are also displayed.
Source: OECD ENV-Linkages model.

StatLink https://stat.link/0id8ch

Plastic pollution encompasses all emissions and risks resulting from the plastics lifecycle. This includes leakage to the environment, GHG emissions, as well as wide variety of other impacts such as resource scarcity, land use, ozone formation and toxicity (Figure 2.10). As discussed in OECD (2022[1]), in the absence of new policies, the environmental and health impacts of plastics will continue to worsen.

Of particular concern for human health is the presence of chemicals that may be present in plastics. Chemical additives are combined with plastic polymers during manufacturing to enhance performance and can include colourants, matting agents, opacifiers and lustre additives to change appearance, inorganic fillers (e.g. carbon or silica) to reinforce the plastic material, thermal stabilizers, plasticizers to render the material pliable and flexible, fire retardants to discourage ignition and burning, and stabilizers to increase resistance to UV degradation (Andrady and Neal, 2009[8]). Overall, more than 16 000 chemicals have been associated with plastics, of which only less than 6% are regulated worldwide (Wagner et al., 2024[9]). More than 4 200 plastic chemicals are of concern because they are persistent, bioaccumulative, mobile, and/or toxic (Wagner et al., 2024[9]).

Human exposure may occur notably during the plastics use phase, e.g. as consumers come in direct contact with food contact materials or consumer products. Exposure can also occur indirectly as humans and biota are exposed to chemicals released from plastics, exposure to microplastics via ingestion or inhalation. Workers who handle plastics are also at risk of chemical exposure. The hazardous properties of these chemicals include carcinogenicity, mutagenicity, reproductive toxicity, specific target organ toxicity, endocrine disruption, ecotoxicity, bioaccumulation potential, environmental persistence and mobility, including the potential for long-range environmental transport to remote locations (UNEP and BRS Secretariat, 2023[10]; Landrigan et al., 2023[11]).

Figure 2.10. Lifecycle impacts are projected to amplify for all polymers

Impacts per million tonne (Mt) of polymer in 2060

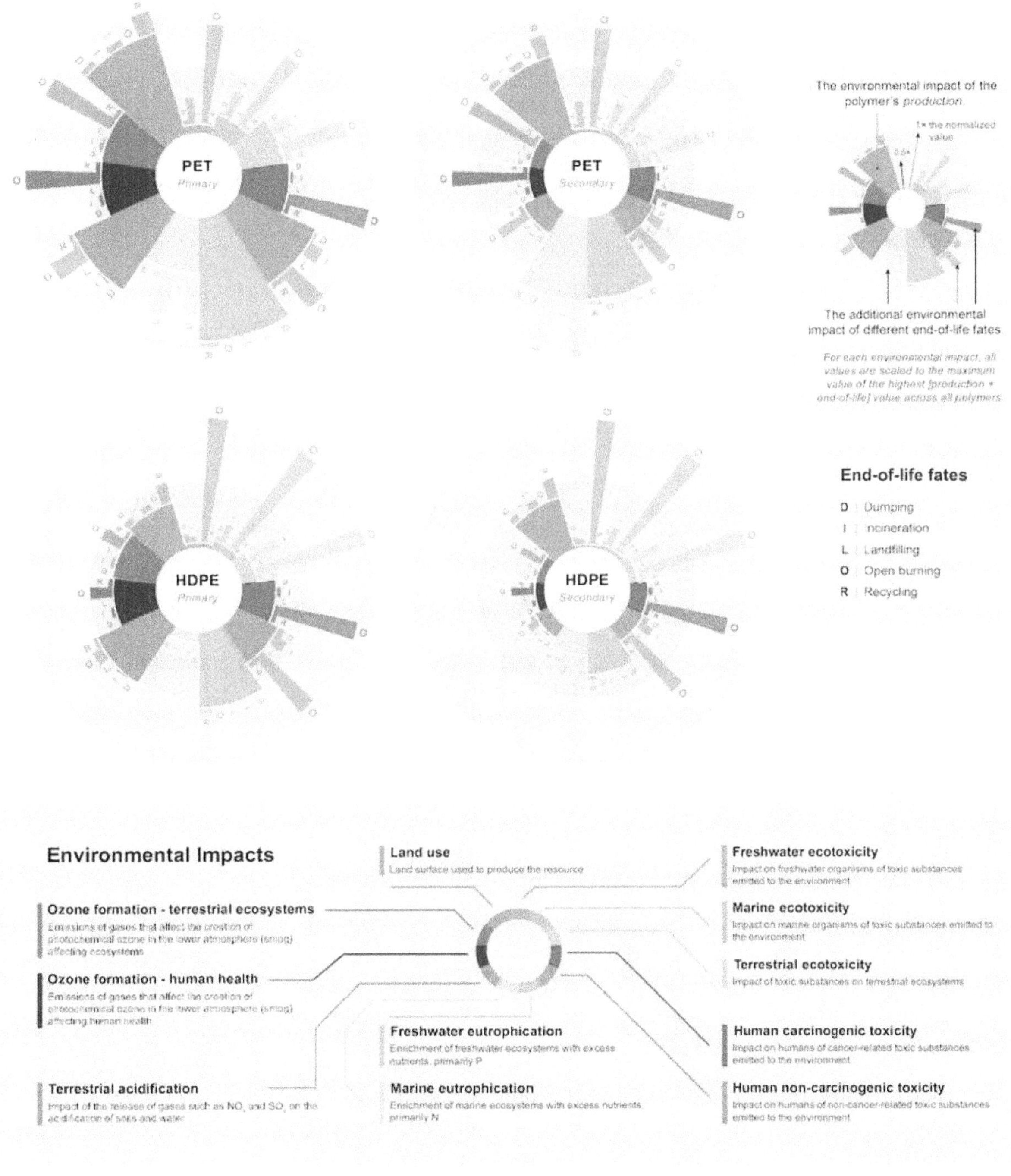

Note: Results from a global level lifecycle assessment (LCA) for a previous version of the *Baseline* scenario in the Global Plastics Outlook.
Source: (OECD, 2022[1]).

References

Andrady, A. and M. Neal (2009), "Applications and societal benefits of plastics", *Philos Trans R Soc Lond B Biol Sci.*, Vol. 364/1526, pp. 1977-84, https://doi.org/10.1098/rstb.2008.0304. [8]

European Commission, DG for Research and Innovation (2021), *Biodegradability of plastics in the open environment,* Publications Office of the European Union, https://doi.org/10.2777/690248. [3]

IEA (2023), *China's petrochemical surge is driving global oil demand growth*, https://www.iea.org/commentaries/china-s-petrochemical-surge-is-driving-global-oil-demand-growth, Licence: CC BY 4.0 (accessed on 4 March 2024). [6]

IEA (2023), *Oil 2023*, https://www.iea.org/reports/oil-2023. [7]

Karali, N., N. Khanna and N. Shah (2024), *Climate Impact of Primary Plastic Production.*, https://escholarship.org/uc/item/12s624vf. [5]

Landrigan et al. (2023), "The Minderoo-Monaco Commission on Plastics and Human Health", *Ann.als of Global Health*, Vol. 89 (1)/23, https://doi.org/10.5334/aogh.4056. [11]

Lebreton, L. (2024), *Quantitative analysis of aquatic leakage for multiple scenarios based on ENV-Linkages*, unpublished. [4]

OECD (2022), *Global Plastics Outlook: Economic Drivers, Environmental Impacts and Policy Options*, OECD Publishing, Paris, https://doi.org/10.1787/de747aef-en. [2]

OECD (2022), *Global Plastics Outlook: Policy Scenarios to 2060*, OECD Publishing, Paris, https://doi.org/10.1787/aa1edf33-en. [1]

UNEP and BRS Secretariat (2023), *Chemicals in Plastics: A Technical Report.* [10]

Wagner, M. et al. (2024), *State of the science on plastic chemicals - Identifying and addressing chemicals and polymers of concern*, https://doi.org/10.5281/zenodo.10701706. [9]

Notes

[1] There is a strong link between socio-economic development and materials use, including plastics, as materials are an important input for all production processes. The OECD's Global Plastics Outlook (2022[1]) details projections to 2060 for socio-economic trends underlying the *Baseline* scenario, including the evolution in regional populations, gross domestic product, the structure of the economy and production technologies.

[2] The modelling framework is not capable of tracking substitutions between polymers over time at the application level and thus polymer growth rates are driven by the growth rates of the applications, which are in turn linked to the growth of the associated economic activities.

[3] Similarly, some plastic litter is collected after littering, e.g. through street sweeping, and then still sorted and treated. Uncollected litter is included in mismanaged waste.

3 Modelling policy packages to mitigate plastic pollution

This chapter describes the policy levers used in the various scenarios to revert the trends expected in the *Baseline* scenario and chart pathways for eliminating plastic pollution. It highlights how the modelling analysis combines ten different policy instruments, grouped into four policy pillars (curb production and demand, design for circularity, enhance recycling and close leakage pathways), in the design of alternative policy scenarios with various degrees of policy ambition. Policy scenarios are characterised by different levels of stringency, lifecycle scope and geographical coverage of the ten policies modelled.

3.1. Introduction

Growing awareness of the adverse impacts associated with the plastics lifecycle has led policymakers and governments worldwide to seek out effective policy instruments that could counter the current unsustainable trends described in Chapter 2. In this sense, a range of policy interventions that can mitigate plastics-related adverse impacts, including the leakage of plastic waste and litter to the environment, are available to policymakers.

Figure 3.1. Policy levers to reduce plastic pollution

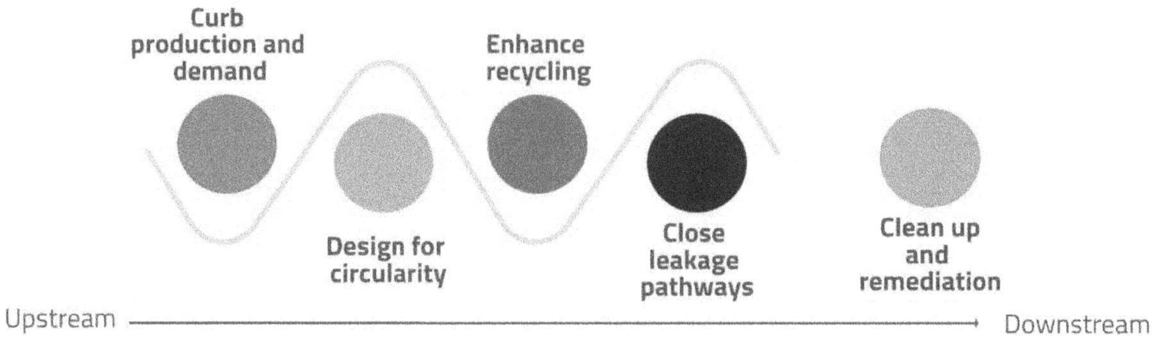

Source: Authors' own elaboration.

Countries have a wide array of policy tools at their disposal to mitigate plastic pollution. As described in Chapter 1, policy interventions influence several stages of the plastics lifecycle and can be grouped into four core policy pillars:[1]

1. **Curb production and demand**: restrain production and demand at sustainable levels. Existing and potential policy instruments that could achieve this objective include avoiding the production and use of unnecessary and problematic plastics, such as via bans, standards, phaseouts or taxes; promoting longer product lifespans; mandatory reuse systems and a shift of demand to services; taxes and regulations applying to all plastics to discourage the production of primary polymers; removal of fossil fuel subsidies. Controls on the production of virgin plastics, e.g. of specific polymers, could also be an effective strategy for reducing environmental impacts associated with the upstream segments of the plastics lifecycle, as well as curbing plastics use and slowing the flow of plastics through the economy.
2. **Design for circularity**: make production process for plastics more circular, for instance via restrictions or phaseouts on problematic materials and hazardous chemicals; Extended Producer Responsibility (EPR) with fee modulation; recycled content standards; eco-design criteria for reuse of packaging and durables, or to improve repairability and substitution away from plastics (where environmentally beneficial); eco-design criteria to prevent microplastic leakage during product use.
3. **Enhance recycling**: close material loops by improving separate collection, sorting and recycling of plastic waste. Relevant instruments include landfill and incineration taxes, EPR for packaging and durables; deposit-refund schemes (DRS), pay-as-you-throw schemes.
4. **Close leakage pathways**: decrease losses into the environment, including by setting up well-functioning collection systems and treatment infrastructure; enhancing municipal litter management; addressing sea-based leakage sources, such as abandoned, lost or discarded fishing gear; improving end-of-pipe capture (e.g. wastewater treatment); improving policies to mitigate the leakage of microplastics, such as upstream interventions to mitigate pellet loss during manufacturing and transport, eco-design measures to reduce microplastics emissions, or downstream interventions to capture emitted microplastics.

A fifth lever concerns **clean up and remediation**, i.e. the removal of plastic from the environment (e.g. via collection on beaches or via the installation of river litter booms that capture plastics) and the mitigation of associated risks. Evaluation of this approach is not included in the policy scenarios used in this report, which focus on the objective of preventing plastic leakage to the environment, and is left for future analysis.

While a wide range of policies could be employed by countries to reduce plastic pollution, only a selection of the instruments listed above has been used in the development of policy scenarios presented in the next sections. Section 3.2 introduces the policy scenarios, including the policy mix modelled and the degrees of policy ambition across the various scenarios.

Alternative policy measures vary in focus: some policy instruments are specific to plastics (e.g. single-use plastic bans and taxes), while others address a wider spectrum of waste or material types (e.g. landfill taxes that discourage disposal of solid waste and promote recycling more generally). There are also opportunities to leverage sectoral policies, such as those related to chemicals or waste management as well as policies designed to address specific externalities, like carbon taxes.

No single policy instrument operates effectively in isolation, and individual measures should constitute part of broader policy mixes that combine mutually reinforcing and complementary tools. Certain policies (e.g. EPR schemes) can contribute to pursuing multiple policy objectives. Economic instruments, such as EPR approaches and plastics, landfill and incineration taxes, work in tandem with regulations, such as product bans, product standards for eco-design, mandatory separate collection of waste and landfill bans. Enabling policies are of central importance in a comprehensive policy approach, including investments in research and development, information, education, nudging and stakeholder alliances.

Countries will need to expand and strengthen policy packages and select the instruments from across the four levers above that are best suited to their specific circumstances. Some countries may require the establishment of efficient waste collection and treatment systems as the most critical first step towards safe and effective plastic waste management. Meanwhile, countries with well-established waste management systems may focus more on internalising negative externalities more effectively, for instance via the use of advanced policy instruments such as pay-as-you-throw schemes or EPR schemes with modulated fees. Overall, a single blueprint to apply to all countries does not exist: rather a multitude of tailored approaches will need to be developed according to the environmental, economic and social features of specific country contexts, contingent on the stringency required to achieve global ambitions.

3.2. Policy scenarios to chart alternative paths to eliminating plastic pollution

The analysis in this report considers alternative policy scenarios that reflect issues and positions that have arisen in the context of ongoing international negotiations for a legally binding instrument to end plastic pollution. The policy scenarios modelled in this analysis vary in terms of their geographical coverage, the stringency of their domestic policy mixes, as well as the scope of policy coverage along the plastics lifecycle.

In the complex international landscape, countries offer diverging perspectives on the possible elements of a global instrument on plastic pollution, including with respect to its scope and the foreseen policy measures to implement. Some countries call for comprehensive approaches targeting all lifecycle stages, while others would prioritise downstream interventions (such as improving waste collection, sorting, treatment and municipal litter management) and opt for less stringent interventions upstream and midstream (such as curbing production and demand and designing for circularity). Similarly, enhanced policy action could be limited to a subset of countries that implement more ambitious policies than other countries. Finally, negotiations could result in global action with a broad coverage of policies along the plastics lifecycle and significant global engagement, but with limited policy stringency.

Specifically, three hypothetical scenarios with partial ambition are simulated to reflect the implications of specific directions the treaty that is being negotiated could pursue:

- The ***Global Downstream High stringency*** policy scenario reflects a possible outcome of treaty negotiations focused on targets and approaches for waste management (i.e. pillar 3 on enhancing recycling, and pillar 4 on closing leakage pathways). This includes stringent policies to improve waste collection, sorting, recycling as well as litter collection and municipal litter clean-up. Policy action to curb production and demand and to design for circularity is limited to current policies (i.e. no additional action is taken on pillars 1 and 2).
- The ***Advanced economies Lifecycle High stringency*** policy scenario models a situation where, in the absence of common, global targets, only select countries enhance policy stringency along the lifecycle of plastics. More specifically, a group of advanced economies (approximated as OECD and European Union countries) implement policies with a high level of policy stringency across all four policy pillars, while other countries do not go beyond the improvements already expected in the *Baseline* scenario.
- The ***Global Lifecycle Low stringency*** policy scenario reflects a possible outcome of the treaty negotiations with broad lifecycle coverage but low policy stringency. This scenario models additional, but more incremental policy action in all countries across all four pillars, but with limited policy stringency.

Two additional hypothetical policy scenarios are constructed that combine multiple aspects of the scenarios presented above. These integrated, high ambition scenarios entail more stringent policy action taken in all world regions and along multiple stages of the plastics lifecycle.

- The ***Global Lifecycle Mixed stringency*** policy scenario combines the three individual scenarios outlined above. It reflects a treaty outcome characterised by moderate alignment across countries on the lifecycle scope of policies. Countries in this scenario agree to pursue all three aspects of the partial ambition scenarios above, but do not move beyond these. Advanced economies implement policies with high stringency throughout the plastics lifecycle (aligned with *Advanced economies Lifecycle High stringency*), while other countries implement high stringency for pillars 3 and 4 (aligned with *Global Downstream High stringency*) and limited stringency for pillars 1 and 2 (aligned with *Global Lifecycle Low stringency*).
- The ***Global Lifecycle High stringency*** [*Global Ambition*] policy scenario models a comprehensive and co-ordinated approach that entails a global ramp up of policy action across the lifecycle of plastics, aligned with the shared objective of ending plastic pollution by 2040. In the model, this is reflected as the (narrower) target to mitigate plastic waste mismanagement and end macroplastic leakage by 2040.[2] Compared to the *Global Lifecycle Mixed stringency* scenario, more stringent upstream and midstream policies would be implemented in non-OECD, non-EU countries, thus aligning their degree of policy ambition for all four policy pillars with the ambitions of the Advanced economies.

3.2.1. Policy scenario set-up

A simple visual representation of the various scenarios is given in Figure 3.2. In the *Baseline* scenario, only current policies are adopted. The three scenarios with limited co-ordination differ in geographical and lifecycle scope on which policy stringency focuses. The *Global Downstream High stringency* scenario limits the lifecycle scope to a focus on downstream measures with global coverage. The *Advanced economies Lifecycle High stringency* scenario covers policies targeting multiple stages of the plastics lifecycle, but in a limited group of countries. The *Global Lifecycle Low stringency* scenario is characterised by full regional coverage and lifecycle scope but less ambitious policy stringency. The *Global Lifecycle Mixed stringency* scenario combines elements of these three partial ambition scenarios, but leaves a stringency gap for upstream and midstream measures in the countries that are not part of the *Advanced economies Lifecycle High stringency* scenario. Finally, the only scenario with full policy stringency across all policy pillars in all regions is the *Global Lifecycle High stringency* [*Global Ambition*] scenario.

Figure 3.2. Visual summary of the policy scenarios

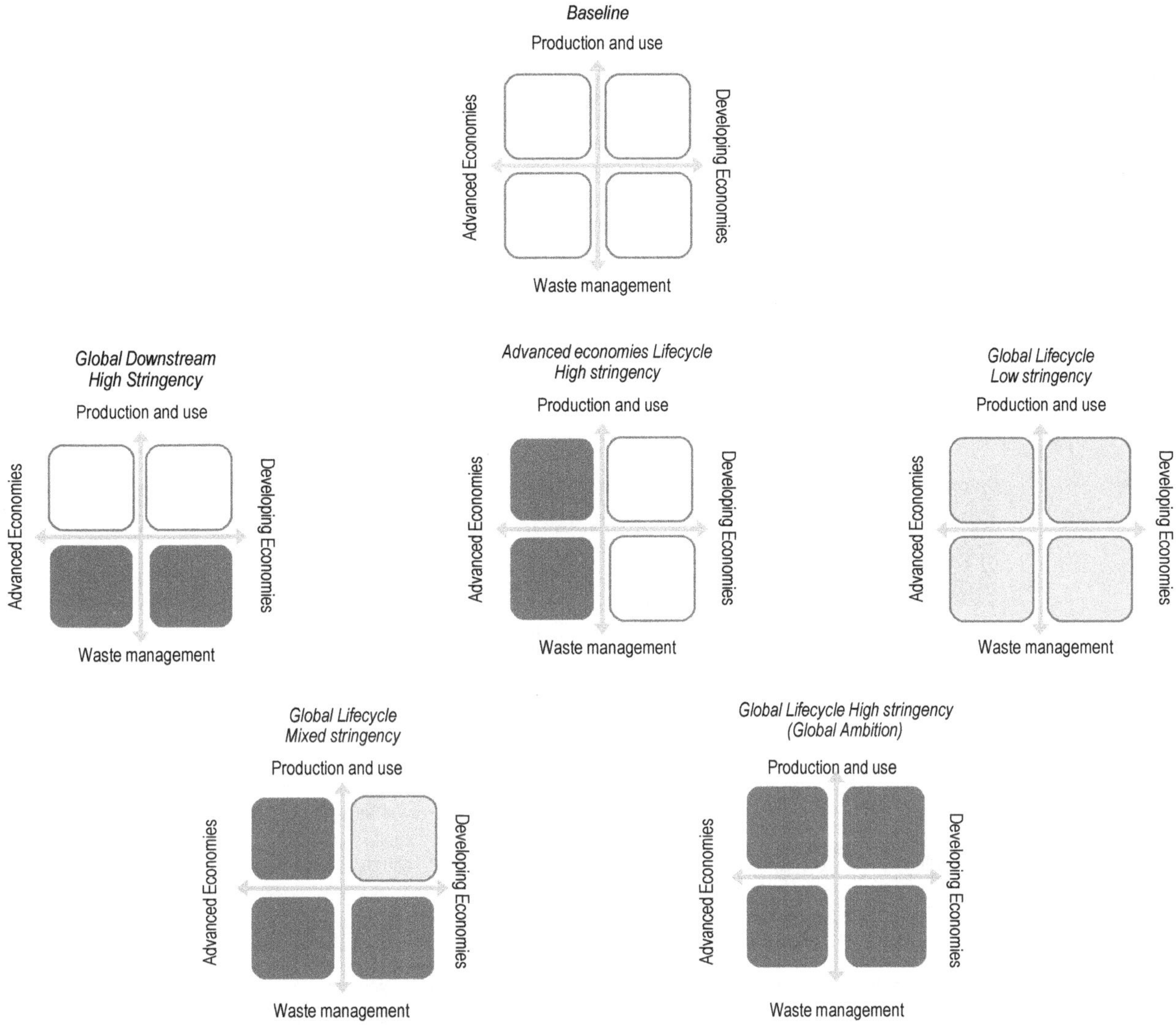

Note: Empty boxes reflect current policy assumptions, light shaded boxes reflect limited policy stringency and dark shaded boxes reflect high policy stringency.
Source: Authors' own elaboration.

3.2.2. Policy instruments modelled

Although degrees of policy stringency and geographical coverage of the policy package vary across scenarios, all scenarios involve (a subset of) ten policy instruments across the four key policy pillars: curb production and demand, design for circularity, enhance recycling and close leakage pathways. The ten different instruments used in the policy scenarios are presented in Figure 3.3. Depending on the scenario, the ten policy instruments or a subset of those are quantified to provide inputs to the modelling. The quantification in the *Global Lifecycle High stringency* [*Global Ambition*] scenario is also provided in Figure 3.3 as an example, while details on the quantification of the other scenarios are presented in Annex B.

Figure 3.3. Policy instruments modelled in the policy scenarios

	Curb production and demand		Design for circularity		
Policy instrument	Packaging plastics tax	Non-packaging plastics tax	Eco-design for durability and repair	Bans on select single-use plastics	Substitute away from plastics
Stringency modelled in Global Lifecycle High stringency [Global Ambition]	**Global:** USD 1 000/tonne by 2030, doubling by 2040	**Global:** USD 750/tonne by 2030, doubling by 2040	**Global:** 15% lifespan increase by 2030, constant after; 10-20% decrease in demand for durables by 2030, constant after; like increase in demand for repair services	**Global:** Phase-out of primary plastics for selected consumer products by 2030	**Global:** 17% reduction of plastics use in production by 2030 with compensating increase in use of other inputs, constant thereafter

	Enhance recycling			Close leakage pathways	
Policy instrument	Recycled content targets	Enhance recycling rates	EPR for packaging, electronics, automotive and wearable apparel	Improved waste collection	Improved litter management
Stringency modelled in Global Lifecycle High stringency [Global Ambition]	**Global:** 30% target by 2040	*Targets* **EU, Japan, Korea:** 60% by 2030, 80% by 2060 **Rest of OECD, China:** 60% by 2040 **Rest of non-OECD:** 45% by 2040	**Global:** Tax on plastics inputs USD 300/tonne by 2030, constant after; 30% point increase in recycling by 2040; waste sector subsidy such that instrument is budget neutral	**Global:** All waste is adequately collected and managed by 2040	**Global:** Increase in collection rates between 5%-points (high-income countries) and 10%-points (low-income countries) by 2040

Note: The choice of policy instruments modelled in the policy scenarios is not intended to be prescriptive, but rather indicative of a potential set of effective instruments that could be implemented. For instance, the packaging tax translates into roughly EUR 0.90 per kilogramme, and could be interpreted as a shadow-price for alternative instruments to curb production and demand. Furthermore, in the pillar "Design for circularity", the ban on single-use plastics models measures to restrict or reduce the use of avoidable or unnecessary plastics. In the policy scenarios that include it, the measure is modelled as a 20% global reduction in the use of polypropylene (PP) in consumer and institutional products, based on a representative set of consumer products covered by the European Union's Single Use Plastic Directive (e.g. plastic bags, straws, cutlery). In practice, measures to restrict avoidable or unnecessary plastics could have a coverage that varies across different countries.
Source: Authors' own elaboration.

The policy scenarios presented in this report present the consequences of different configurations of policy mixes. For modelling purposes, they are based on a representative set of ten policy instruments (see Figure 3.3). These instruments constitute a cost-effective benchmark against which countries can evaluate alternative instruments. Bringing together the dimensions of the policy pillars and the policy scenarios, Figure 3.4 presents a schematic overview of the implied stringency of the various policy scenarios by pillar. These outcomes are presented using indicators that are – at least roughly – representative of the ambitions of the different pillars in terms of policy stringency.[3] If alternative policy instruments are chosen, these implied stringencies can be a guide to the required ambition level of alternative policy choices.

Figure 3.4. Overview of the implied policy stringency of the different pillars in the policy scenarios

		Curb production and demand	Design for circularity	Enhance recycling	Close leakage pathways
	Indicator	Primary plastics use	Plastics intensity	Recycling rate	Macroplastic leakage
Limited ambition scenarios	**Global Downstream High stringency**	***Global:*** Current policies	***Global:*** Current policies	***Global:*** Quadruple to 42%	***Advanced economies:*** Eliminate ***Other economies:*** 30% below 2020
Limited ambition scenarios	**Advanced economies Lifecycle High stringency**	***Advanced economies:*** Stabilise below 2020 ***Other economies:*** Current policies	***Advanced economies:*** 25% below 2020 ***Other economies:*** Current policies	***Advanced economies:*** Quadruple to 46% ***Other economies:*** Current policies	***Advanced economies:*** Eliminate ***Other economies:*** Current policies
Limited ambition scenarios	**Global Lifecycle Low stringency**	***Advanced economies:*** 15% above 2020 ***Other economies:*** 65% above 2020	***Global:*** 10% below 2020	***Advanced economies:*** Triple to 29% ***Other economies:*** Double to 22%	***Advanced economies:*** Eliminate ***Other economies:*** 25% above 2020
Integrated, high ambition scenarios	**Global Lifecycle Mixed stringency**	***Advanced economies:*** Stabilise below 2020 ***Other economies:*** 65% above 2020	***Advanced economies:*** 25% below 2020 ***Other economies:*** 10% below 2020	***Global:*** Quadruple to 42%	***Advanced economies:*** Eliminate ***Other economies:*** 30% below 2020
Integrated, high ambition scenarios	**Global Lifecycle High stringency [Global Ambition]**	***Global:*** Stabilise below 2020	***Global:*** 25% below 2020	***Global:*** Quadruple to 42%	***Global:*** Eliminate

Notes: 1. "Advanced econ." reflects the group of countries that have a high ambition level in the *Advanced economies Lifecycle High stringency* scenario; they are by assumption approximated as OECD and non-OECD European Union in the model. "Other econ." reflects countries not included in the "Advanced economies" group.
2. Plastics intensity (tonnes/USD) refers to the intensity of plastics use relative to GDP. It is a normalised indicator that allows for comparison of plastics use across countries and regions and over time.
Source: Authors' own elaboration.

3.3. Overview of the modelling framework for the projections of plastic flows

The modelling of economic flows, plastics use, plastic waste and environmental impacts involves several steps, as illustrated in Figure 3.5. Plastics production and use is linked to sectoral and regional economic projections, which drive the evolution of plastics use over time. Volumes of plastics are then used to calculate generated waste based on product lifespans of different applications. Trade in plastics is also taken into account. The amount of waste generated is further broken down by waste end-of-life fate, i.e. collected for recycling, recycled, incinerated, landfilled, mismanaged and littered waste, taking into account differences across regions. Calculation of waste treatment fates also includes an assessment of recycling losses, i.e. plastic that is collected for recycling but is in the end incinerated or landfilled, as well as a reattribution of collected litter to other fates. Finally, projections are made for a subset of environmental impacts, including leakage of macroplastics to the terrestrial environment, leakage to aquatic environments and emissions of greenhouse gases (GHG).

The analysis relies on a suite of modelling tools. More specifically, projections of the economic flows, plastics production and use, plastic waste, and greenhouse gas emissions rely the OECD ENV-Linkages model, while projections of aquatic leakage rely on calculations made by Lebreton (2024[1]). These modelling tools are described in more detail in Annex A.

Figure 3.5. Methodological steps in the modelling framework

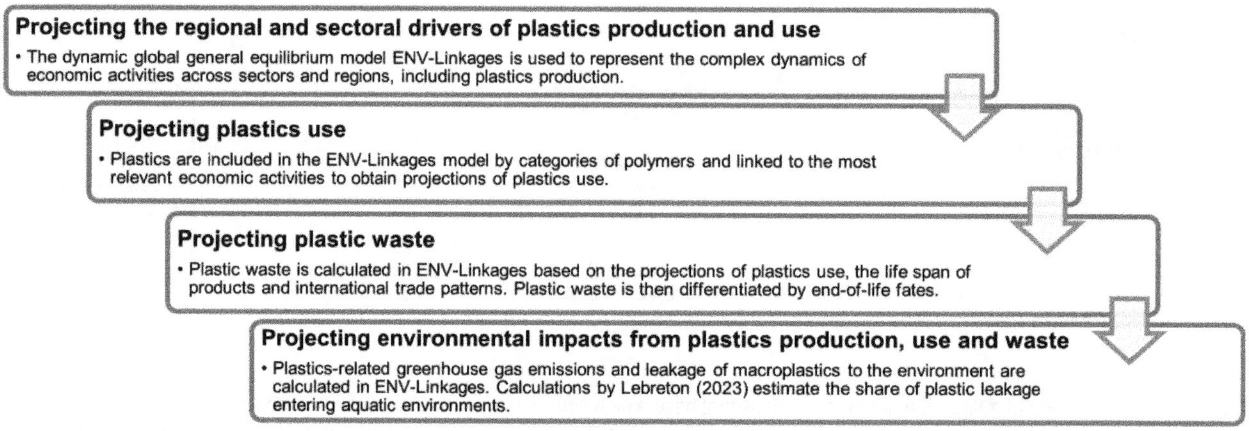

Source: Authors' own elaboration.

A detailed description of the treatment of plastics in the model is provided in OECD (2022[2]). Plastics flows are differentiated by polymer and application (Table 3.1).

Table 3.1. Mapping of plastics use by application to economic sectors

Input sectors	Applications	Output sectors	Polymers*
Plastic products	Building & Construction	Construction	ABS, ASA, SAN; Bioplastics; HDPE; LDPE, LLDPE; PP; PS; PUR; PVC; Other
	Consumer & Institutional products	Accommodation and food service activities; Air transport; Education; Health; Insurance; Lumber; Non-metallic minerals; Business services; Other manufacturing; Public services; Land transport; Pulp, paper and publishing; Real estate; Textile; Water transport	ABS, ASA, SAN; Bioplastics; HDPE; LDPE, LLDPE; PP; PS; PUR; PVC; Other
	Electrical/Electronic	Electrical equipment; electronics	ABS, ASA, SAN; Bioplastics; HDPE; LDPE, LLDPE; PP; PS; PUR; PVC; Other
	Industrial/Machinery	Fabricated metal products; iron and steel; nonferrous metal; Machinery and equipment	HDPE; LDPE, LLDPE; PP; PUR
	Packaging	Food products; Chemical products	Bioplastics; HDPE; LDPE, LLDPE; PET; PP; PS; PUR; PVC; Other
	Personal care products	Chemical products	HDPE; PET
	Transportation - other	Motor vehicles; Public services; Other transport equipment	ABS, ASA, SAN; Bioplastics; Fibres; HDPE; LDPE, LLDPE; PP; PUR; PVC; Other
	Other	Other sectors	Other
Chemicals	Marine coatings	Other manufacturing, other transport equipment	Marine coatings
	Road markings	Construction	Road markings
	Textile sector - clothing	Textiles	Bioplastics; fibres
	Textile sector - other	Textiles	Fibres
	Transportation - tyres	Plastic products	Elastomers (tyres)

Note: ABS = acrylonitrile butadiene styrene; ASA = acrylonitrile styrene acrylate; HDPE = high-density polyethylene; LDPE = low-density polyethylene; LLDPE = linear low-density polyethylene; PET = polyethylene terephthalate; PP = polypropylene; PS = polystyrene; PUR = polyurethane; PVC = polyvinyl chloride; SAN = styrene acrylonitrile.
Source: OECD ENV-Linkages model.

Regional leakage of macroplastics to the environment is calculated using the methodology described in OECD (2022[2]). Specifically, macroplastic leakage stems from three distinct sources: (i) leakage of mismanaged waste, (ii) leakage of littered items and (iii) leakage from marine activities. The former two sources of leakage respond to changes in waste management systems, while the latter is proportional to marine economic activities (and is thus similar across scenarios). Finally, note that providing projections of microplastic leakage and projections of the regional production of plastics extend beyond the scope of the current analysis, although the modelling framework does account for global projections of plastics production (see Box 1.1 in Chapter 1).

References

Lebreton, L. (2024), *Quantitative analysis of aquatic leakage for multiple scenarios based on ENV-Linkages*, unpublished. [1]

OECD (2022), *Global Plastics Outlook: Economic Drivers, Environmental Impacts and Policy Options*, OECD Publishing, Paris, https://doi.org/10.1787/de747aef-en. [3]

OECD (2022), *Modelling plastics in ENV-Linkages: A novel approach to projecting future plastics use and waste*, https://www.oecd.org/environment/plastics/Technical-Report-Modelling-plastics-in-ENV-Linkages.pdf. [2]

Notes

[1] This list is adapted from the policy roadmap presented in (OECD, 2022[3]).

[2] A variant of the *Global Lifecycle High stringency* [*Global Ambition*] scenario is the *Global Lifecycle Delayed stringency* scenario. The latter models the implementation of the policy package of the *Global Lifecycle High stringency* scenario over an extended timeframe, towards a 2060 target for the elimination of leakage.

[3] These indicators are thus not inputs in the scenario implementation, but outputs that reflect the stringency of the ten policy instruments. The numerical implementation of the policy scenarios in the modelling framework is done for the ten instruments and details of their implementation are presented in Figure 3.3 for the *Global Lifecycle High stringency* [*Global Ambition*] scenario and in Annex B for all scenarios.

4 Implications of policy scenarios with partial ambition

This chapter explores modelling scenarios with partial global ambition, defined in terms of limited policy stringency, partial coverage of the policies along the lifecycle of plastics, or incomplete global geographical coverage of policy measures. It presents projections of the plastics lifecycle for each scenario, highlighting that policy action can significantly reduce plastics use and environmental impacts below levels expected in the *Baseline* scenario by 2040, but all partial ambition scenarios presented in this chapter fall short of eliminating the leakage of plastics to the environment.

4.1. Introduction

This chapter explores modelling scenarios that reflect stylised views of possible outcomes of the international negotiations when global ambition is partial. Each scenario is characterised by different levels of stringency across the various policy pillars, but all fall short of eliminating global plastic leakage by 2040.[1] Specifically, the scenarios investigate the consequences for plastics use, waste and leakage from policy action that Figure 4.1:

- is limited to downstream policies only (the *Global Downstream High stringency* policy scenario):[2]
- has geographical coverage limited to a group of advanced economies, approximated as OECD and non-OECD EU countries (the *Advanced economies Lifecycle High stringency* policy scenario):
- encompasses all lifecycle stages and all countries, but with limited stringency (the *Global Lifecycle Low stringency* policy scenario).

Figure 4.1. Policy scenarios with partial ambition

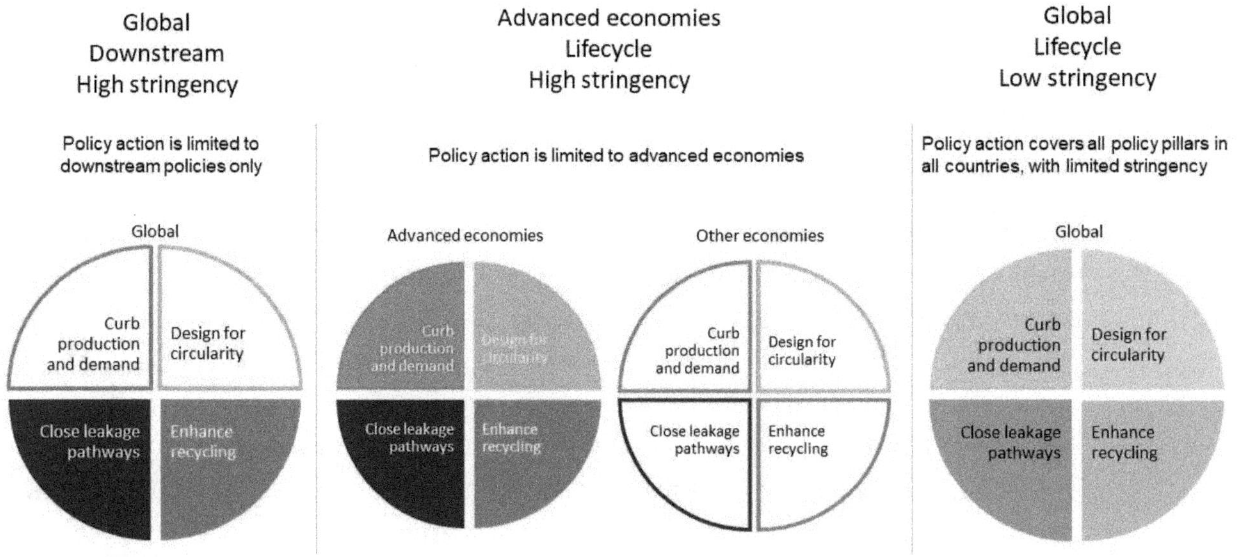

Source: Authors' own elaboration

4.2. In the absence of strong, common commitments for reduction, plastics use and waste generation is at best slowed compared to the *Baseline*

The three partial ambition scenarios vary significantly in the stringency of policy measures to curb production and demand and to improve design for circularity (the policy pillars that most directly affect plastics production and use). As a result, the effects on regional plastics exhibit significant differences across these scenarios. All three scenarios reduce plastics use – and waste generation – below *Baseline* levels in 2040, but these reductions tend to be quite limited and are furthermore insufficient to overcome growth in plastics use and waste in the *Baseline* compared to 2020 levels (Figure 4.2). The *Global Downstream High stringency* scenario does not contain any policies to curb production and demand and design for circularity. Some downstream policies, such as enhancing recycling, do affect plastics use by increasing the costs for primary plastics and by subsidising secondary plastics, however these effects are limited globally to 4.5% for plastics use and less than 3% for waste generation.

A comparison between use and waste generation in advanced economies in the *Advanced economies Lifecycle High stringency* and *Global Downstream High stringency* scenarios sheds light on the importance of upstream and midstream interventions in the policy mix, notably policies to curb production and demand and to foster eco-design. As expected, in the *Advanced economies Lifecycle High stringency* scenario, plastics use and waste are significantly reduced in OECD and EU countries in 2040 (by 28% and 22% relative to the *Baseline*, respectively), but remain largely unchanged in non-OECD, non-EU countries (+0.3% and -5%, respectively). The positive aspect of this result is that there is no significant leakage effect whereby ambitious policies in the advanced economies would lead to shifts in economic production that boost plastics use in other countries. Thus, the demand reductions in OECD and EU countries are effective and not mitigated by increases elsewhere. In fact, the policies to reduce demand in advanced economies lead to (i) a spillover effect of eco-design that extends the lifetimes of products globally and not only in advanced countries,[3] (ii) a reduction of plastics embedded in exports to other countries and (iii) a reduction in plastic waste exported to other countries.

Although the *Global Lifecycle Low stringency* scenario envisions enhanced policies across the plastics lifecycle, the scenario projects only modest decreases in plastics use (10%) and waste generation (7%) below *Baseline* levels in 2040. Somewhat larger reductions are observed in OECD countries, reflecting their higher capacity to implement stringent policies. Plastics use and waste generation levels would still increase in this scenario by 2040 (by 53% and 59%, respectively, compared to 2020 levels).

Figure 4.2. Reductions in plastics use and waste below *Baseline* levels remain modest in the partial ambition scenarios

Percentage deviation from the *Baseline* in 2040

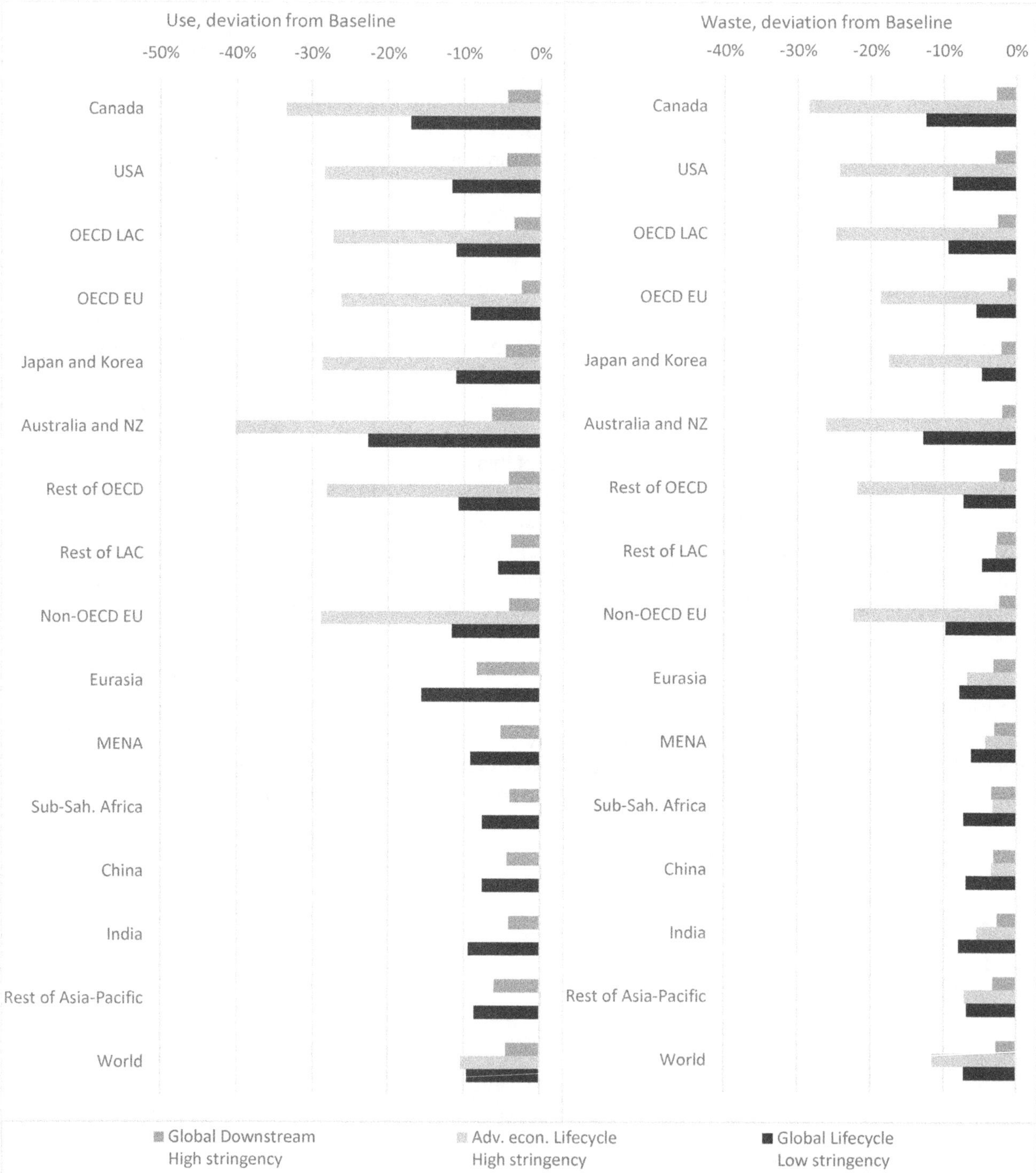

Note: "Adv. econ." stands for Advanced economies.
Source: OECD ENV-Linkages model.

StatLink https://stat.link/3j48uy

Plastics intensity, measured as plastics use (in million tonnes) divided by GDP (in million USD), can be used as an indicator of efficiency in the production and use of plastics in the economy. Improvements in plastics intensity reflect a decoupling of economic activity from plastics production and use, and is thus an indirect indicator of the effectiveness of the policy pillar on designing for circularity. In line with projections for plastics use, the largest gains in plastics intensity are achieved in scenarios that contain measures to curb production and demand and to enhance eco-design. Specifically, the *Advanced economies Lifecycle High stringency* scenario leads to a significant reduction in plastics intensity in OECD countries, but virtually none in non-OECD countries. The early implementation of selected policies by 2030 – most notably the plastics tax and EPR schemes – significantly contribute to rapidly reductions in plastics intensity, with some additional effects occurring the subsequent decade. The *Global Downstream High stringency* scenario does not directly aim at upstream demand control, but has indirect effects on plastics use that also affect plastics intensity, as policies to enhance recycling make primary plastics production more expensive (see above). The *Global Lifecycle Low stringency* scenario reduces plastics intensity more than the *Global Downstream High stringency* scenario, especially after 2030, when the effects from the upstream policies begin to manifest.

Figure 4.3. Policy action can amplify the decreasing trend in plastics intensity

Plastics use per unit of GDP, in tonnes of plastics per unit of sectoral output in USD (t/USD)

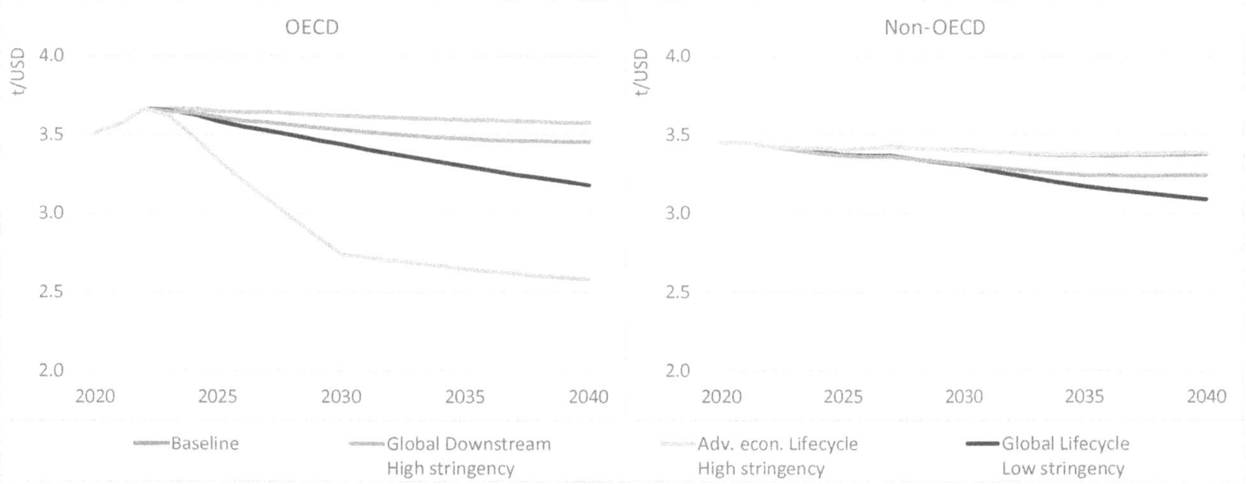

Note: The gradual decline in plastics intensity is driven by technological progress and structural change, as discussed in Chapter 2.
Source: OECD ENV-Linkages model.

StatLink https://stat.link/ysmx8c

4.3. The level and direction of policy ambition matters for waste treatment outcomes

The partial ambition scenarios all result in total waste volumes that are below *Baseline* levels in 2040, but well in excess of 2020 levels (as discussed above). With current policies (i.e. the *Baseline* scenario), this would mean increases in volumes of waste being recycled, incinerated and landfilled, but also increased volumes of mismanaged waste. Waste management shares, i.e. end-of-life fate shares, change only marginally in the *Baseline* scenario, including the reduction in the share of waste that is mismanaged in developing countries, due to rising income levels.[4] If the policy agreement is combined with limited international co-ordination and support for actions downstream in the plastics lifecycle, there may be risks of insufficient technical and financing support to manage waste effectively. Importantly, capacity building required in a number of developing countries to establish well-functioning waste management systems, including adopting the necessary policy and regulatory frameworks, set up strong governance mechanisms and ensure stable financing that cover the operational costs of waste collection and sorting.

Recycling output in all three partial ambition scenarios is projected to increase compared to the *Baseline* scenario owing to the implementation of policies that incentivise both the supply and demand of recycled plastics (e.g. recycled content requirements, recycling targets, EPR schemes). The global share of waste that is recycled increases from 9.5% in 2020 to 14% in 2040 in the *Baseline* scenario, 41% in the *Global Downstream High stringency* scenario, 27% in the *Advanced economies Lifecycle High stringency* scenario and 25% in the *Global Lifecycle Low stringency* scenario (Figure 4.4).[5] The largest increases in recycling output are foreseen in the *Global Downstream High stringency* scenario, thanks to a combination of significant improvements in waste collection, ambitious expansion of recycling infrastructure and a lack of measures to reduce waste streams. Specifically in non-OECD countries combined, the share of waste that is collected for recycling increases from 10% in 2020 to 38% in 2040 in the *Global Downstream High stringency* scenario. This also implies that significant scrap is available in this scenario to induce a shift from primary to secondary production, and thus most of the global growth in plastics use in this scenario is actually covered by secondary plastics.

In contrast, in OECD and EU countries the *Advanced economies Lifecycle High stringency* scenario achieves the same increase in recycling shares as the *Global Downstream High stringency* scenario, reaching 46% for this group of countries in both cases. The *Global Lifecycle Low stringency* scenario is less ambitious, reaching a recycling rate of 29% in OECD countries, and 22% in non-OECD countries. These findings illustrate that the broad agreement modelled in this scenario is indeed relatively shallow, resulting in less than a tripling of the recycling rate at the global level, versus a more than quadrupling in the *Global Downstream High stringency* scenario.

Another outcome of interest pertaining to end-of-life fate categories is mismanaged waste. The policy scenarios with the most stringent downstream policies achieve the best outcomes with respect to this measure. Specifically, the *Global Downstream High stringency* scenario reduces mismanaged waste in non-OECD countries from 81 million tonnes (Mt) in 2020 to 54 Mt in 2040 (a reduction of 55% compared to the *Baseline* level of 119 Mt in 2040), resulting in 9% of total waste that will remain mismanaged. The lack of measures to curb production and demand, and to slow down waste generation, implies that technical and economic barriers to collecting, sorting and (sanitarily) landfilling plastic waste in countries that have high levels of mismanaged waste in the *Baseline* scenario may prevent a full elimination of plastic leakage. This effect is also visible when comparing the *Global Downstream High stringency* scenario and the *Advanced economies Lifecycle High stringency* scenario for OECD regions: the latter scenario is more effective as it combines reductions in waste generation with improved collection and treatment. This results in virtually all mismanaged waste in OECD countries being eliminated in the *Advanced economies Lifecycle High stringency* scenario (with less than 1.5 Mt remaining in 2040), and a significant reduction in the *Global Downstream High stringency* scenario, with less than 3.5 Mt remaining in OECD countries (compared to almost 7 Mt in the *Baseline*). The main reason that some mismanaged waste remains in the *Advanced economies Lifecycle High stringency* scenario is that not all plastic waste can be collected; some streams evade the management system, such as waste from road markings, ghost fishing gear and uncollected litter.

Although the *Global Lifecycle Low stringency* scenario contains several incentives to reduce mismanaged waste below 2020 levels in all regions, significant amounts of mismanaged waste remain, especially in non-OECD countries: 50 Mt in 2040 vs 72 Mt in 2020.

Figure 4.4. Plastic waste end-of-life shares continue to diverge significantly across regions in the partial ambition scenarios

Shares of waste management categories as a percent of waste generated in 2040, by region

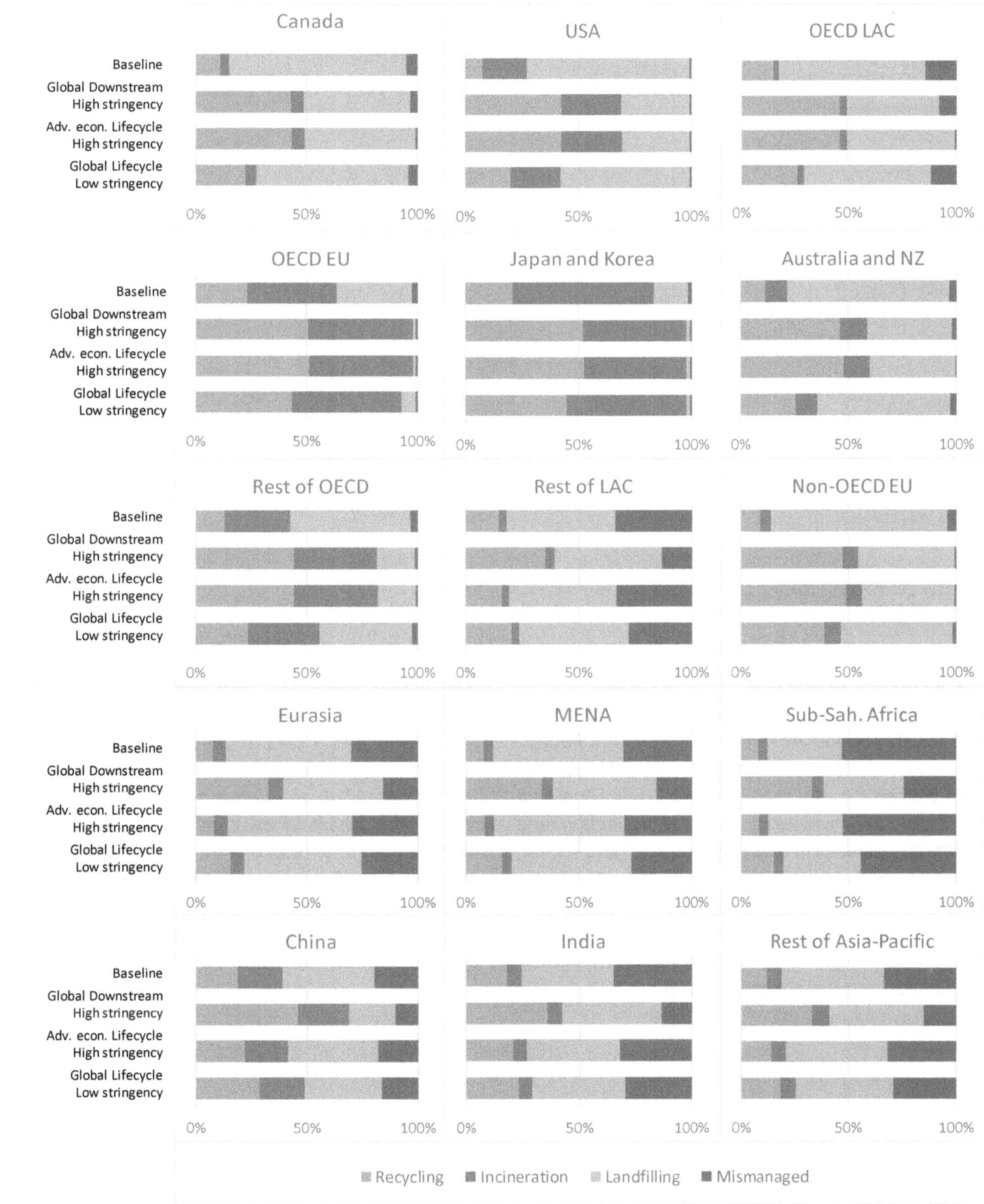

Source: OECD ENV-Linkages model.

StatLink https://stat.link/pi01a3

Figure 4.5. Improvements in waste collection, sorting and recycling are pivotal to enabling greater availability of secondary plastics

Secondary plastics in use in 2040 in million tonnes (Mt) across partial ambition scenarios, compared to 2020 levels and *Baseline*

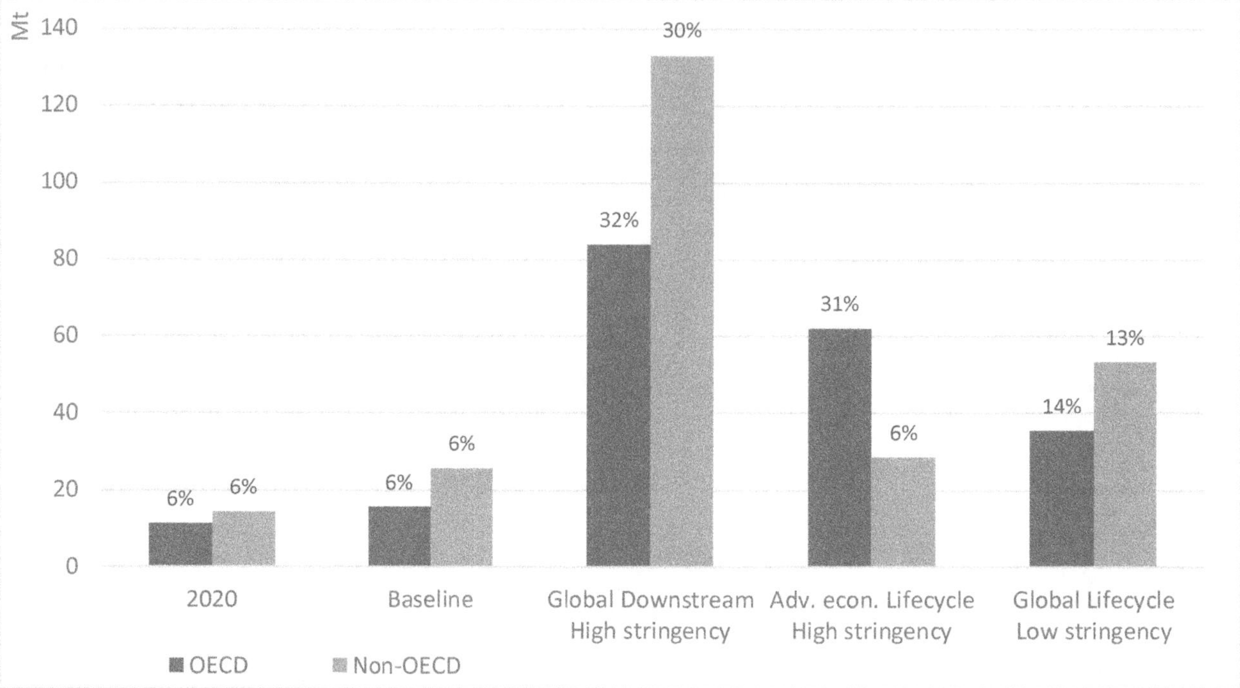

Note: The percentages above the bars present the share of secondary in total use.
Source: OECD ENV-Linkages model.

StatLink https://stat.link/5kqjd9

The increased supply of scrap in the policy scenarios modelled also allows for an expansion of secondary plastics production (Figure 4.5). Global demand for secondary plastics in 2040 is projected to be 3.5 times that in 2020 in the *Advanced economies Lifecycle High stringency* and *Global Lifecycle Low stringency* scenarios, and 8.5 times that in 2020 in the *Global Downstream High stringency* scenario (equalling more than 5 times the *Baseline* level for 2040). The *Global Downstream High stringency* scenario projects very significant improvements in waste collection and recycling that result in an increase in the share of secondary plastics in overall production and demand, from less than 6% in 2020 to more than 30% in 2040. This reflects the supply push for the transition to secondary plastics. The recycled content target policy in turn implies a demand pull for secondary plastics. For OECD countries, the share of secondary plastics is about as large in the *Advanced economies Lifecycle High stringency* scenario (31%) as in the *Global Downstream High stringency* scenario (32%), but the volume of secondary plastics is lower, as demand for plastics and the supply of scrap are both lower.

4.4. Significant plastic leakage remains in the scenarios with partial ambition

In the absence of more significant reductions of total plastics use at the global level (see Figure 4.2), improvements in recycling and secondary plastics production (see Figure 4.5) would remain insufficient to prevent growth in primary plastics production (Figure 4.6, left-hand panel). Hence, the environmental and human health effects associated with primary plastics production, such as dependence on fossil-based feedstock, production-related greenhouse gas (GHG) emissions and exposure to chemicals of concern, would remain significant. Furthermore, the significant remaining volume of mismanaged waste (Figure 4.6, right panel) implies that plastics continue to leak to terrestrial and aquatic environments.

Figure 4.6. The partial ambition scenarios at best slow down primary plastics use and cannot eliminate mismanaged plastic waste globally

In million tonnes (Mt)

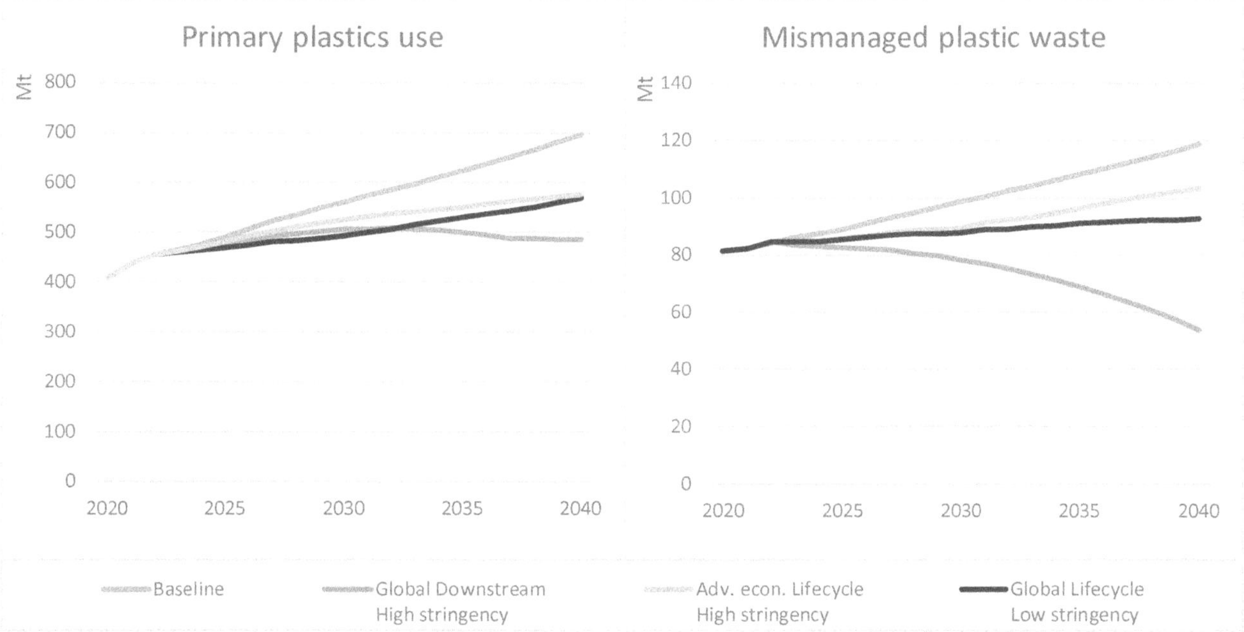

Source: OECD ENV-Linkages model.

StatLink https://stat.link/ebm27i

Of the three partial ambition scenarios, the *Global Downstream High stringency* scenario performs best in terms of limiting growth in GHG emissions from production and conversion (Figure 4.7). Although total plastics demand increases significantly from 2020 levels, a significant share of production comes from secondary plastics, and the GHG emissions from production and conversion are lower than in other scenarios. However, large waste volumes and high recycling rates combine to substantially increase the GHG emissions associated with end-of life waste management. Furthermore, in the absence of policies to curb primary production (which is the main driver of GHG emissions), the contribution of plastics to GHG emissions continues to increase substantially compared to 2020 levels: GHG emissions grow by 30% in 2040 (from 1.8 gigatonnes of carbon dioxide equivalent [$GtCO_2e$] in 2020 to 2.3 $GtCO_2e$). The other two scenarios perform similarly, closing the gap by roughly half between *Baseline* growth and stabilisation at 2020 levels.

Figure 4.7. The partial ambition scenarios increase annual plastics-related GHG emissions by almost one-third above 2020 levels

Greenhouse gas emissions from the plastics lifecycle in gigatonnes carbon dioxide equivalent ($GtCO_2e$)

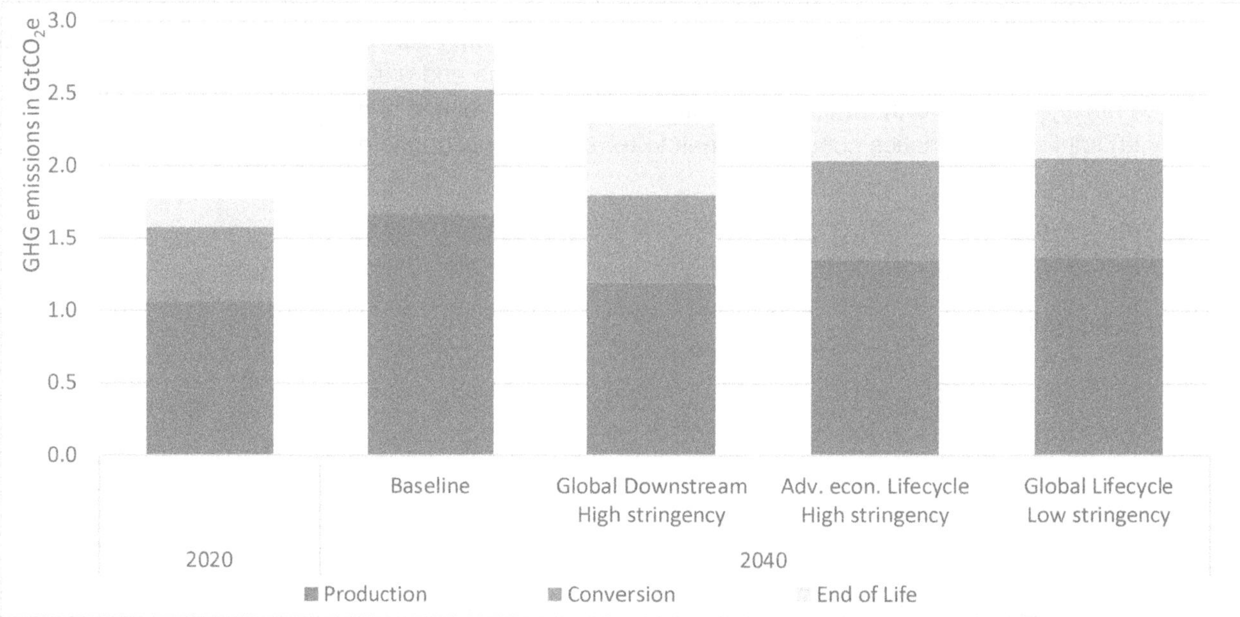

Source: OECD ENV-Linkages model.

StatLink https://stat.link/98l0ab

The efforts modelled in non-OECD countries to improve waste management – including collection, sorting and treatment – in the *Global Lifecycle Low stringency* and especially in the *Global Downstream High stringency* scenarios would be responsible for a large part of global reductions in plastic leakage below *Baseline* levels (Figure 4.8). The enhanced stringency of downstream policies in OECD and non-OECD countries combined in the *Global Downstream High stringency* scenario could prevent 129 Mt of additional plastics leaking to the environment between 2020-2040 compared to *Baseline*, which projects cumulative plastic leakage of 519 Mt between 2020 and 2040. Thus, a cumulative 390 Mt of plastics would still leak to the environment between 2020 and 2040 despite stringent downstream measures to enhance recycling and close leakage pathways. With annal leakage still well above 10 Mt in 2040, further leakage would also occur after 2040.

In the other partial ambition scenarios, the avoided leakage remains limited to 41 Mt in the *Advanced economies Lifecycle High stringency* scenario and 58 Mt in the *Global Lifecycle Low stringency* scenario. In both scenarios, leakage of plastics to the environment does not stabilise over time, and thus the associated environmental burden would continue to grow after 2040. In the *Advanced economies Lifecycle High stringency* scenario, stringent policy action is limited to countries that already have low shares of mismanaged waste in the *Baseline* scenario. While there are some positive spillover effects from Advanced economy policies on plastic waste generation in other countries, these effects are limited, and – in contrast to the *Global Downstream High stringency* scenario – the *Advanced economies Lifecycle High stringency* scenario assumes developing countries are not incentivised to take ambitious action to close leakage pathways. In the *Global Lifecycle Low stringency* scenario, the main cause for increasing plastic leakage over time is a lack of policy stringency. Even if a broad agreement covering all four policy pillars was reached and implemented by all countries, low policy stringency of the measures implemented would result in a failure to stabilise global plastic leakage, let alone eliminate further leakage.

Figure 4.8. Strong advancements in waste collection and treatment are necessary to reduce plastic leakage below 2020 levels

Leakage of plastics to the environment in million tonnes (Mt)

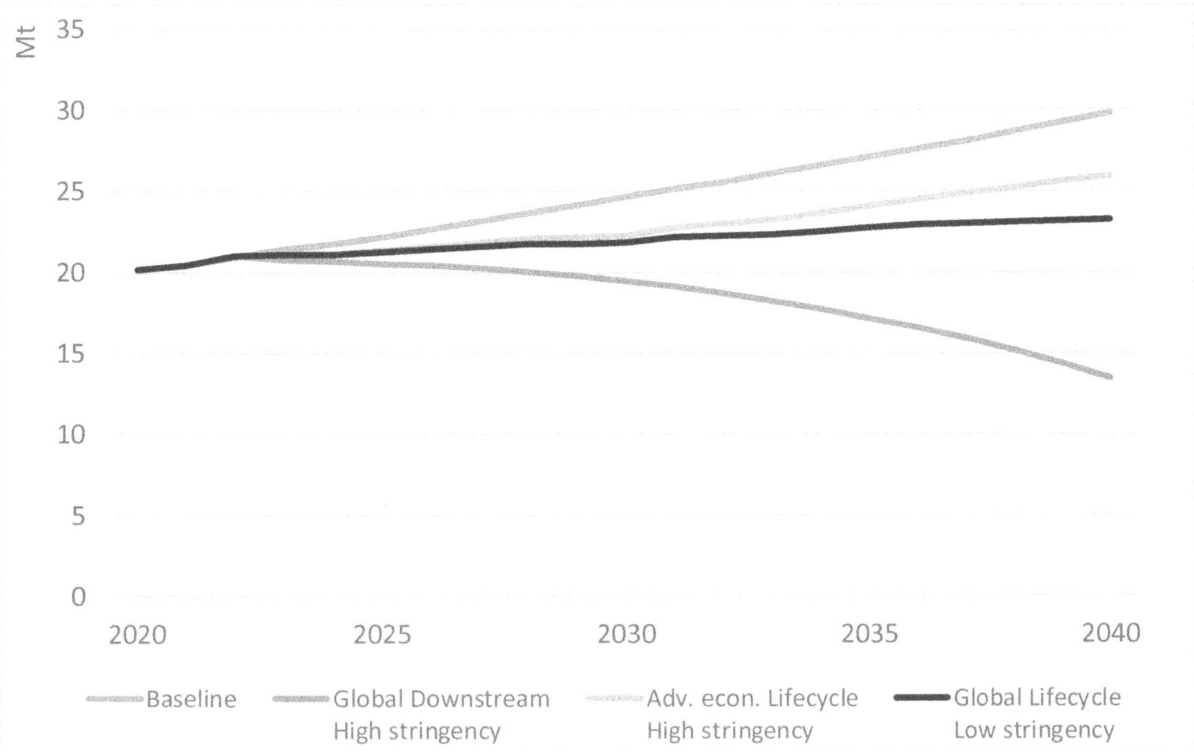

Source: OECD ENV-Linkages model.

StatLink https://stat.link/5107cm

Overall, strategies that do not include global policy action with high stringency for all four policy pillars, offer limited potential to reverse current trends. In the absence of broad stringent actions, the international community would fall far short the goal of eliminating plastic pollution for the foreseeable future.

Notes

[1] The details of the numerical implementation of the policy scenarios in the modelling framework are presented in Annex B.

[2] In line with the scenario descriptions in Chapters 1 and 3, a white background reflects current policies (as in the *Baseline* scenario); a semi-transparent background reflects low policy stringency and a fully coloured background reflects high policy stringency. Unlike in Figure 1.1 (Chapter 1) and Figure 3.2 (Chapter 3), here the different pillars are made explicit.

[3] This is a model assumption reflecting the fact that technological advances tend to spill over to other countries, especially when a sufficient segment of the global market is implicated by such advances.

[4] "Mismanaged" is included as a waste management category for accounting purposes; by assumption, no management costs are associated with this end-of-life fate.

[5] Significant technical breakthroughs may be required to achieve the strong improvements in recycling envisioned in the scenarios modelled. These challenges are further discussed in Section 7.2 of Chapter 7.

5 Implications of policy scenarios with high ambition

This chapter investigates two ambitious scenarios that have global coverage of policies targeting multiple stages of the plastics lifecycle. The results highlight that high policy stringency for all four pillars is essential to eliminate plastic leakage by 2040 and reduce primary plastics use below 2020 levels, which is important to also contain greenhouse gas emissions. The chapter highlights the environmental benefits of global ambition with a horizon to 2040, and the trade-offs associated with slower policy action.

5.1. Introduction

In the *Global Lifecycle Mixed stringency* policy scenario, countries agree on pursuing all three directions of the partial ambition scenarios, but fail to go beyond this. Stringent policy action at upstream and midstream stages of the plastics lifecycle (i.e. the curb production and demand and eco-design pillars) is limited to advanced economies (approximated as OECD and EU countries). Other regions implement upstream and midstream policies with limited stringency, while downstream policies (i.e. the enhance recycling and close leakage pathways pillars) are implemented with high stringency in all countries.[1]

The *Global Lifecycle High stringency* [*Global Ambition*] policy scenario closes the final gaps in policy stringency. This comprehensive and co-ordinated approach goes beyond the *Global Lifecycle Mixed stringency* scenario by implementing the ten policy instruments with high stringency in all regions, reflecting a high level of collaboration to eliminate plastic leakage. This entails a global strengthening of policy action throughout the plastics lifecycle, in view of a shared target to end macroplastic leakage by 2040. This scenario can potentially be used as a strategic guide to chart a path towards the elimination of global plastic pollution before the middle of the century.[2]

Figure 5.1 presents a visual representation of the two high ambition policy scenarios.

Figure 5.1. Policy scenarios with high ambition

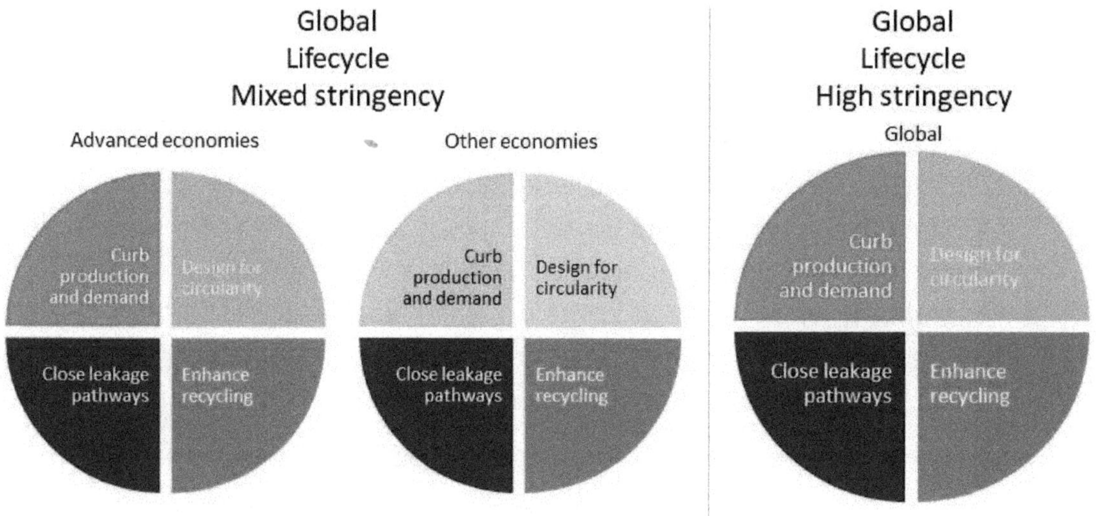

Source: Authors' own elaboration.

5.2. Ambitious integrated policies can largely decouple economic activity and plastics use

In both high ambition scenarios, all countries adopt policies to curb production and demand and to improve the design of products for circularity. Thus, these integrated scenarios improve on the partial ambition policy scenarios discussed in Chapter 4. A key difference between the two high ambition scenarios is the level of stringency of the upstream and midstream policies for countries outside the OECD and EU. In the *Global Lifecycle Mixed stringency* policy scenario, the policies implemented in these countries are limited to the lower stringency levels of the *Global Lifecycle Low stringency* policy scenario, while in the *Global Lifecycle High stringency* [*Global Ambition*] scenario, all countries implement strict policies for all four policy pillars to ensure a balance between efforts upstream and downstream in the value chain.

Global primary plastics use is projected to roughly stabilise at 2020 levels by 2040 in the *Global Lifecycle Mixed stringency* scenario (Figure 5.2). A significant reduction is projected in the *Global Lifecycle High stringency* [*Global Ambition*] scenario, with reductions below 2020 levels in most regions: 46 Mt below the 2020 level in OECD countries combined and 14 Mt below the 2020 level in non-OECD countries combined. These reductions lead to environmental benefits from the reduced scale of primary plastics production, including reduced greenhouse gas (GHG) emissions.[3]

Figure 5.2. Policy measures affecting production, demand and product design are pivotal to reducing primary plastics production and use below 2020 levels

Percentage change in primary plastics use in 2040 compared to 2020 levels

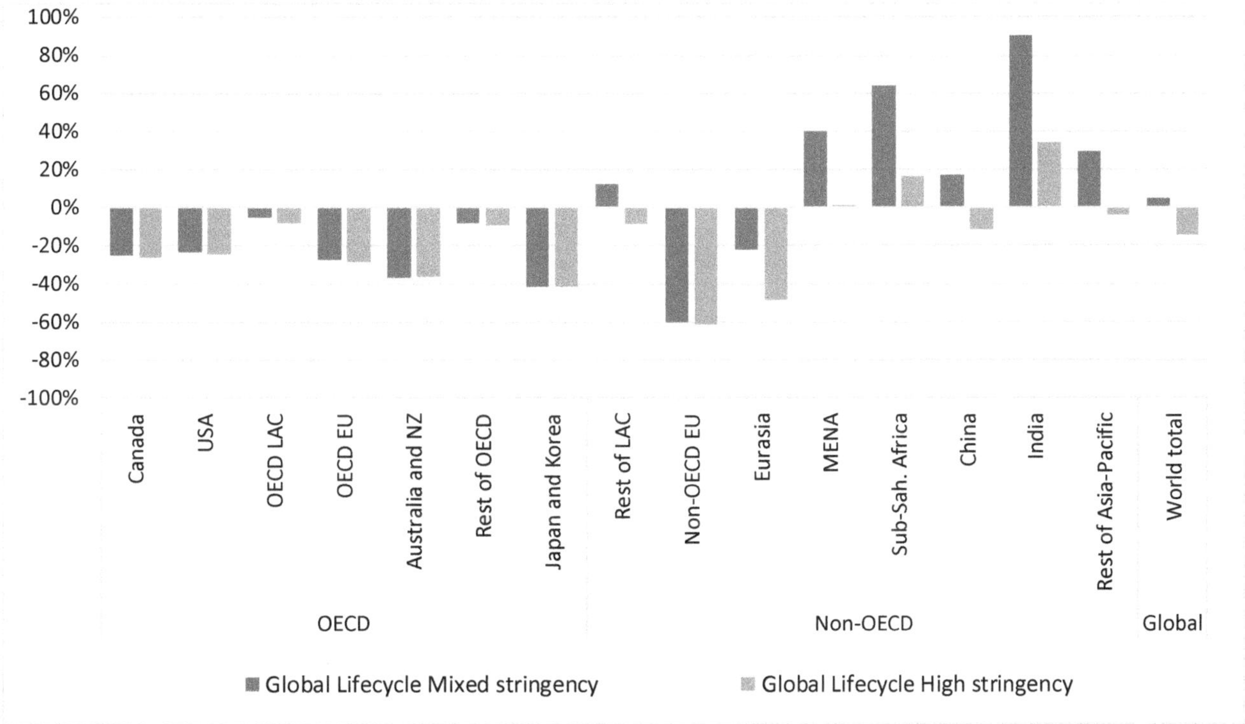

Source: OECD ENV-Linkages model.

StatLink https://stat.link/k9fndw

In the *Global Lifecycle Mixed stringency* scenario, primary plastics use in non-OECD countries would continue to grow, increasing to 286 Mt by 2040 as policy stringency remains limited to the levels of the *Global Lifecycle Low stringency* scenario. In comparison, primary plastics use in non-OECD countries in the *Baseline* scenario would grow from 227 Mt in 2020 to 435 Mt in 2040. Significant reductions of primary plastics in OECD countries below *Baseline* levels (which is very similar in both high ambition scenarios) can to some extent compensate for growth in non-OECD countries and deliver a near stabilisation of global primary plastics use. However, regional shifts in plastics use could worsen plastic pollution if larger shares of plastics end up as waste in countries with less developed waste management systems.

As the policies take time to be fully implemented, total plastics use and plastic waste continue to grow beyond 2020 levels (Figure 5.3). With stringent measures in place to generate scrap for secondary plastics production, the growth of total plastics use is met through growth in secondary plastics, while primary plastics use remains roughly constant (see Figure 5.2). Secondary plastics production increases especially after 2030, once recycling capacity is built up. The increases in plastic waste tend to be a bit larger than in plastics use, driven by the long lifetime of certain plastics applications and thus a delayed effect of policies on waste volumes. In the *Global Lifecycle Mixed stringency* scenario, global plastics use increases from 435 million tonnes (Mt) in 2020 to 626 Mt in 2040 (an increase of 43%). In the *Global Lifecycle High stringency* [*Global Ambition*] scenario, plastics use in 2040 is lower, at 508 Mt (17% above 2020 levels). The *Global Lifecycle High stringency* [*Global Ambition*] scenario thus avoids 228 Mt of plastics use compared to the *Baseline* scenario, and a reduction of 31%. Most of the reduction is achieved by 2030, through the early implementation of policies to curb production and demand as well as EPR schemes.

Figure 5.3. Even the most ambitious policy scenarios fail to stabilise global plastics use and waste in the long run

Global plastics use (left-hand panel) and waste (right-hand panel) in million tonnes (Mt)

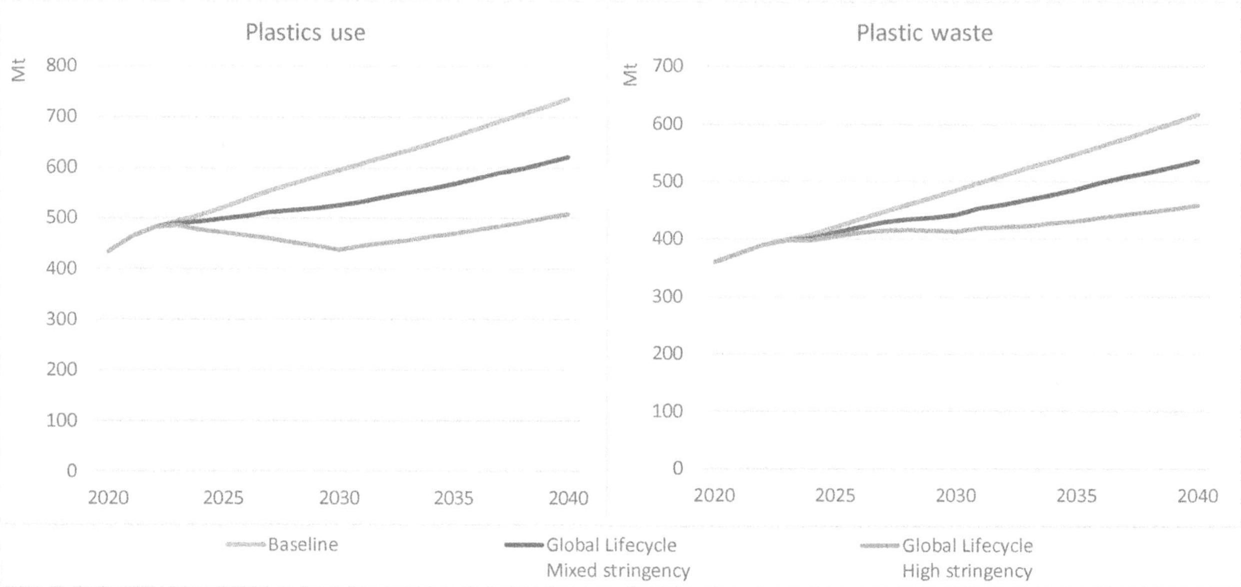

Source: OECD ENV-Linkages model.

StatLink https://stat.link/yasvwr

The main reason for the increase in plastics use after 2030 is that the *Global Lifecycle High stringency* [*Global Ambition*] scenario does not explicitly target total plastics use. Rather, it aims to reduce plastic pollution by curbing production and demand and increasing the share of secondary plastics (i.e. to reduce pollution associated with primary plastics production), to improve eco-design for circularity and to eliminate mismanaged plastic waste (i.e. to minimise plastic leakage). Further emphasis on policy measures to reduce total plastics use rather than primary plastics production could lead to excessive costs (see Chapter 6). The *Global Lifecycle High stringency* [*Global Ambition*] scenario aims to strike a balance between these elements.

Global plastic waste follows total plastics use, with a delay that depends on the lifetime of the associated plastics applications. On the one hand, eco-design policies contribute to lengthening the lifetime of applications, thus further postponing plastic waste generation – and postponing the benefits of curbing plastics production and demand. This is especially visible in Figure 5.3 by comparing the effect of the *Global Lifecycle High stringency* [*Global Ambition*] policy scenario on the trend in use with that on the trend in waste, with much stronger reductions in plastics use by 2030 than in plastic waste. On the other hand, a large part of plastics use is associated with applications that are short-lived, such as packaging, and thus the trends in plastic waste are rather similar to those of plastics use (see Chapter 2).

Not all applications grow equally fast over time, and different polymers and applications are affected through their links to economic sectors and the policies imposed (Figure 5.4). The largest reductions plastics use in 2040 in the *Global Lifecycle High stringency* [*Global Ambition*] scenario (relative to the *Baseline* scenario) pertain to applications with longer lifetimes, notably Transportation (-46% compared to the *Baseline* in 2040) and Buildings and Construction (-39% compared to the *Baseline*). Reductions in packaging are limited to 24%, from 139 Mt in 2020 to 234 Mt in 2040 in the *Baseline* and 179 Mt in *Global Lifecycle High stringency* [*Global Ambition*]. For all applications, reductions are somewhat larger in non-OECD countries than in OECD countries.

Figure 5.4. Globally ambitious policies affect the composition of plastics use by application

Plastics production and use by application in million tonnes (Mt), *Global Lifecycle High stringency* [*Global Ambition*] scenario

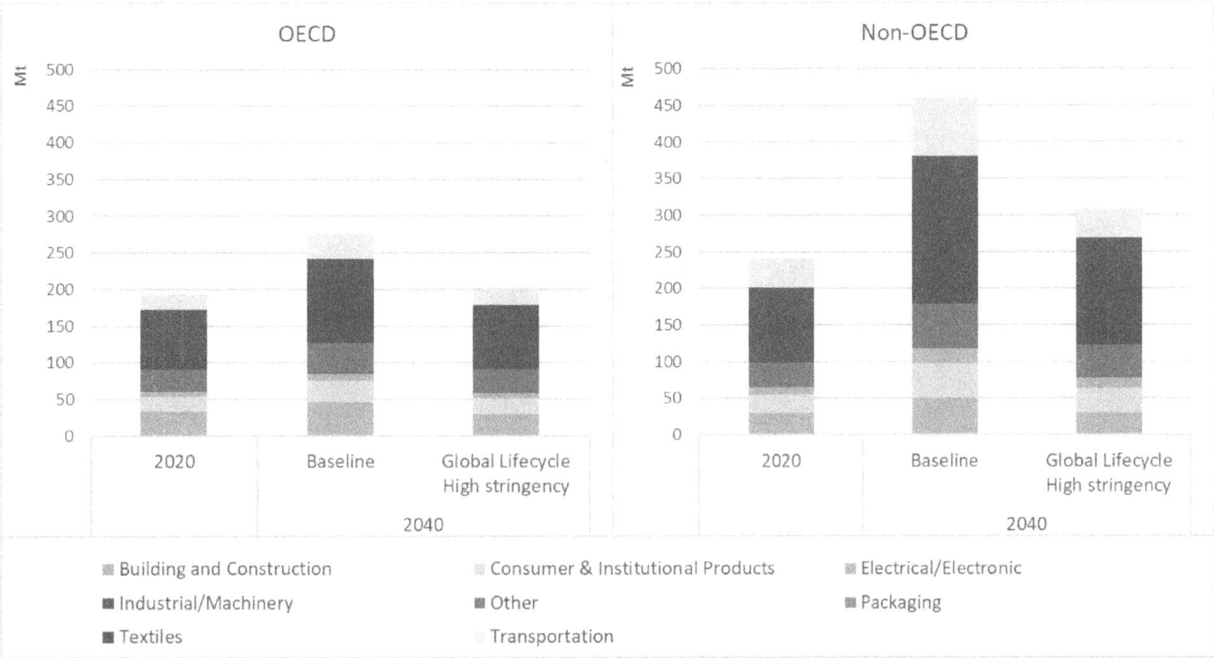

Source: OECD ENV-Linkages model.

StatLink https://stat.link/i32coe

Continued economic growth in all scenarios, and significantly lower levels of plastics use relative to *Baseline* levels imply an improvement in the plastics intensity of the economy (Figure 5.5). Over time, the plastics intensity in the *Baseline* scenario does not change much, although there is a slight trend towards stronger growth in plastics use than in GDP in OECD countries, and the opposite trend in non-OECD countries. The latter is driven by the rapid expansion of economic sectors that don't rely heavily on plastics, such as services, whereas the structure of OECD economies is more stable.

Both of the high ambition policy scenarios considered here can reduce plastics intensity between 2020 and 2040, but the *Global Lifecycle High stringency* [*Global Ambition*] scenario is more effective than the *Global Lifecycle Mixed stringency* scenario due to the additional efforts undertaken to curb production and demand in non-OECD countries. A more than 30% reduction in plastics intensity relative to 2020 levels (and 2040 *Baseline* levels) demonstrate that with targeted policies, economic growth can largely be decoupled from an increased reliance on plastics.

Figure 5.5. Stringent measures to curb production and demand are required to reduce plastics intensity and decouple economic activity from plastics use

Plastics intensity in tonnes of plastics use per unit of sectoral output in USD (t/USD)

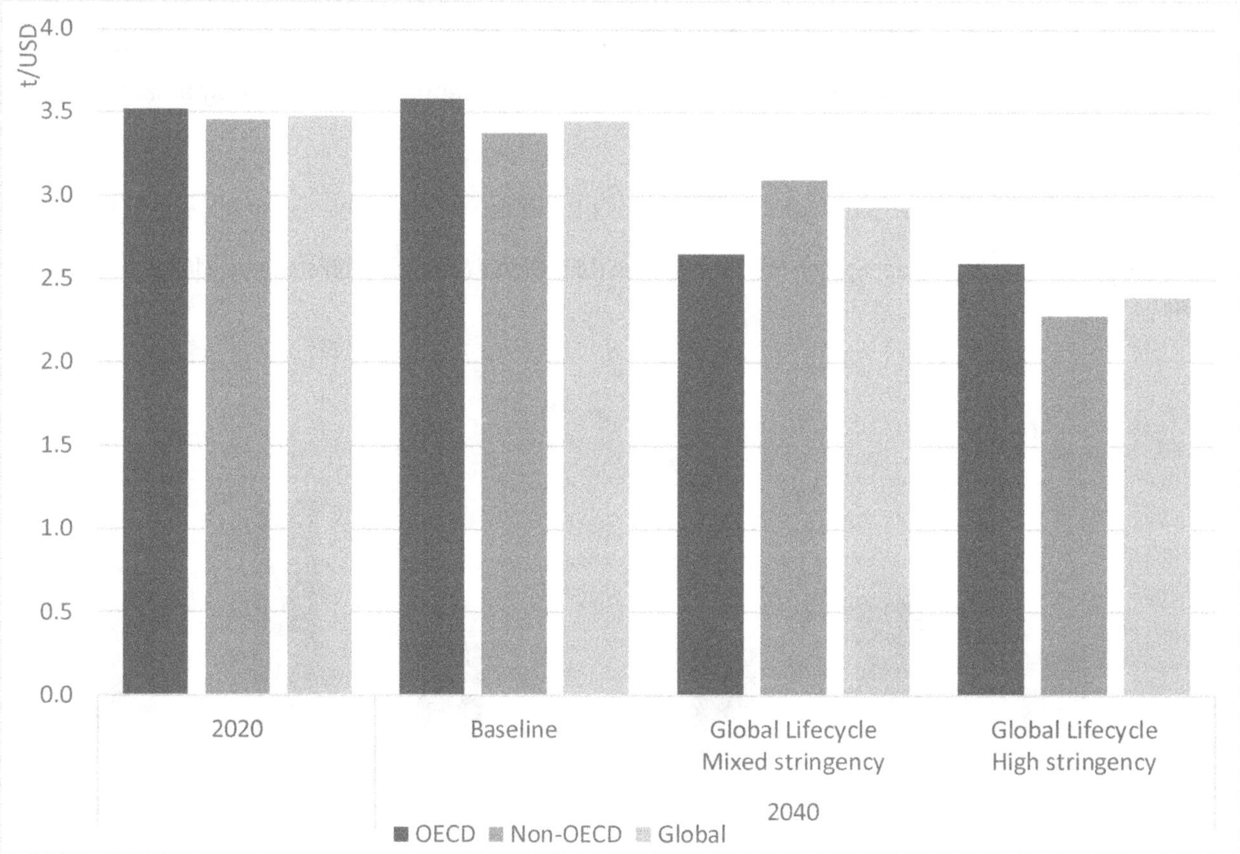

Source: OECD ENV-Linkages model.

StatLink https://stat.link/5akeyn

5.3. Interventions throughout the plastics lifecycle in all countries are required to eliminate mismanaged plastic waste by 2040

While most developed countries already have pervasive municipal waste collection and treatment systems, this is not the case in many developing countries. An urgent expansion of waste collection systems is a crucial prerequisite to reduce mismanaged waste, as waste that is not collected is mostly mismanaged and may end up in natural environments or be burned informally, leading to serious adverse consequences for human health and ecosystems. At the same time, a scale-up of waste management infrastructure is required around the world, in OECD and non-OECD countries alike, to support recycling. The *Global Lifecycle High stringency* [*Global Ambition*] scenario would achieve an almost total elimination of mismanaged waste by 2040 (see Figure 5.6). Mismanaged waste shares are already steadily reduced in the *Baseline*, as countries grow richer and can afford better waste management, but this policy package overcomes significant *Baseline* growth in the amounts of plastics that are mismanaged annually.

The prevention of waste generation by 2040 (relative to *Baseline* levels) would help to relieve the burden on waste management systems around the globe. In contrast to the *Global Lifecycle High stringency* [*Global Ambition*] scenario, the *Global Lifecycle Mixed stringency* scenario cannot eliminate all mismanaged waste (dashed yellow line in Figure 5.6), as the total generation of plastic waste is significantly larger and there are limits to the scaling up of recycling facilities in developing countries. Such challenges also exist in the *Global Lifecycle High stringency* [*Global Ambition*] scenario (see Chapter 7), but the improved balance between the four policy pillars is essential for the feasibility of the ambitious targets in the high ambition scenarios.

Figure 5.6. Global Ambition entails rapid reductions in mismanaged waste and strong increases in recycling

Shares of end-of-life fates for plastic waste, *Global Lifecycle High stringency* [*Global Ambition*]

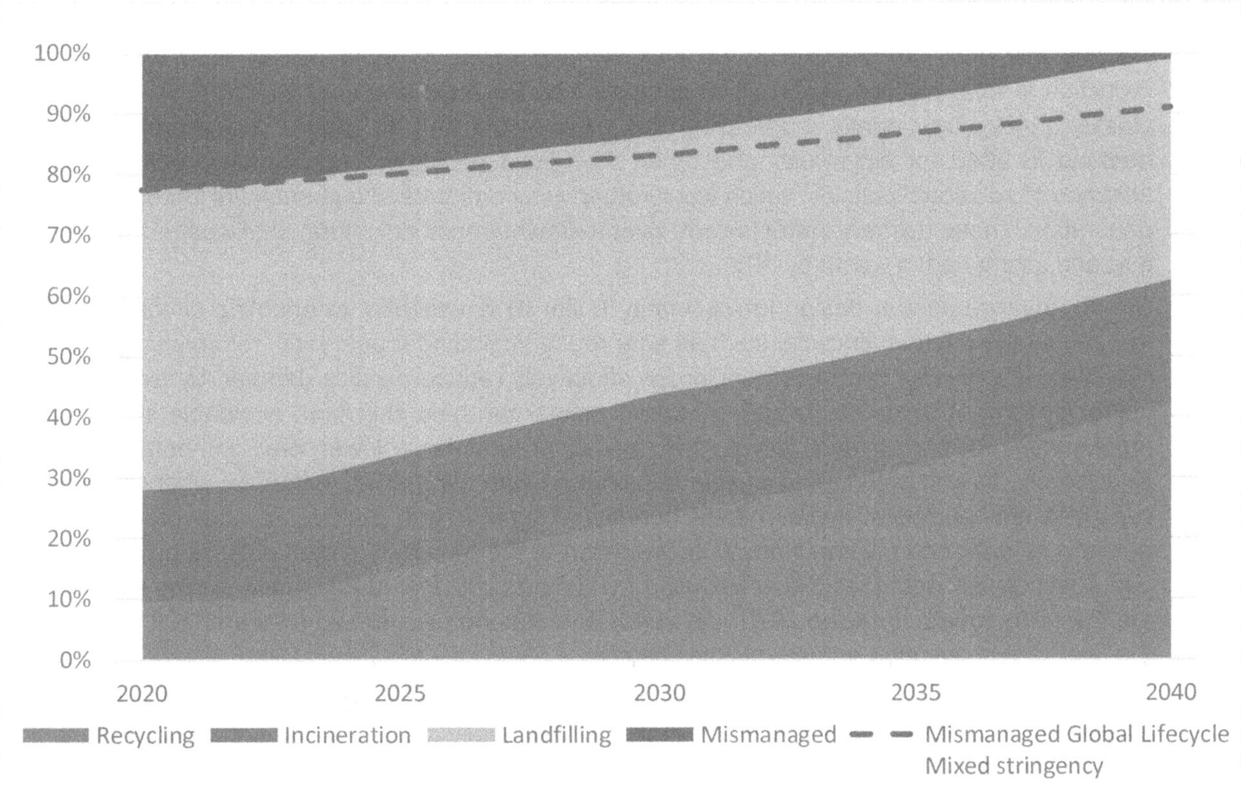

Note: The dashed line shows the remaining mismanaged waste in the *Global Lifecycle Mixed stringency* scenario, for comparison. Recycling shares are very similar across both scenarios (and therefore not shown here for the *Global Lifecycle Mixed stringency* scenario).
Source: OECD ENV-Linkages model.

StatLink https://stat.link/qlsy4p

Both high ambition policy scenarios lead to a very significant increase in recycling rates, with the share of waste that is recycled climbing to 42% by 2040, a more than quadrupling of 2020 levels (Figure 5.6). Such rapid increases in recycling allow for the generation of scrap that is essential for making the transition from primary to secondary plastics production. Achieving such considerable increases in recycling rates would require overcoming very significant challenges, as recycling rates remain currently low for several polymers and in many low- and middle- income countries. This is further discussed in Chapter 7.

Despite the effectiveness of the high ambition policy packages in reducing plastic waste generation, the resulting levels of plastic waste remain high enough to facilitate the use of scrap in secondary plastics production, provided that international markets for scrap are facilitated and recycling losses are reduced. As a result, while annual plastics production is projected to grow modestly from 2020 levels, both high ambition scenarios ensure that secondary plastics can accommodate the additional demand. As a result, demand for primary plastics would fall in 2040 relative to 2020 in the *Global Lifecycle High stringency* [*Global Ambition*] and would roughly stabilise over this time period in the *Global Lifecycle Mixed stringency* scenario.

5.4. Each policy pillar is essential in reducing plastic waste mismanagement and overall pollution

Policies that curb production and demand and foster design for circularity contribute to 27% of the overall reductions in mismanaged waste achieved by 2040 in the *Global Lifecycle High stringency* [*Global Ambition*] scenario relative to the *Baseline* scenario (Figure 5.7). Importantly, the combination of extended lifespans for durable products, facilitated by improved eco-design and support for reuse and repair, generate reductions in the demand for (and thus production of) plastics. More specifically, reductions are achieved through a combination of the four policy pillars:

- Policies that curb plastics production and demand (pillar I) would deliver a 97 Mt (i.e. 13%) reduction in total plastics use in 2040 compared to *Baseline* levels, of which 95 Mt are primary plastics (14%). Importantly, addressing this pillar would help to reduce the sharp increase in demand in 2040 for single-use and other short-lived packaging applications projected in the absence of additional policies, which would otherwise contribute to a substantial increase in waste generation. These upstream effects carry over to downstream indicators: total waste is reduced by 8%, and mismanaged waste by 10%.
- Strong advancement in design for circularity (pillar II) is essential to enabling circular solutions throughout the plastics lifecycle, such as safe reuse (including repair, refill, refurbishing, etc.) and recycling. In this way, improved design can effectively reduce plastics demand by expanding the useful lifespan of products. Targeted bans or taxes can help shift from avoidable short-lived or problematic plastics to alternatives that are safer and bear lower environmental footprints. Additionally, design criteria can enable substitution with alternative materials, where such shifts can yield environmental and/or health benefits. Together with policies to curb production and demand, this second pillar induces a deceleration in the growth of global plastics production and use. Plastics use would fall below *Baseline* by 208 Mt (28%) in 2040, compensating two-thirds of the *Baseline* growth between 2020 and 2040. The second pillar would also add 105 Mt (15%) to the first pillar in avoiding primary plastics use.
- The eco-design for circularity also contributes significantly to reducing total waste and mismanaged waste. Total waste is reduced by 94 Mt (15%), substantially more than the contribution of the first pillar to curb production and demand. A key driver of these reductions is the extension of the lifetimes of plastics applications. While this pillar does not directly improve waste management shares, mismanaged waste is reduced by 19 Mt (16%) due to a reduction in the overall generation of plastic waste, globally.
- Enhancing recycling (pillar III) has very limited effects on total plastics use (20 Mt or less than 3%), but the impact on primary plastics use is much larger (145 Mt or 21%), as recycling policies induce a shift from primary to secondary plastics use. Similarly, the effect on total waste is small (12 Mt or 2%), but more significant in reducing mismanaged waste (31 Mt or 26%), as a larger share of collected waste is diverted towards recycling, thus reducing mismanaged waste such as open pit burning.
- Finally, the policies to close leakage pathways (pillar IV) focus on eliminating mismanaged waste, and are essential in this regard, reducing mismanaged waste by 53 Mt or 44%. However, the effects of such policies on other variables is virtually zero (less than 1 Mt for each). The upstream effects of improved waste management come through the effect of increased waste management costs on national income and thus economic activity. The fact that the effect is very small is therefore positive, highlighting that the macroeconomic consequences of closing leakage pathways are small (see Chapter 6).

Together, policy action in these four pillars facilitate the transition to more circular plastics use, as (upstream) secondary plastics production rises in parallel to the increased availability of scrap from (downstream) recycling efforts. The global implementation of policies across these four pillars with policy stringency aligned with the *Global Lifecycle High stringency* [*Global Ambition*] scenario would require overcoming large governance, economic and technical challenges, as further discussed in Chapter 7.

Figure 5.7. All policy pillars contribute to eliminating mismanaged plastic waste by 2040

Contribution of each policy pillar to reductions in plastic flows, all expressed in percentage change compared to the *Baseline* in 2040, *Global Lifecycle High stringency* [*Global Ambition*] scenario

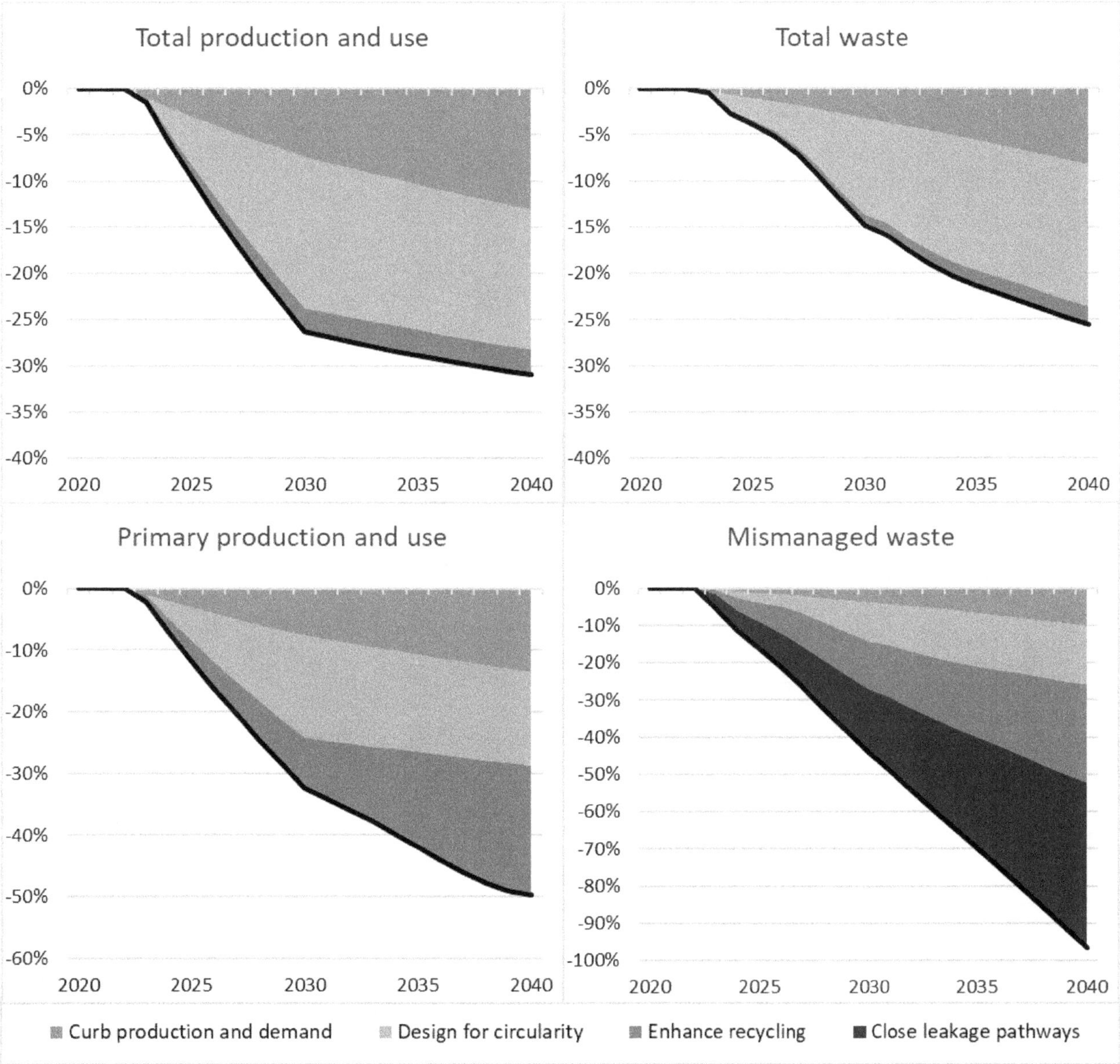

Source: OECD ENV-Linkages model.

StatLink https://stat.link/d08iec

The *Global Lifecycle High stringency* [*Global Ambition*] scenario projects a peak in global primary plastics use in 2022 (Figure 5.8). The rapid and global implementation of policies to curb production and demand and improve design for circularity lead to a decoupling of economic growth from primary plastics use, resulting in a significant decline in primary and total plastics use by 2030. After 2030, when recycling systems have larger capacity – as indicated by an increasing recycling rate – and when more scrap is available, secondary plastics use continues to grow, more than offsetting the continued shrink of primary plastics use. A corresponding decrease in the use of primary plastics production is expected to lead to environmental benefits, including reduced GHG emissions. This transition to secondary plastics production and use is generally associated with smaller environmental impacts, despite the required increases in recycling activities (OECD, 2022[1]).

Figure 5.8. Global Ambition reduces primary plastics production below 2020 levels

Global plastics production and use in million tonnes (Mt) (left axis) and global average recycling rate (right axis), *Global Lifecycle High stringency* [*Global Ambition*]

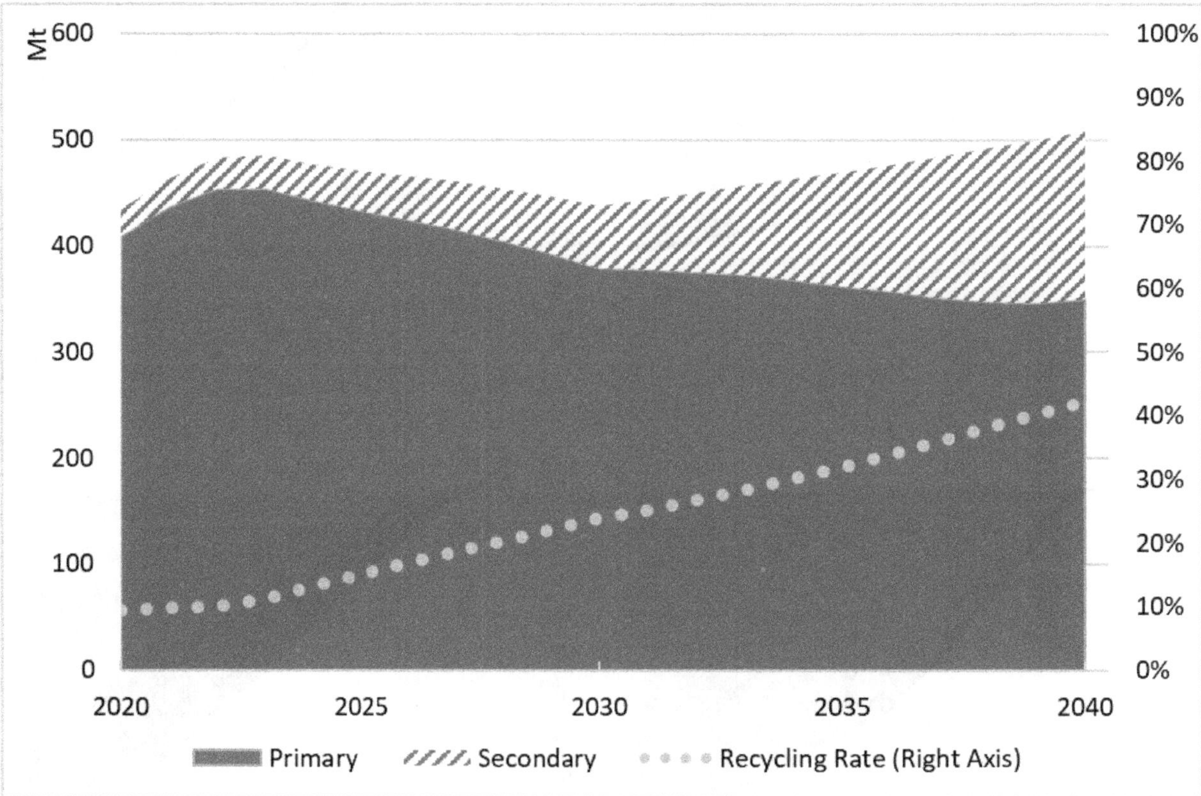

Source: OECD ENV-Linkages model.

StatLink https://stat.link/fgseqy

5.5. Strategies to halt microplastic leakage will also be required

Microplastic (roughly speaking, plastics smaller than 5 mm) pollution is an emerging threat to ecosystem and human health. Owing to their small size, microplastics are particularly likely to be ingested by aquatic species, and they have been found in the digestive tracts of several aquatic and terrestrial species. Growing microplastic pollution constitutes a reason of concern for the environment and human health, including due to the potential for microplastics to act as a carrier of hazardous substances.

Microplastics are generally categorised into three main types (OECD, 2021[2]):

- **Primary microplastics**, which include: i) manufactured microplastics, such as plastic pellets that may enter the environment due to accidental spills occurring during production, transport and storage, and ii) microplastics intentionally added to products, such as microbeads in cosmetics or scrubbing agents.
- **Use-based secondary microplastics**, which originate from the degradation of plastics occurring during use. This includes for instance microplastics from the wear and tear of vehicle tyres on road surfaces, paints, synthetic textiles or shoe soles.
- **Degradation-based secondary microplastics**, which originate from the degradation and fragmentation of larger pieces of plastics, including after leakage to the environment.

Leakage of (primary and use-based secondary) microplastics is projected to worsen in all regions in the *Baseline* scenario, from 2.7 Mt in 2020 to 4.1 Mt in 2040 (for the categories for which estimations are possible) (OECD, 2022[1]). As discussed in (OECD, 2022[1]), microplastic leakage continues to increase with rising income levels, although some saturation occurs at higher levels of income. In contrast, macroplastic leakage per capita tends to decrease in middle- and high-income countries due to improvements in waste management systems. Interventions to address the emission and leakage of microplastics are generally less advanced, as this form of pollution occurs throughout the product lifecycle and policy action remains limited by a currently limited understanding of the problem and the possible interventions to address it.

While the environmental and human health risks associated with microplastics are still being investigated, extensive documentation of exposure routes and the associated potential for widespread risks and irreversible harm caused call for policy intervention to mitigate pollution levels and risks. It has been argued that microplastics are contaminants for which no safe threshold for emissions can be identified, and that even if a safe threshold exists, it will inevitably be surpassed due to the continued accumulation and persistence of microplastics in the environment (Nordic Council of Ministers, 2022[3]). Mitigation action should be proportional, consistent with existing policy frameworks, based on adequate cost-benefit analysis considerations and sufficiently flexible to encourage scientific research and innovation in mitigation solutions.

Given the potential for widespread ecosystem and human health impacts of microplastics, policies that can specifically mitigate microplastic leakage will need to form an important part of the policy mix, to ensure effective mitigation of microplastic pollution (OECD, 2021[2]). While the reduction of mismanaged waste and hence macroplastic leakage envisioned in the *Global Lifecycle High stringency* [*Global Ambition*] scenario could mitigate the generation of degradation-based secondary microplastics from additional pollution, leakage of microplastics would persist. In the absence of additional policies to target microplastics, reductions in microplastic leakage would be limited to those stemming from reductions in the plastics intensity of the economy and from expected improvements in end-of-pipe capture (e.g. via wastewater and stormwater collection and treatment).[4]

Possible approaches and policy measures for the mitigation of microplastic leakage may include:

- Bans or restrictions on intentionally added microplastics.
- Eco-design criteria to minimise the tendency of products to generate microplastics.
- Behavioural change to uptake best practices by consumers (e.g. eco-driving) as well as industry (e.g. in the handling of pre-production pellets).
- End-of-pipe approaches, such as improved wastewater, stormwater and road runoff management and treatment to retain emitted microplastics before they enter the environment.
- Standards or best-available techniques to advance the implementation of technologies and processes that prevent the release of microplastics to the environment (e.g. industrial, commercial, and domestic filters).
- Clean-up of plastic pollution can also contribute to reducing microplastics in the environment, although it is currently unclear how this could be done in a cost-effective manner and at a large scale, as discussed in Section 7.4 in Chapter 7.

The most cost-effective way to tackle microplastics is likely the implementation of a mix of policy tools targeting several mitigation entry points along the product lifecycle. Measures aimed at minimising the emission of microplastics at their source are likely to have the largest mitigation potential. Especially for intentionally added microplastics as well as for diffuse sources of pollution (e.g. tyre wear particles, airborne textile microfibres), prevention is often more cost-effective than treatment options downstream. At the same time, given the variety of entry pathways, interventions upstream cannot entirely alleviate the risk of microplastic pollution of the water cycle. Thus, these will likely need to be supplemented by effective end-of-pipe solutions, such as the improved collection and treatment of stormwater, road runoff and wastewater.

Overall, while there is a need for further research on the cost-effectiveness of the measures identified above and the potential for unintended consequences, the need for further research should not justify delays in action. Select countries have already implemented bans or restrictions on microplastics intentionally added to products, as has been done in the EU for a wide range of products (including granular infill materials in sports turfs, cosmetics, detergents, fertilisers, glitter, etc.). Important gains can also be made with respect to reducing microplastic leakage by exploiting or adapting existing measures in other policy areas. For instance, reductions in passenger vehicle use and shifts towards more sustainable transport modes, generally driven by a need to reduce GHG emissions and air pollution, can contribute significantly to mitigating microplastics emissions from road transport (OECD, 2020[4]). Similarly, certain end-of-pipe mitigation options, such as improved wastewater treatment technologies or nature-based solutions, primarily designed to manage other pollutants or risks of flooding can generate significant co-benefits for microplastic pollution mitigation.

5.6. The environmental benefits of global ambition by 2040

5.6.1. Globally co-ordinated policy action can bring significant environmental benefits by 2040

Plastic pollution represents a multifaceted challenge with a wide range of adverse impacts that go beyond the visible presence of plastics in the environment. Risks for human health may notably arise from exposure to hazardous chemicals or microplastics. Plastics in the environment may disrupt ecosystems, act as vectors for invasive species, and affect fisheries and tourism. The *Global Lifecycle High stringency* [*Global Ambition*] scenario illustrates a viable pathway to achieve significant global benefits for present and future generations.

Figure 5.9. Global Ambition delivers the largest environmental benefits

Projections for plastics leakage to the environment in million tonnes and for stocks in aquatic environments (Mt) and greenhouse gas (GHG) emissions from the plastics lifecycle in gigatonnes of carbon dioxide equivalent ($GtCO_2e$)

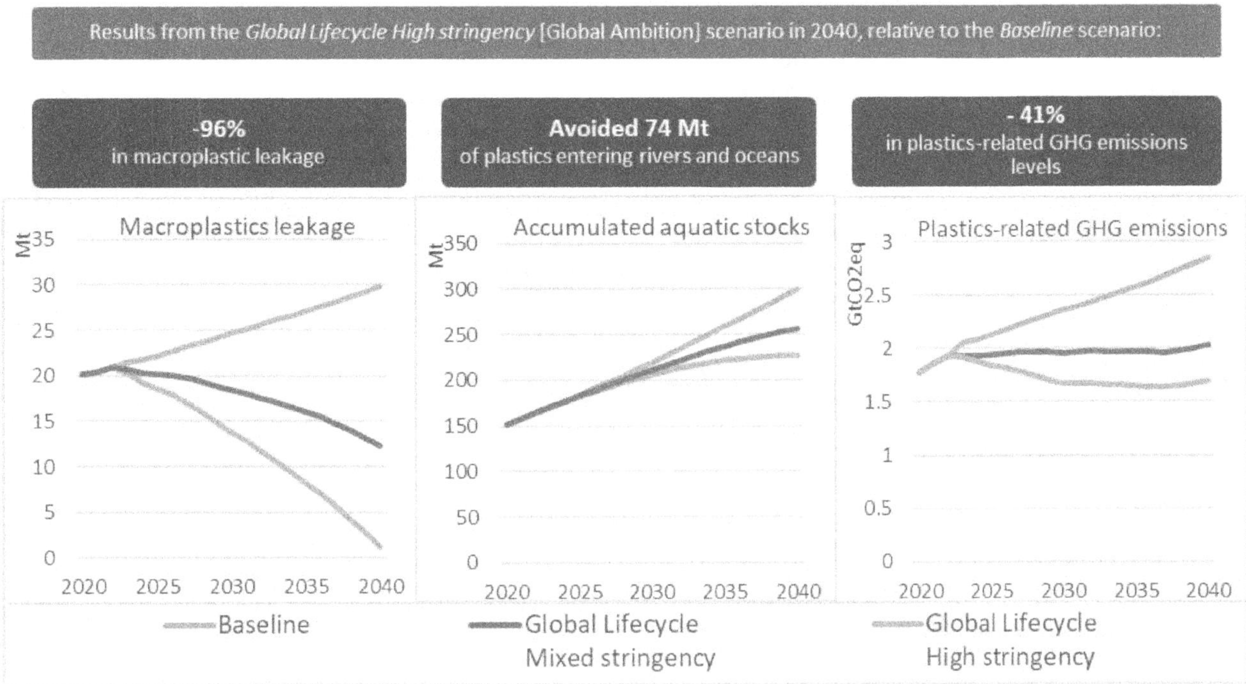

Sources: OECD ENV-Linkages model and (Lebreton, 2024[5]), based on OECD ENV-Linkages model projections.

StatLink https://stat.link/cvzspt

The comprehensive mix of waste prevention measures and improvements in waste collection and management envisioned in the *Global Lifecycle High stringency* [*Global Ambition*] scenario can achieve a reduction in plastic leakage of more than 95% by 2040 compared to *Baseline*. The combination of the most ambitious policies in a globally concerted manner would deliver an almost immediate fall in the leakage of macroplastics to the environment, due to the reduction of short-lived plastics applications and improved waste management, especially increased waste collection. The leakage that remains in 2040 mainly comes from uncollected litter, a stream that evades waste management systems. Microplastic leakage also remains largely unaddressed by this policy mix and addressing this type of plastic pollution will require additional, targeted policy interventions. Overall, the total amount of leakage that is avoided between 2020 and 2040 when moving from the *Baseline* scenario to the *Global Lifecycle High stringency* [*Global Ambition*] scenario amounts to 246 Mt. Even with the rapid implementation of this policy package, however, a total of 273 Mt of plastics will still leak to the environment between 2020 and 2040.

Virtually eliminating plastic leakage to the environment by 2040 is a challenging target that requires interventions at all stages of the lifecycle of plastics, globally and achieving it hinges on the assumption that countries are willing and able to co-ordinate their efforts. Co-ordination could include, for example, technology transfer (e.g. advanced recycling technologies), agreeing on the phase out of problematic or avoidable plastic products or harmful chemicals, developing harmonised criteria and guidelines for design for circularity, scaling up international markets for scrap and secondary plastics, and co-ordinating the implementation of reuse systems, for instance via harmonised design standards and certification and labelling requirements. For comparison, in the *Global Lifecycle Mixed stringency* scenario, where limited international co-ordination on upstream interventions hinders the potential of at least some of these interventions, an additional 175 Mt of waste would be generated in 2040 (over 2020 levels) and 49 Mt would be mismanaged. Approximately 12 Mt of plastic leakage would persist in 2040 and a path to near-zero charted only by 2060, amplifying plastic pollution and lifecycle impacts.

The *Global Lifecycle High stringency* [*Global Ambition*] scenario achieves very significant reductions of the accumulated stock of plastics in aquatic environments compared to *Baseline* levels, preventing up to 64 Mt and 11 Mt of plastics from being added to existing stocks in rivers and oceans, respectively. Although all major trajectories of plastics in aquatic environments are significantly reduced in this scenario relative to the *Baseline* scenario (Figure 5.10), accumulated stocks of macroplastics in rivers and oceans will nevertheless be significantly higher in 2040 than in 2020 (226 Mt of total accumulation between 2020 and 2040 instead of 301 Mt in the *Baseline* scenario). This is despite the most ambitious global action modelled. By 2040, plastics continue to be transported from rivers to oceans, while leakage to rivers from terrestrial environments is largely eliminated. Thus, some flows, in particular plastics floating in rivers, can become negative, indicating that there are more plastics flowing from rivers into oceans than there are entering rivers.

Figure 5.10. Even if Global Ambition nearly eliminates aquatic plastic leakage, plastics in rivers and oceans continue to accumulate until 2040

Plastic leakage to aquatic environments in million tonnes (Mt), in 2020 and in 2040 in the *Baseline* and *Global Lifecycle High stringency* [*Global Ambition*] scenarios

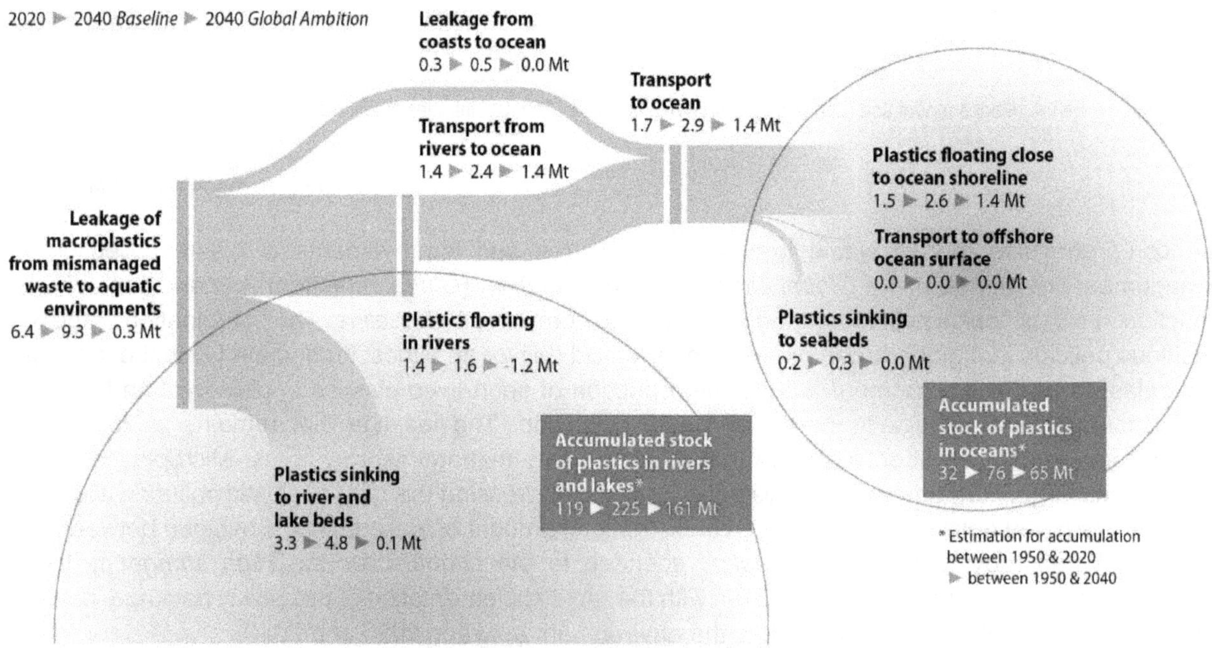

Source: (Lebreton, 2024[5]), based on OECD ENV-Linkages model projections.

The *Global Lifecycle High stringency* [*Global Ambition*] scenario is also likely to deliver considerable benefits for human health due in large part due to a reduction in improper waste disposal practices, such as air pollution from open pit burning. Chemicals of concern would be phased out to reduce risks for human health and the environment and to facilitate recycling and reuse. Policies to address microplastic leakage will also be essential in mitigating adverse health and environmental outcomes, as already discussed in Section 0.

5.6.2. Globally co-ordinated policy action can stabilise plastic-related GHG emissions

The plastics lifecycle is closely linked to climate change, due to the fossil-based origins of most plastics and the domination of fossil-based primary plastics in current production and use. As discussed in (OECD, 2022[1]), a reduction in GHG emissions related to the lifecycle of plastics is essential for achieving ambitious climate scenarios, including net-zero emissions scenarios. Implementing the *Global Lifecycle High stringency* [*Global Ambition*] scenario could achieve a 41% reduction in plastics-related GHG emission levels (1.7 $GtCO_2e$ in 2040 versus 2.8 $GtCO_2e$ in the *Baseline* scenario; see Figure 5.11, panel A) and prevent significant increases compared to 2020 levels. This reduction in emissions is the net result of a decrease in emissions associated with the production and conversion of primary plastics and an increase in emissions associated with enhanced recycling (panel B). Changes in emissions associated with mismanaged waste, such as those from open pit burning, could not be quantified, but are expected to be significantly lower in this policy scenario thanks to important reductions in mismanaged waste. Nonetheless, the remaining emissions are not aligned with the ambitions of the Paris Agreement, and thus the plastics policy package should be complemented by dedicated mitigation actions to further reduce GHG emissions associated with plastics.

Figure 5.11. Global Ambition could limit plastics-related GHG emissions to 2020 levels by 2040

Panel A. Greenhouse gas emissions from the plastics lifecycle in gigatonnes carbon dioxide equivalent (GtCO2e), by lifecycle stage

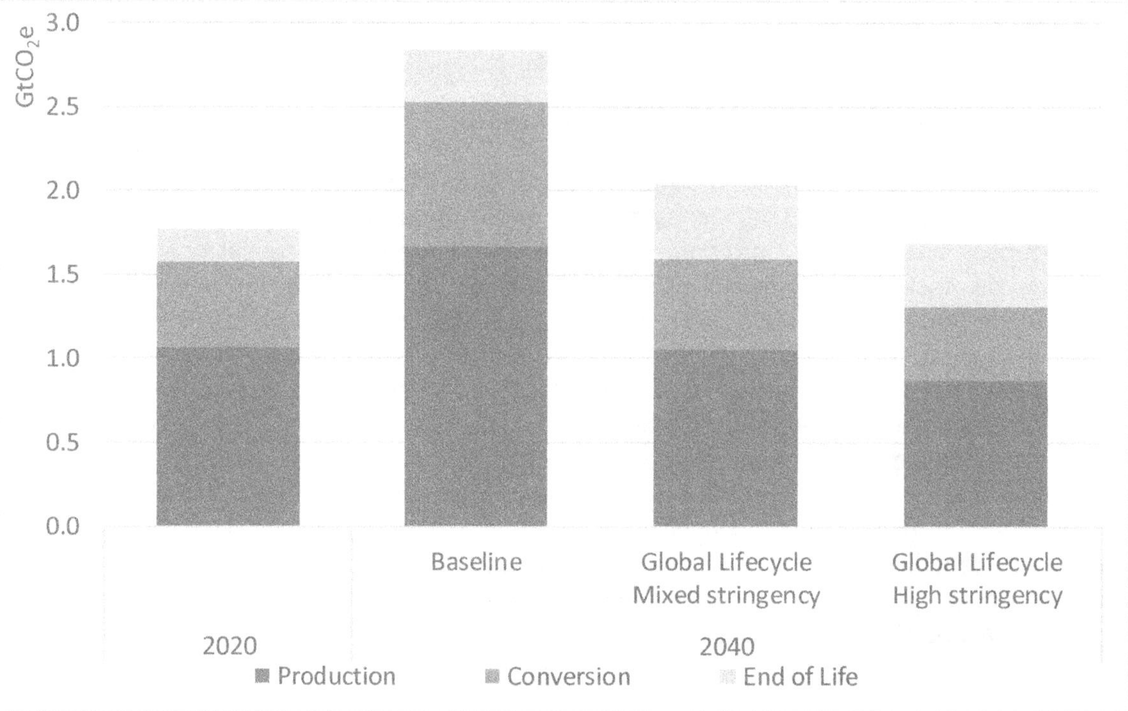

Panel B. Percentage deviation from the Baseline scenario, Global Lifecycle High stringency [Global Ambition] scenario, by contribution of different policy pillars

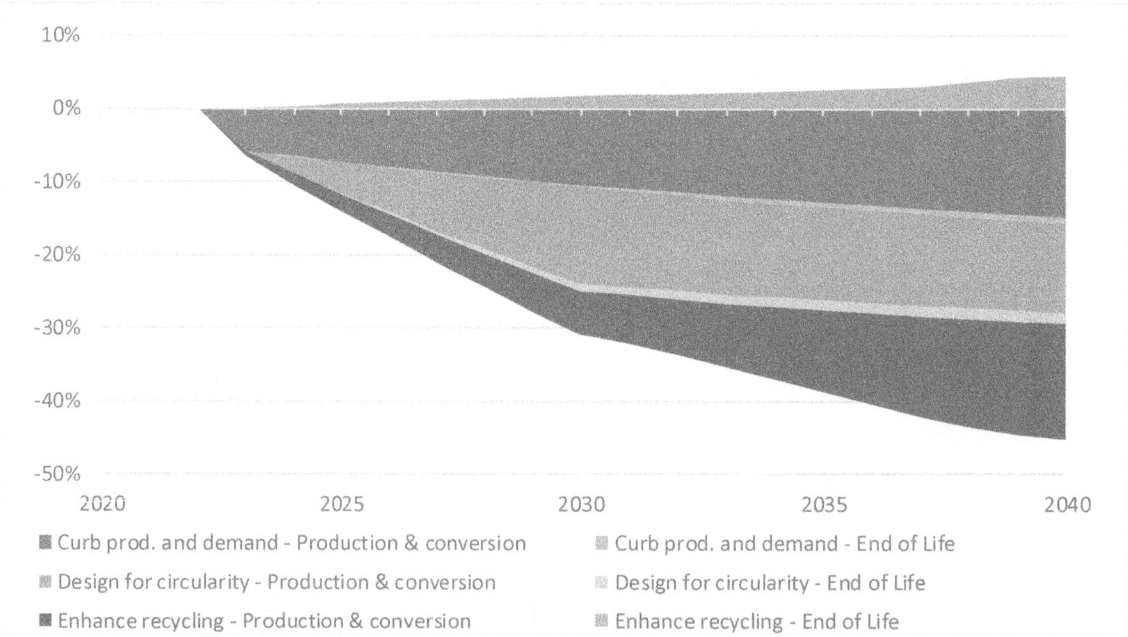

Note: Changes in emissions from the fourth pillar, associated with changes in mismanaged waste, cannot be quantified and are therefore not included in the figure.
Source: OECD ENV-Linkages model.

StatLink https://stat.link/7x8p2m

Public policies to mitigate climate change and curb plastic pollution have generally developed independently. However, the links between plastics policies and climate change mitigation policies can be strengthened to more effectively exploit synergies (OECD, 2023[6]). Combining plastics policies with ambitious mitigation policies further incentivises a shift away from primary plastics production and could reduce plastics-related emissions to below 2020 levels. Specifically, mitigation policies can disincentivise the use of fossil fuel energy in plastics production, conversion and waste management towards less carbon-intensive alternatives, including electrification, especially when the power sector is also decarbonised. Combined, these policies offer synergies that can reduce plastics-related GHG emissions; plastics policies can reduce the production of plastics, while mitigation policies can reduce the GHG intensity of the remaining production. At the end-of-life stage for plastic, there is a trade-off, however, in the form of the emissions associated with plastics recycling, which are not negligible.

References

Lebreton, L. (2024), *Quantitative analysis of aquatic leakage for multiple scenarios based on ENV-Linkages*, unpublished. [5]

Nordic Council of Ministers (2022), *Addressing microplastics in a global agreement on plastic pollution*, https://pub.norden.org/temanord2022-566. [3]

OECD (2023), *Climate change and plastics pollution: synergies between two crucial environmental challenges*, https://www.oecd.org/environment/plastics/Policy-Highlights-Climate-change-and-plastics-pollution-Synergies-between-two-crucial-environmental-challenges.pdf. [6]

OECD (2022), *Global Plastics Outlook: Policy Scenarios to 2060*, OECD Publishing, Paris, https://doi.org/10.1787/aa1edf33-en. [1]

OECD (2021), *Policies to Reduce Microplastics Pollution in Water: Focus on Textiles and Tyres*, OECD Publishing, Paris, https://doi.org/10.1787/7ec7e5ef-en. [2]

OECD (2020), *Non-exhaust Particulate Emissions from Road Transport: An Ignored Environmental Policy Challenge*, OECD Publishing, Paris, https://doi.org/10.1787/4a4dc6ca-en. [4]

Notes

[1] The details of the numerical implementation of the policy scenarios in the modelling framework are presented in Annex B.

[2] Fully eliminating plastic pollution would involve additional considerations, including addressing legacy plastics in the environment, emissions beyond greenhouse gases, as well as chemicals and human health concerns.

[3] As discussed in Section 5.6.2, GHG emissions do not fall below 2020 levels, as the policy packages do not explicitly focus on reducing emissions, suggesting that the inclusion of climate mitigation policies and targets in policy scenarios would be required to further reduce GHG emissions.

[4] This has not been included in the current modelling analysis, but only in the Global Plastics Outlook (2022[1]). The "Global Ambition" scenario presented in the Global Plastics Outlook also included a set of policies to mitigate microplastic leakage. However, due to data and information limitations, these were mostly limited to bans on microplastics intentionally added to products.

6 Comparison of costs across scenarios

This chapter presents the economic consequences of the policy scenarios explored in the previous chapters. It focuses on macroeconomic implications as indicated by the change in Gross Domestic Product (GDP), as well as the changes in costs for the collection, sorting and treatment of plastic waste. It highlights that a balanced package that combines policy action to reduce plastics use and waste flows with improved waste management is more cost-effective than policy scenarios that focus purely on downstream policy actions.

6.1. Introduction

The implementation of policies modelled in the policy scenarios presented in the previous chapters comes at a cost to the economy. For instance, increasing the collection of plastic waste has a cost, recycling tends to be more expensive than landfilling or incineration and taxes on plastics lead to higher prices.[1] One possible exception is the policy pillar on eco-design, which mostly entails facilitating better design, and enabling shifts from shorter-lived products to products with a longer lifetime and repair services. It would thus involve reduced economic activity (and value added) in some sectors, but a compensating increase in economic activity (and value added) in other sectors.

Generally, macroeconomic costs implied by a policy increase with its stringency. Economic impacts also depend on the type of policy instrument chosen to achieve the ambitions of a specific policy pillar: choosing alternative instruments in the policy mix could significantly alter the economic implications. The policies chosen in this report rely heavily on economic instruments, as these can be considered a cost-effective benchmark against which alternative policy options, such as regulatory measures, can be evaluated. Furthermore, the policy instruments modelled are the same across all scenarios (albeit with differing levels of stringency), allowing for a comparison of costs across scenarios.

This chapter presents and compares the macroeconomic costs of the ten policy instruments modelled in each policy scenario. The environmental costs of inaction are not within the scope of this chapter.

6.2. Policy packages that target all stages of the plastics lifecycle are more cost-effective at the macroeconomic level

Reduced ambition in policies across the plastics lifecycle could generally lead to lower macroeconomic consequences of policy packages, but this would translate into additional economic costs if the policy package is unbalanced (i.e. characterised by a focus on selected interventions along certain stages of the lifecycle only) and into higher environmental costs (Figure 6.1). The *Global Lifecycle Low stringency* scenario represents the outcome of a less ambitious international agreement. While a lower level of policy stringency may reduce costs relative to higher policy stringency (in the narrow sense of GDP impacts excluding avoided costs of inaction), lower policy stringency also reduces the benefits of policy action, including lower waste management costs when waste volumes decline. The *Global Downstream High stringency* and *Advanced economies Lifecycle High stringency* scenarios show that an unbalanced policy package can lead to excessive costs, including due to costs of waste management that would be higher in the presence of larger plastics production, use and waste.

Figure 6.1. Global Ambition combines large environmental benefits with modest macroeconomic costs

Percentage change in GDP (left axis) and in plastic leakage (right axis) compared to the *Baseline* in 2040

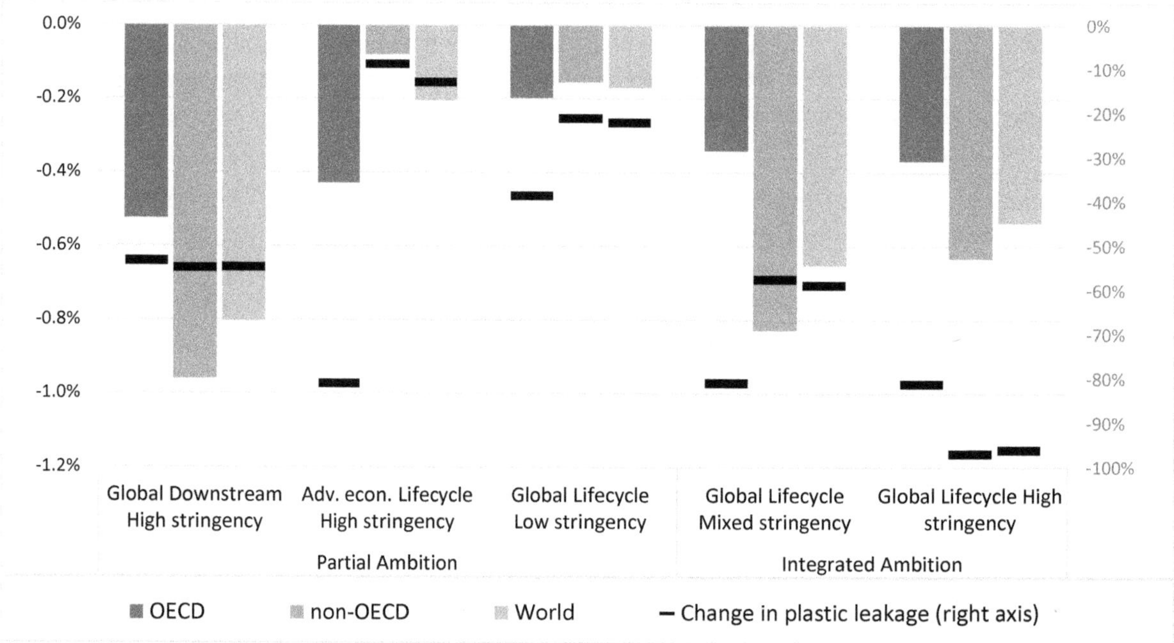

Note: The lower reduction in leakage in OECD countries compared to non-OECD countries in the *Global Lifecycle Mixed stringency* and *Global Lifecycle High stringency* [*Global Ambition*] scenarios reflects their lower share of mismanaged waste, not a lower ambition level.
Source: OECD ENV-Linkages model.

StatLink https://stat.link/c69p7y

The *Global Lifecycle Mixed stringency* scenario, which bundles the policy actions contained in the three partial ambition scenarios, also leads to larger macroeconomic costs than necessary, especially in non-OECD countries. In this scenario, non-OECD countries focus on downstream action, and thus combine ambitious targets for recycling and plastic waste management with large volumes of plastic waste generation. This implies significant costs, as well as persistent plastic leakage.

For OECD countries, both the level of ambition and the macroeconomic costs are comparable across the three most ambitious scenarios (*Advanced economies Lifecycle High stringency*, *Global Lifecycle Mixed stringency* and the *Global Lifecycle High stringency* [*Global Ambition*]), as all involve the implementation of stringent policies in OECD countries. However, the two high ambition policy scenarios come at a lower macroeconomic cost in OECD countries compared to non-OECD countries because the policy packages are more balanced across regions. As a result, firms do not lose as much competitive position relative to their non-OECD competitors.

The macroeconomic consequences of the ambitious package of policies envisioned in the *Global Lifecycle High stringency* [*Global Ambition*] scenario are limited to 0.5% of global GDP by 2040. These macroeconomic costs only reflect costs that could be included in the modelling framework, i.e. the expected costs of implementing the envisioned policy instruments and their indirect economic effects. However, substantial economic benefits would materialise from reduced pressures on the environment and human health along the plastics lifecycle. Even if such economic benefits have not been quantitatively assessed within the scope of this analysis, it is expected that they would largely offset the quantified costs of implementing the considered policy packages (OECD, 2022[1]).

While global costs are modest overall in the *Global Lifecycle High stringency* [*Global Ambition*] scenario, especially in light of the strong environmental benefits, macroeconomic costs are on balance higher in non-OECD countries (slightly more than 0.6% loss in GDP compared to the *Baseline* scenario in 2040) than in OECD countries (less than 0.4% GDP loss). One driver of this is the less developed waste management systems in place in many developing countries, and the costs implied in improving these systems (see also Section 6.3). Section 7.5 in Chapter 7 will dive deeper into the support needed for policy action in developing countries, including financing.

Significant differences in the macroeconomic impacts of the *Global Lifecycle High stringency* [*Global Ambition*] scenario are evident across policy pillars.[2] Policies to enhance recycling are the largest contributors to macroeconomic costs, and are comprised of both improving waste management systems to increase recycling rates, as well as establishing recycled content targets. Depending on the country, a tax-and-subsidy scheme implemented in the model to reduce primary plastics and stimulate secondary plastics comes at a higher cost of plastic products for consumers.[3]

Policies to design for circularity include some policies that can bring both economic and environmental benefits, as they focus on improving the economic efficiency of plastics use (i.e. reducing the plastics intensity of the economy) and shifting economic activity towards more durable goods and repair services. These measures are not profitable in the *Baseline* scenario, where plastics remain cheap, but they become cost-effective when combined with policies that increase the costs of primary plastics use (e.g. plastic taxes contained in the curb production and demand pillar).

The macroeconomic costs associated with the curb production and demand pillar, i.e. the taxes on plastics and packaging, lead to a small reduction in GDP as consumers and industry shift away from using cheap plastics. The macroeconomic effect of this shift is particularly strong in non-OECD countries, such as developing countries in Sub-Saharan Africa and Asia. The plastics intensity of these economies is on average higher than in OECD countries (see Chapter 2), mostly due to relatively low GDP levels and a less diversified economy with a smaller share of services. Thus, increased costs from taxes on plastics use are more difficult to avoid by adjusting economic activity towards less plastics-intensive sectors. Furthermore, economic development tends to be associated with a boom in infrastructure development and construction, typically accompanied by significant plastics use, before shifting toward a more services-oriented economy and a resulting decline in plastics intensity.[4]

Finally, the projected macroeconomic costs associated with closing leakage pathways, the fourth pillar of the policy package, are rather small. As explained in detail in Section 6.3, this policy pillar induces higher costs for collecting, sorting and treating waste. However, the incremental costs of implementing policies in this pillar, after other policies have already contributed to lowering total waste streams, are very modest, especially at the macroeconomic level.

Figure 6.2. The macroeconomic costs of Global Ambition vary by policy pillar and region

Contribution of policy pillars to variations in global GDP in percentage changes compared to the *Baseline*, *Global Lifecycle High stringency* [*Global Ambition*] scenario

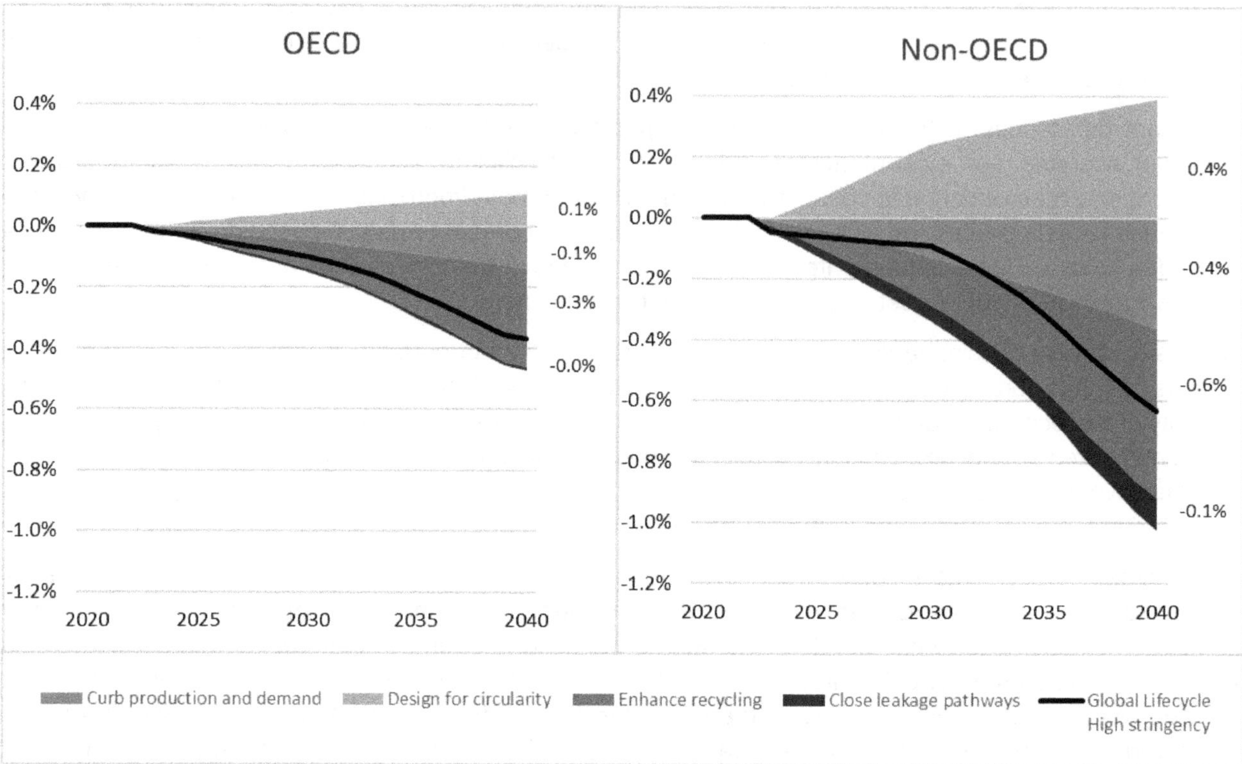

Source: OECD ENV-Linkages model.

StatLink https://stat.link/k5d8o2

6.3. Non-OECD countries face higher investment needs to enhance waste management

Enhancing waste collection, sorting and treatment, i.e. improving waste management, accounts for a substantial portion of the macroeconomic costs of the policy scenarios, as shown in the analysis of the macroeconomic costs by policy pillar above. In the *Baseline* scenario, OECD countries would already jointly invest more than USD 1 trillion in plastic waste management between 2020 and 2040. Non-OECD countries would invest a similar amount, amounting to USD 2.1 trillion globally (Figure 6.3; see also Figure 6.4, Panel A). A large portion of these costs are related to waste collection, which is characterised by relatively low unit costs that constitute a sizeable amount in aggregate. Further treatment of plastic waste for incineration or recycling has higher unit costs but significantly lower volumes. Furthermore, per-capita costs of plastic waste management vary widely across countries, with relatively high costs in the USA and Canada, and the lowest costs in Sub-Saharan Africa.

Figure 6.3. Waste management costs under business-as-usual are dominated by collection costs

Per capita cumulative waste management costs for 2020-2040 by region and category in USD, *Baseline* scenario

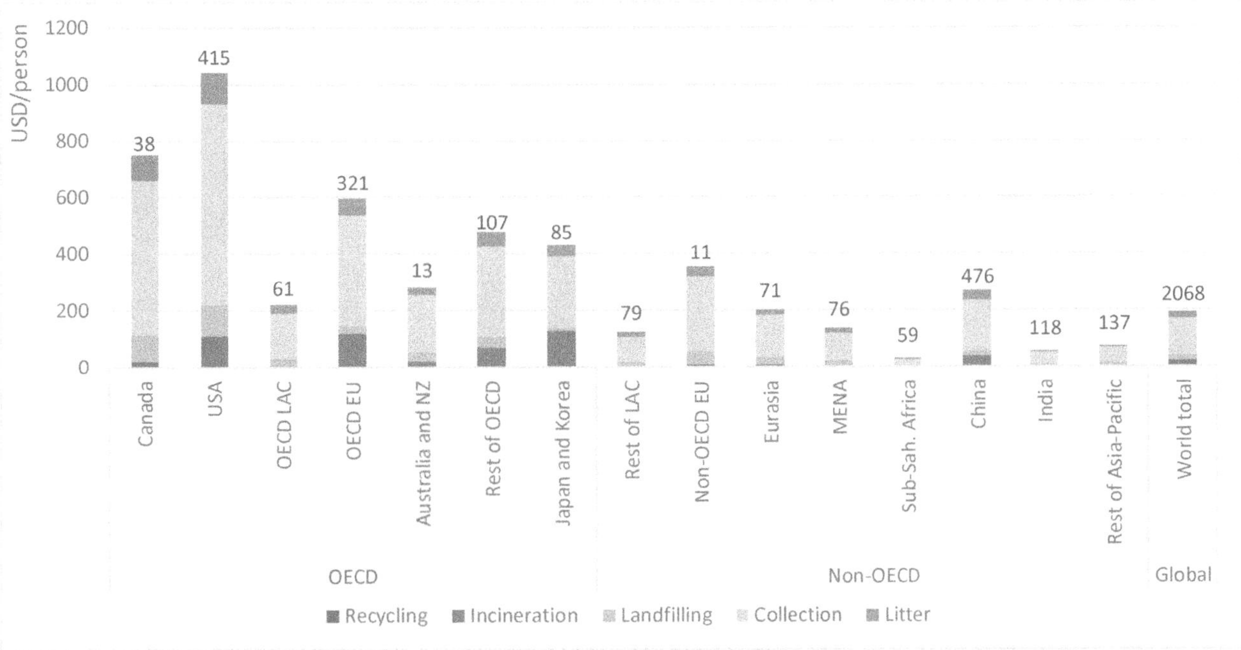

Note: Total cumulative waste management costs are presented as data labels above the bars.
Source: OECD ENV-Linkages model.

StatLink https://stat.link/3w5bjh

Policy packages have two distinct effects on waste management costs (Figure 6.4). On the one hand, the upstream and midstream policy measures can reduce total plastic waste volumes, thereby reducing the costs of collection, sorting and treatment. On the other hand, downstream policy measures imply that larger shares of waste (and litter) are collected and that more expensive waste management options are used, such as for recycling. The changes in waste management costs incurred in the policy scenarios, also referred to as "investment needs", are calculated as the difference in costs between the policy scenario and the *Baseline* scenario, and are attributed to different waste management categories, namely recycling, incineration, (sanitary) landfilling, collection and municipal litter collection.

Figure 6.4. Focusing on downstream policies leads to high costs of collecting large volumes of waste

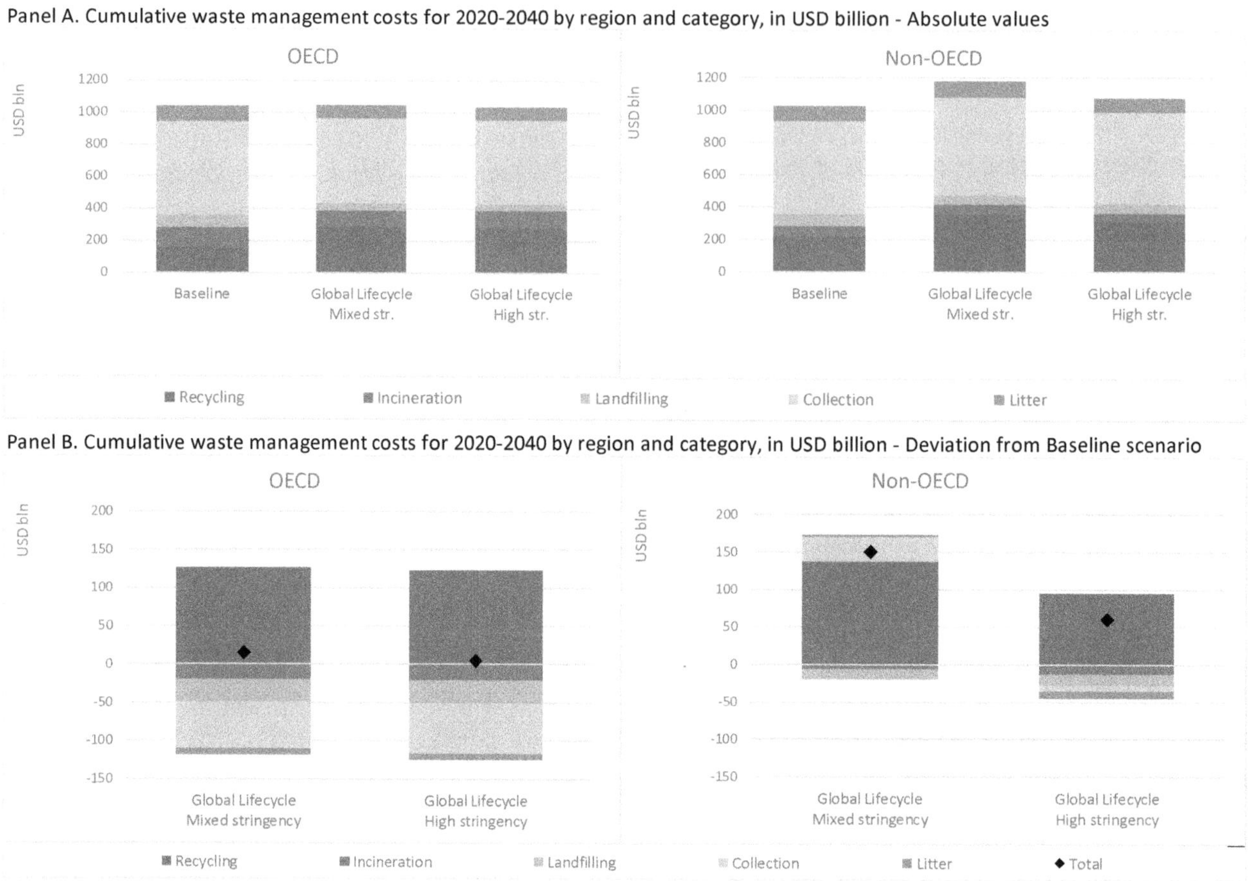

Source: OECD ENV-Linkages model.

StatLink https://stat.link/qfshp1

On balance, the net policy-induced changes in plastic waste management costs tend to be small in OECD countries, but positive in most non-OECD countries. In the former, cost increases are almost exclusively due to increased recycling, while in many emerging and developing economies significant increased costs are also entailed for the collection of plastic waste, especially in the absence of sufficient upstream and midstream measures to reduce waste volumes.

For OECD countries, where mismanaged waste levels are already minimal in the *Baseline*, the additional costs are concentrated in recycling activities, amounting to more than USD 120 billion between 2020 and 2040 in both the *Global Lifecycle Mixed stringency* and *Global Lifecycle High stringency* [*Global Ambition*] scenarios. These values don't represent a net cost due to the fact that upstream and midstream measures also reduce waste volumes and thus lower the operational costs of waste management. The same result applies to China.

Growth in waste generation in the *Global Lifecycle Mixed stringency* scenario exacerbates the scale of the problem to be managed and threatens to strain waste collection and management systems, especially in rapidly growing low- and middle- income economies. As plastics use and waste remain unchecked, some countries face considerably higher costs and investment needs, while plastic leakage persists. In the *Global Lifecycle Mixed stringency* scenario, the costs required to establish needed waste management systems in non-OECD countries at requisite scales (i.e. the costs associated with recycling waste collection and litter management), would reach USD 174 billion, while the avoided costs of incineration and landfilling is limited to USD 20 billion.

In countries with significant mismanaged waste shares in the *Baseline* scenario, such as those in Sub-Saharan Africa and emerging economies and developing countries in Asia (Rest of Asia region), increased collection costs outweigh the lower waste volumes even in the *Global Lifecycle High stringency* [*Global Ambition*] scenario, leading to a total cost increase of USD 18 billion in Sub-Saharan Africa and USD 14 billion in Rest of Asia (Figure 6.5). Nevertheless, the effects of combining measures all along the lifecycle contribute to limiting increases in the net costs of waste collection, sorting and treatment in non-OECD countries in the *Global Lifecycle High stringency* [*Global Ambition*] scenario. The net costs of waste management increase by a relatively modest USD 50 billion in this scenario over *Baseline* levels. Box 6.1 further illustrates how changes in waste management costs are associated with the different policy pillars.

Figure 6.5. Reduced waste volumes largely offset increased waste management costs in many countries in the *Global Lifecycle High stringency* [*Global Ambition*] scenario

Cumulative waste management costs for 2020-2040 by category in deviation from the Baseline scenario (in USD billion), *Global Lifecycle High stringency* [*Global Ambition*] scenario

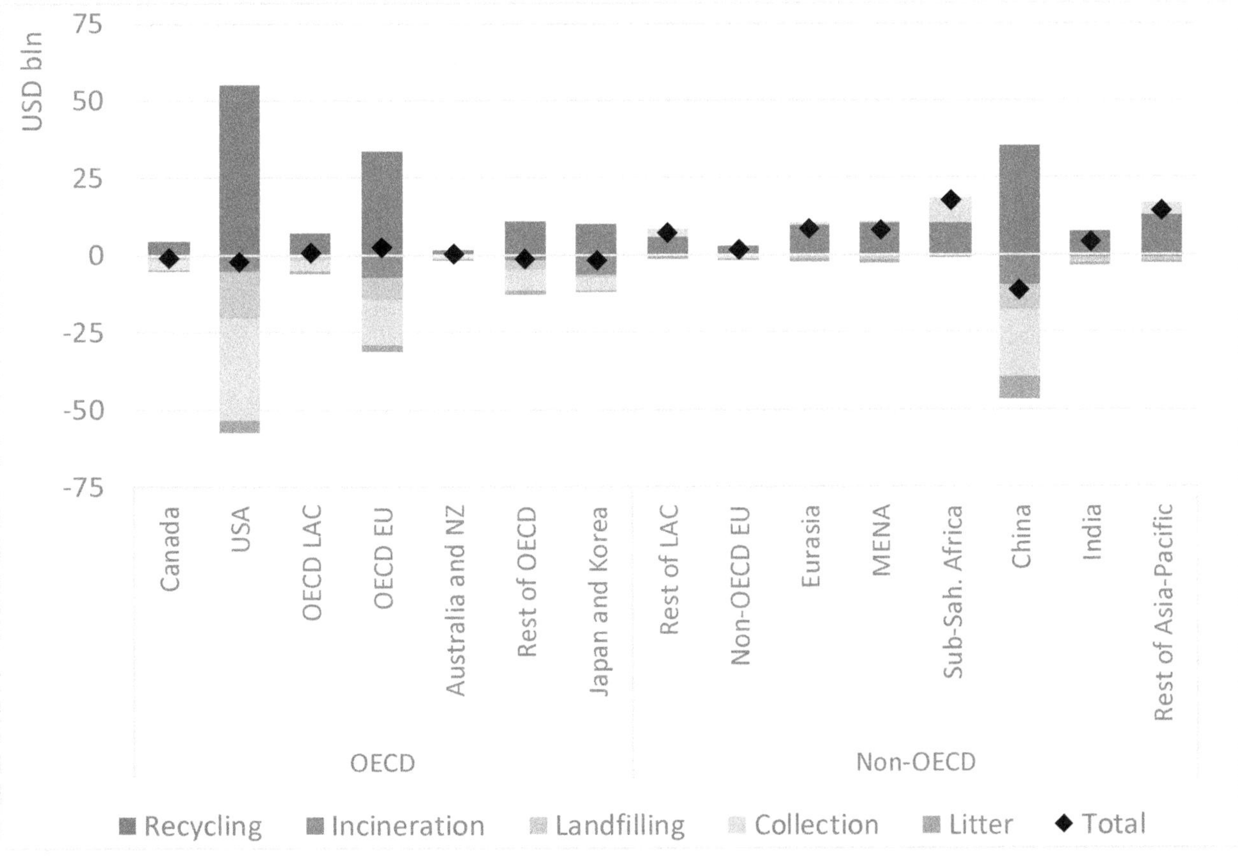

Source: OECD ENV-Linkages model.

StatLink https://stat.link/yf5sle

Finally, technical uncertainties could complicate the viability of over-reliance on downstream measures and increase the costs of policy implementation beyond the projections presented here. Technological constraints, including the time needed to establish sanitary landfills or recycling facilities, may impede their rapid development. Additionally, as the *Global Lifecycle High stringency* [*Global Ambition*] scenario assumes rapid recycling expansion across all regions, concerns emerge regarding the availability of sufficient scrap materials and the functioning of international scrap markets to sustain this ambitious recycling effort.

In conclusion, although prioritising downstream policy interventions has the potential to contain mismanaged waste, this approach is likely to fall short in tackling the root drivers of plastic pollution. This is due in part to the significantly higher investment needed to manage growing amounts of waste and the possible technical constraints that could hinder the development of advanced waste management systems. Considerable uncertainty exists regarding the possible viability and cost-effectiveness of a downstream-oriented strategy. Downstream-focused strategies in low- and middle- income countries hinge on assumptions that nations that currently lack robust waste management collection and management systems can swiftly implement the necessary policies and investments. A shared recognition of the need for whole-of-lifecycle approaches is likely to be the most cost-effective strategy to achieving the global goal of eliminating plastic pollution.

Box 6.1. Allocating changes in waste management costs to policies sheds light on the effort needed to close leakage pathways

Changes in plastic waste incineration costs as presented in Figure 6.5 are driven by three factors: (i) total waste volumes decline as a result of upstream and midstream policy measures (to curb production and demand and to enhance eco-design); (ii) the share of waste that is incinerated declines due to policies to enhance recycling; and (iii) closing leakage pathways implies higher waste collection rates as well as lower litter loss rates, thus increasing the amount of waste that is treated (Figure 6.5). Figure 6.6 decomposes waste management costs according to these three policy effects.

Figure 6.6. The changes in costs for the different policy pillars largely offset each other

Cumulative waste management costs 2020-2040 by policy driver, deviation from the *Baseline* scenario (in USD billion)

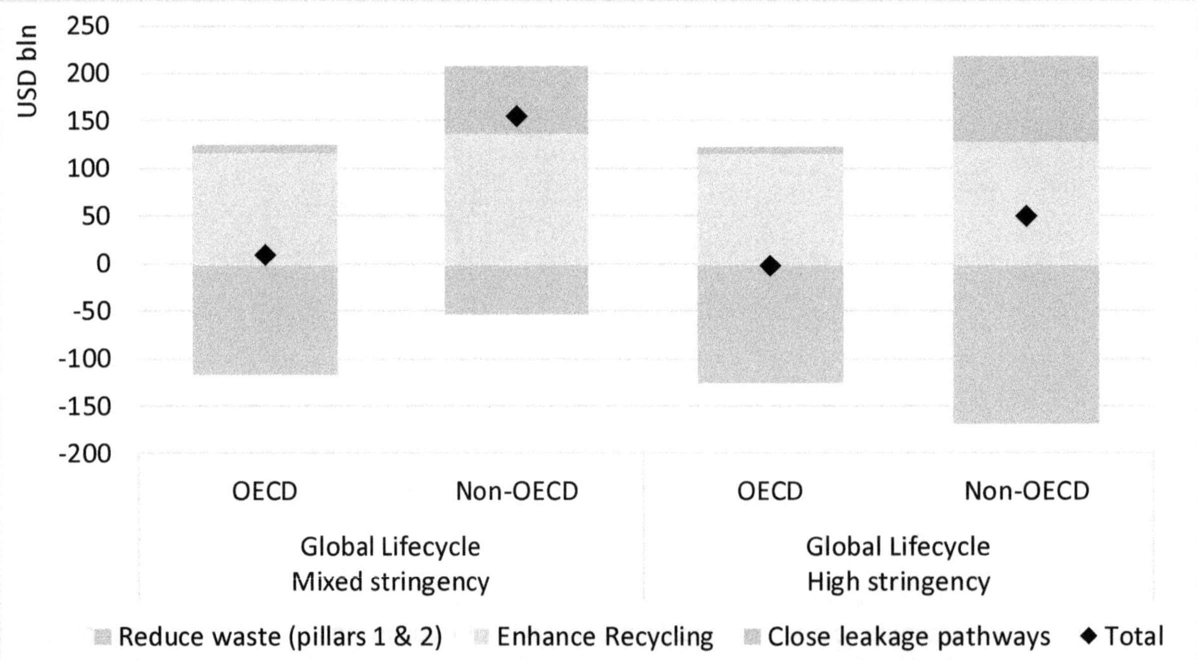

Note: Totals are identical to those in Figure 6.5.
Source: OECD ENV-Linkages model.

StatLink https://stat.link/vc7yn8

Especially in countries with currently minimal mismanaged waste shares, the effects of the upstream and midstream policies to reduce waste are roughly similar to the negative cost categories in Figure 6.5, as the reduction in incineration costs is largely driven by the reduction in the total generation of plastic waste.

However, in countries with significant levels of mismanaged waste, the cost savings from upstream and midstream policies are larger than the change in waste collection costs suggested in Figure 6.5, as the latter are comprised of reduced waste generation (a saving compared to *Baseline*) and increased costs of collection (additional costs, mainly for additional waste collection and recycling, compared to *Baseline*). In the alternative decomposition presented in Figure 6.6, these additional costs reflect the costs associated with closing leakage pathways, defined as the increased costs of collection (incl. litter) and management in absence of the effect of the upstream policies.

Finally, the additional waste management costs associated with enhanced recycling largely consist of the additional recycling costs, which are partially offset by lower incineration and landfilling costs.

The figure above shows that the lower waste management costs in the *Global Lifecycle High stringency* [*Global Ambition*] scenario, relative to the *Global Lifecycle Mixed stringency* scenario, stem from the effect of policies to curb production and demand, and policies to promote the eco-design of products. The costs of enhancing recycling are very similar (as the policy package is largely the same), while the costs associated with closing leakage pathways are somewhat higher, but also more effective as mismanaged waste shares are reduced to zero.

6.4. Co-ordinated approaches can limit the costs of action

Policy packages that focus on downstream measures, especially the *Global Downstream High stringency* scenario, would reduce plastic leakage while total plastic waste increases, leading to a significant increase in total waste management costs. The absence of upstream policy measures is therefore not cost-effective for waste management (Figure 6.7).

Figure 6.7. Balancing upstream, midstream and downstream policies can make policy packages more cost-effective

Percentage change in plastic leakage compared to Baseline in 2040 versus cumulative waste management costs for 2020-2040 (in USD billion)

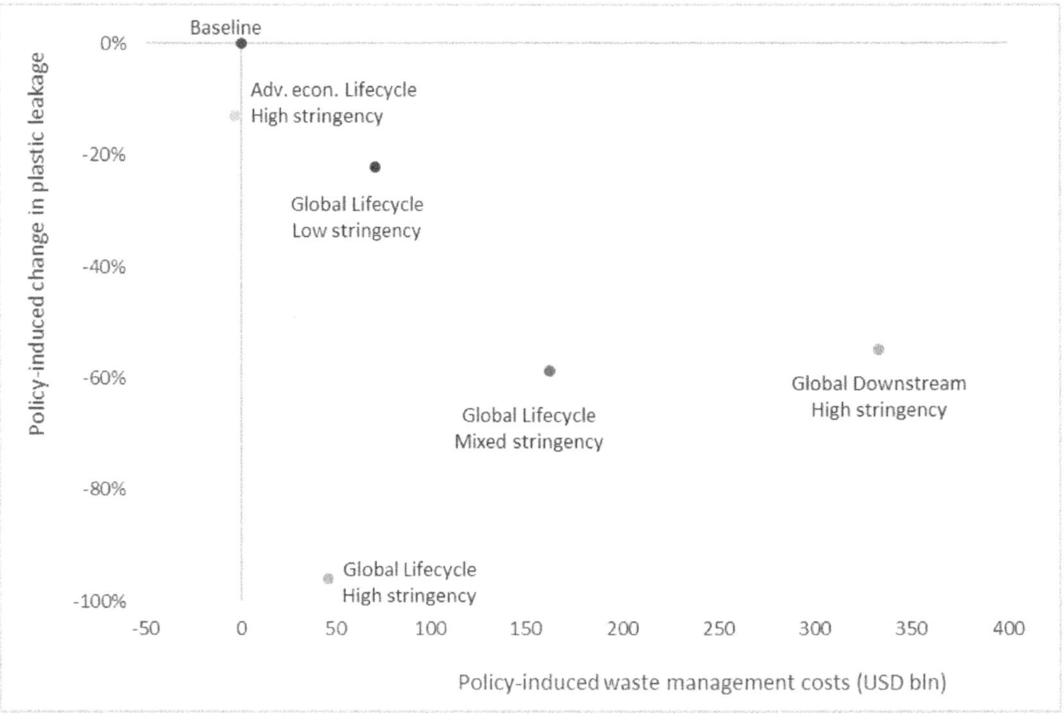

Source: OECD ENV-Linkages model.

StatLink https://stat.link/2897lo

In contrast, high policy ambition throughout the plastics lifecycle in Advanced economies only will have very limited effects on global waste management costs, as most advanced economies already have very high waste collection rates. Correspondingly, reductions in global plastic leakage also remain small. The *Global Lifecycle Low stringency* scenario, which balances measures across all four policy pillars but with partial ambition levels, has impacts that fall somewhere in between.

Combining the three partial ambition scenarios in the *Global Lifecycle Mixed stringency* scenario helps to avoid the largest costs of the pure downstream scenario, by incorporating the ambitious upstream and midstream policies in *Advanced economies Lifecycle High stringency* and the *Global Lifecycle Low stringency* policies for emerging and developing economies. However, this integrated policy scenario cannot eliminate all plastic leakage and is still characterised by an over-reliance on downstream policies.

As a result, the *Global Lifecycle High stringency* [*Global Ambition*] scenario improves the *Global Lifecycle Mixed stringency* scenario by further aligning upstream and midstream policies, eliminating plastic leakage and simultaneously reducing total global waste management costs.

The above findings regarding the cost-effectiveness of balanced policy packages hold at global level, but can still incur costs in countries that have a low capacity to raise the required investment for waste management. Therefore, the globally efficient solution could benefit from flanking policies to help developing countries create capacity for policy implementation and waste management, and to provide international support for the required investments. This issue is discussed further in Chapter 7.

6.5. What would be the economic and environmental implications of slower action?

The speed of policy implementation in the *Global Lifecycle High stringency* [*Global Ambition*] scenario stretches the economy, and especially waste management systems. Targeting an end to plastic pollution after 2040 could potentially lower the transitional costs. The *Global Lifecycle Delayed stringency* policy scenario explores this possibility by modelling the same policy package as the *Global Lifecycle High stringency* [*Global Ambition*] scenario but over a longer timeframe, aligned with a 2060 target for the elimination of macroplastic leakage.[5] Delayed action could generate short term economic benefits but with significant repercussions for plastic pollution and negative effects on the well-being of current and future generations.

Indeed, implementing the policies over a longer timeframe (as in the *Global Lifecycle Delayed stringency* scenario) could limit macroeconomic costs by 2040 to 0.2% of global GDP, compared to 0.5% for *Global Lifecycle High stringency* [*Global Ambition*] (Figure 6.8). Longer-term costs to 2060 would be very similar across both scenarios. Reduced ambition levels by 2040 could contain macroeconomic costs to 2040 in all countries due to slower policy implementation, as well as a slower restructuring of waste management systems. Furthermore, when the ambition to eliminate plastic leakage is delayed, some countries can reap temporary competitiveness gains when they have relatively modest targets and significant capacity to enhance recycling. This is due to the assumption that policy stringency is tightened faster in OECD countries than in non-OECD countries, which causes a smaller rise in production costs for some exporting sectors in Asia (notably China) than in most other regions, allowing them to benefit from the consequent temporary increase in competitiveness (OECD, 2022[1]). This is an exceptional case, however, and is not expected to persist in the long term as countries gradually increase policy stringency to meet the global target. The temporary rise in GDP also does not take into account the externalities associated with a delayed target, namely through missed opportunities to reduce plastics production and plastic waste and to avoid additional leakage to the environment and pollution. These externalities would imply higher clean-up costs in the future, as well as significant negative effects on well-being through health and environmental damages.

Figure 6.8. Slower ambition can half transitional macroeconomic costs in the medium term

Impact on GDP of policy scenarios by region, expressed in percentage change compared to the *Baseline* in 2040

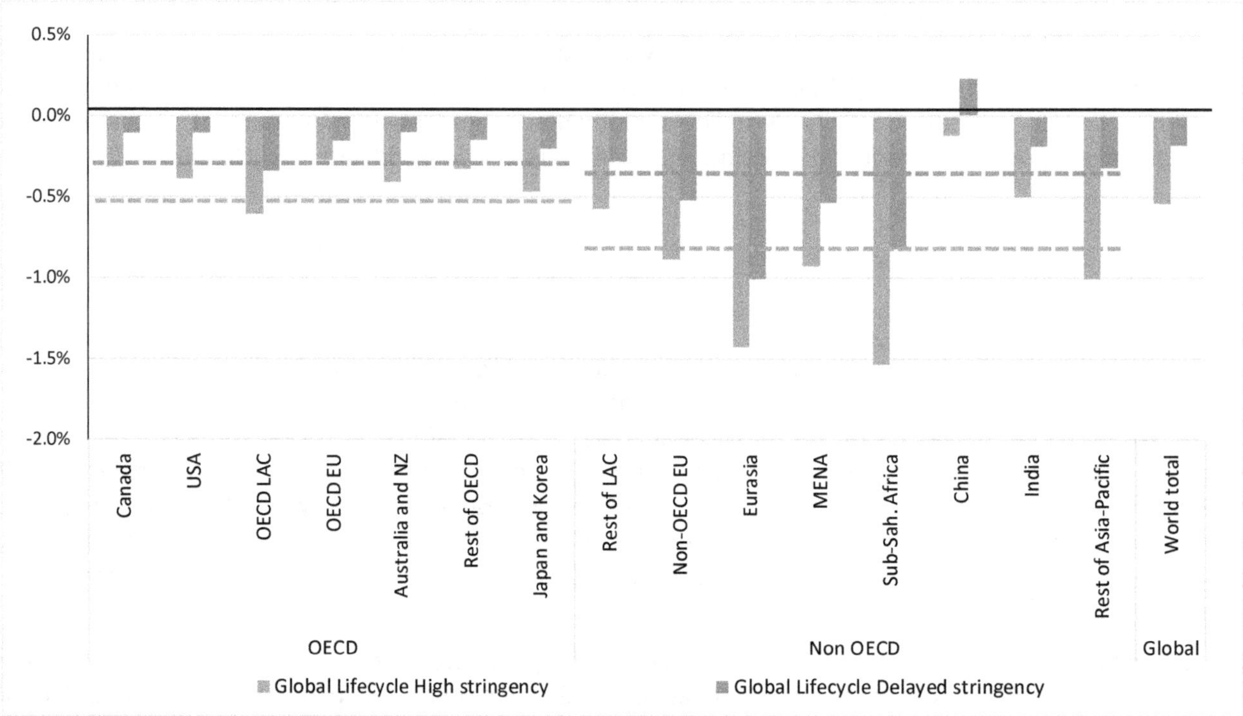

Note: The dashed lines represent average impact on GDP for OECD (left) and non-OECD (right) countries.
Source: OECD ENV-Linkages model.

StatLink https://stat.link/4oya7v

Importantly, delayed action would impose a significantly larger environmental and health burden on present and future generations (Figure 6.9; Box 6.2). Mismanaged waste volumes would fall relatively slowly and 64 million tonnes (Mt) of waste would still be mismanaged in 2040. Similarly, levels of macroplastic leakage would only fall by 1.1% annually over the 2020-2040 period (versus 13% in *Global Lifecycle High stringency* [*Global Ambition*]), meaning that around 16 Mt of macroplastics would still leak into the environment annually by 2040. The slower pathway to zero macroplastic leakage results in an additional 38 Mt of macroplastics accumulated in aquatic environments alone over the 2020-2040 period. As more plastics accumulate in these environments, they tend to degrade into smaller microplastics and become harder, or virtually impossible, to remove and thus the additional aquatic leakage poses more severe environmental consequences. Finally, a slower pathway would also imply an additional 3.9 Gt CO_2-eq. of plastics-related greenhouse gas emissions between 2020 and 2040, compared to *Global Lifecycle High stringency* [*Global Ambition*] scenario.

Figure 6.9. Delayed action amplifies plastic pollution in rivers and oceans

Stocks of macroplastics accumulating in aquatic environments by 2040, million tonnes (Mt)

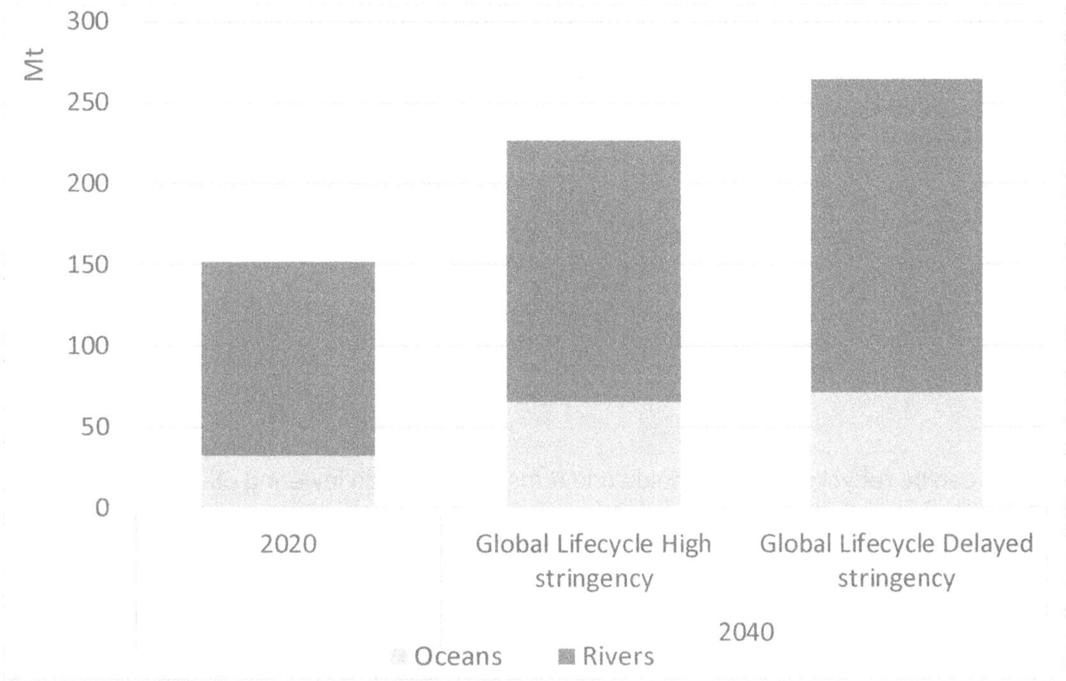

Source: (Lebreton, 2024[2]), based on OECD ENV-Linkages model projections.

StatLink https://stat.link/6hzldt

Box 6.2. The long-term environmental benefits of rapid policy action

Delaying policy ambition from 2040 to 2060 implies that plastic leakage continues after 2040, leading to a range of negative outcomes between 2040 and 2060. These include more plastic accumulated in the environment, including in rivers and oceans, and higher greenhouse gas emissions.

Compared to the *Global Lifecycle High stringency* [Global Ambition] scenario, the *Global Lifecycle Delayed stringency* scenario would result in the following by 2060:

+ 936 Mt additional plastic waste over 2020-2060	**+ 297 Mt** additional plastic leakage over 2020-2060	**+ 7.2 Gt CO_2-e** in GHG emissions levels over 2020-2060	**+ 92 Mt** accumulated plastic stocks in rivers and oceans

Source: OECD ENV-Linkages model.

References

Lebreton, L. (2024), *Quantitative analysis of aquatic leakage for multiple scenarios based on ENV-Linkages*, unpublished. [2]

OECD (2022), *Global Plastics Outlook: Policy Scenarios to 2060*, OECD Publishing, Paris, https://doi.org/10.1787/aa1edf33-en. [1]

Notes

[1] Tax revenues can be recycled to households and firms, e.g. through lowering other taxes or by increasing lump-sum transfers to households. The macroeconomic costs of a tax policy are therefore not the cost of the tax itself, but the costs associated with the tax shift, which are much lower.

[2] The distribution of costs over the various pillars differ across scenarios depending on which pillars are emphasised.

[3] The policy is implemented in the model such that the tax revenues on primary plastics cover the subsidy expenditures on secondary plastics in a manner that is in principle budget-neutral to governments (apart from indirect effects). Depending on the specific country circumstances, however, this may increase or decrease the consumer price of plastics.

[4] The Global Plastics Outlook (OECD, 2022[1]) shows that this inverse U-curve exists for macroplastics, but not for microplastics.

[5] The ambition for the global plastics recycling rate by 2060, as aligned with the Global Plastics Outlook. is higher than the ambition for 2040 in the *Global Lifecycle High stringency* [*Global Ambition*] scenario, reflecting the fact that technological barriers to recycling are likely to diminish over time.

7 Putting the Global Ambition into context: Challenges and priorities

Stringent policy packages implemented globally can facilitate the transition towards a world free of plastic pollution. This chapter discusses challenges and priorities ahead for policymakers in the implementation of policies along the lifecycle of plastics. The chapter also looks at the research efforts that are required to close knowledge gaps and to ensure adequate means of implementation in all countries.

7.1. Introduction

As presented in the previous chapters, global ambition via the implementation of stringent policies across the world and targeting multiple stages of the lifecycle (as modelled in the *Global Lifecycle High stringency* [*Global Ambition*] scenario) could deliver large benefits for the environment, as well as for human well-being. However, the realisation of these benefits rests on the assumption that a number of barriers are overcome. This chapter discusses challenges and priorities ahead for policymakers in the implementation of the four pillars, including policy instruments to curb production and demand and foster eco-design, and policies to enhance recycling and close leakage pathways. The chapter also looks at the research efforts that are required to close knowledge gaps, such as regarding microplastic pollution and the related mitigation measures, and to ensure adequate means of implementation for the successful introduction of stringent policy packages in all world regions.

7.2. Accelerate action to slow plastic flows and foster eco-design

As part of an overall containment of plastics production and use, the *Global Lifecycle High stringency* [*Global Ambition*] scenario would see a dramatic reduction in plastics demand for packaging applications, which is expected to grow by 70% by 2040 in the *Baseline* scenario. Structural changes in the economy will be required in order to achieve significant reductions in plastics demand, for instance to shift from single-use applications to reuse systems. The stylised policy package of the *Global Lifecycle High stringency* [*Global Ambition*] scenario modelled in this report assumes that all countries are capable of and willing to implement taxes on plastics production or use. As also discussed in Chapter 1, to accommodate specific country circumstances, taxes could be avoided if other instruments are found to be equally effective in incentivising a reduction in plastic flows.

7.2.1. Harmonised standards would support the removal or phase down of problematic plastics and the eco-design of plastic products

The identification and gradual removal of avoidable and problematic plastics can play an important role in reducing waste mismanagement and leakage, as well as reducing concerns for human health. More than 140 countries have banned or restricted selected plastic products and packaging, often single-use plastic applications that are known to be particularly prone to littering and leakage to the environment. However, additional efforts are required to identify unsafe plastic items, polymers and additives, as well as to develop solutions that avoid possible unintended risks of substitution. Raubenheimer and Urho (2024[1]) have proposed potential criteria based on a determination of the function or end-use of a product, and whether it is deemed essential or not, as summarised in Figure 7.1.

Incorporating circularity considerations in product design is essential to prolonging product lifespans and to enabling safe reuse, improved repairability, as well as higher recycling rates. However, rethinking product design can present technical and economic barriers. Governments should consider policy frameworks that promote design for circularity and facilitate the adoption of supportive business models.

Figure 7.1. Decision hierarchy for determination of problematic, unnecessary and avoidable products

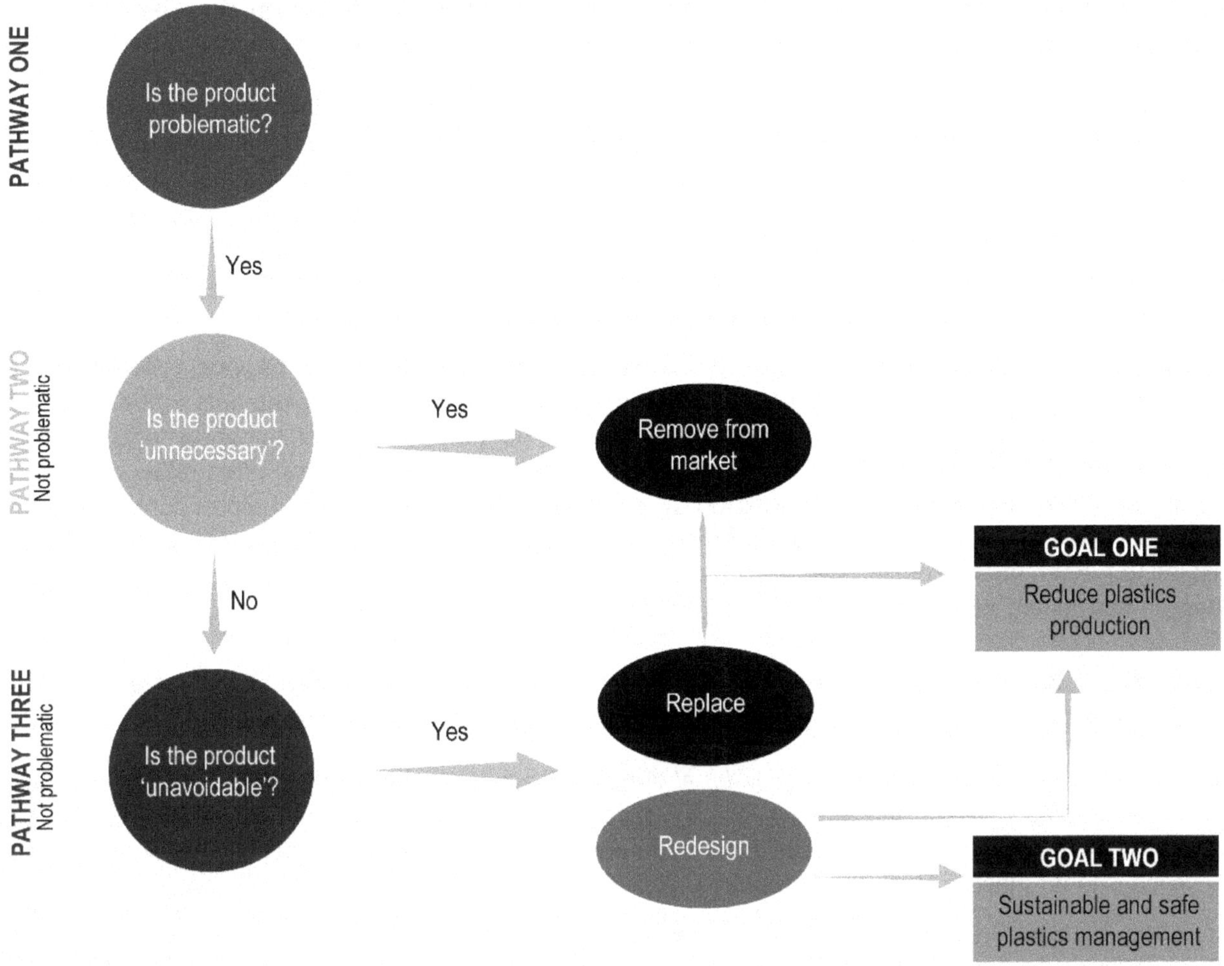

Source: Adapted based on (Raubenheimer and Urho, 2024[1]).

7.2.2. Strong incentives, infrastructural investments and harmonised standards could facilitate the scale-up of reuse systems

Reuse systems offer the promise of reducing plastics demand and waste generation, especially of short-lived plastics applications. Broadly defined, these systems are designed to enable multiple circulations of an item, typically packaging. The consumer benefits from the service provided by the item, e.g. the provision of packaged meals, and then returns it to the provider. As items intended for reuse are generally more resource-intensive than single-use alternatives and dedicated infrastructure and maintenance is required (e.g. washing), the certainty of multiple uses is essential to securing environmental benefits.

While reuse can be implemented in closed loop systems, it is most effective when implemented at scale. To this end, collaboration between industry and different levels of governments is essential to establishing coherent policy frameworks around reuse. Public incentives for reuse and innovation can play a pivotal role in facilitating the expansion and integration of these models on a larger scale, including to incentivise investments in the infrastructure required. Reuse systems must be designed to fit the specific needs of each sector and socio-economic context. At the international level, developing clear definitions of reuse and harmonising criteria could help to establish a clear and enforceable framework, discourage fragmented approaches and foster investments into reuse models.

7.3. Support environmentally sound waste management in all regions

7.3.1. Technical and financial support is required to set up systems for waste collection around the world

As discussed in Chapter 5, progress towards ending plastic pollution will require significant improvements in waste collection and sorting, especially in developing countries. Many low- and middle-income countries tend to have lower use and waste generation levels, in per capita terms, compared to high-income countries. However, they tend to have less-developed waste collection and management services, often with the persistence of practices such as open dumping and burning that exacerbate environmental and human health concerns. Governance challenges as well as limited financial resources currently hinder the rapid development of effective waste management infrastructure in these contexts.

To support the expansion of efficient collection and sorting systems in all world regions, policies such as EPR schemes and waste collection targets have proven to be effective. Improvements in the collection, sorting and treatment of plastic waste are expected to be part of general enhancements in waste management, beyond targeting plastic materials and waste. As waste collection often relies on informal waste pickers, solutions that ensure the integration of the informal sector would help to achieve the high collection rates set out in the *Global Lifecycle High stringency* [*Global Ambition*] scenario, while also mitigating human health concerns for workers and ensuring a just transition. As discussed in the previous chapter, restraining demand for plastics can play a pivotal role in containing the costs of waste collection.

7.3.2. Major technical breakthroughs may be required to achieve the significant improvements in recycling envisioned in the high ambition scenarios

The *Global Lifecycle High stringency* [*Global Ambition*] scenario projects a near-total elimination of mismanaged plastic waste and a major shift to recycling in the end of life treatment of plastics, to cover 42% of waste generated in 2040 (Figure 7.2). This would correspond to a quadrupling of the average global recycling rate for plastics (from 9.5% in 2020).

Currently, both available recycling technologies and the availability of scrap limit the expansion of the transition to secondary plastics. The challenges of mechanical recycling of post-consumer plastic waste vary across waste streams. They include the availability of recycling infrastructure for certain types of plastics (such as for PET), the possible presence of hazardous additives, as well as the need for dismantling operations for complex waste streams (such as those treating electronic and electric equipment) (Landrigan et al., 2023[2]). Achieving the outcomes of the *Global Lifecycle High stringency* [*Global Ambition*] policy scenario will require strong improvements in recycling and reductions of recycling losses (Box 7.1). Scaled investments in recycling technologies, combined with upstream and midstream interventions (including improved design for recycling), are required to expand the sources of viable feedstock for mechanical recycling.

Box 7.1. Not all plastics collected for recycling are recycled

Plastic waste that is collected for recycling frequently includes some non-plastic materials. Moreover, collected plastic waste typically includes a multitude of plastic items and fragments with varying chemical and physical compositions. The degree to which what is collected is useful to plastics reprocessing depends on a range of factors. In general, high income countries implement recycling collection schemes that are designed to yield high material mass through an accessible and simplified system that is easy for people to understand. Conversely, in many low- and middle-income countries, separate waste collection for recycling is carried out by informal workers who selectively collect the most valuable items and objects from waste streams, focusing on quality and concentration rather than high yield. Even with diligent, selective collection, plastic articles contain a multitude of intentionally and non-intentionally appended, entrapped, adhered and entrained materials and objects that must be removed from the dominant plastic before it can be reprocessed.

The estimates and projections presented in this report for the category "recycled plastic waste" refer to plastic waste that has effectively been recycled, i.e. net of recycling losses.

Source: (OECD, 2022[3])

The *Global Lifecycle High stringency* [*Global Ambition*] scenario relies on the assumption that high recycling rates can be attained for all waste streams and polymers, including those that are barely recycled at present, via mechanical recycling technologies.[1] This implies that major technical breakthroughs may be required to enable the large-scale switch from primary to secondary plastics for all polymers and achieve the consequential reductions in environmental impacts. Should these substantial technical breakthroughs fail to materialise, meeting the ambitions of the policy package will require heightened ambition in other parts of the policy package, for instance via induced reductions in the use of hard-to-recycle polymers or more significant reductions in plastics demand.

Figure 7.2. Global Ambition requires significant technological advancements in recycling

Average global recycling rate

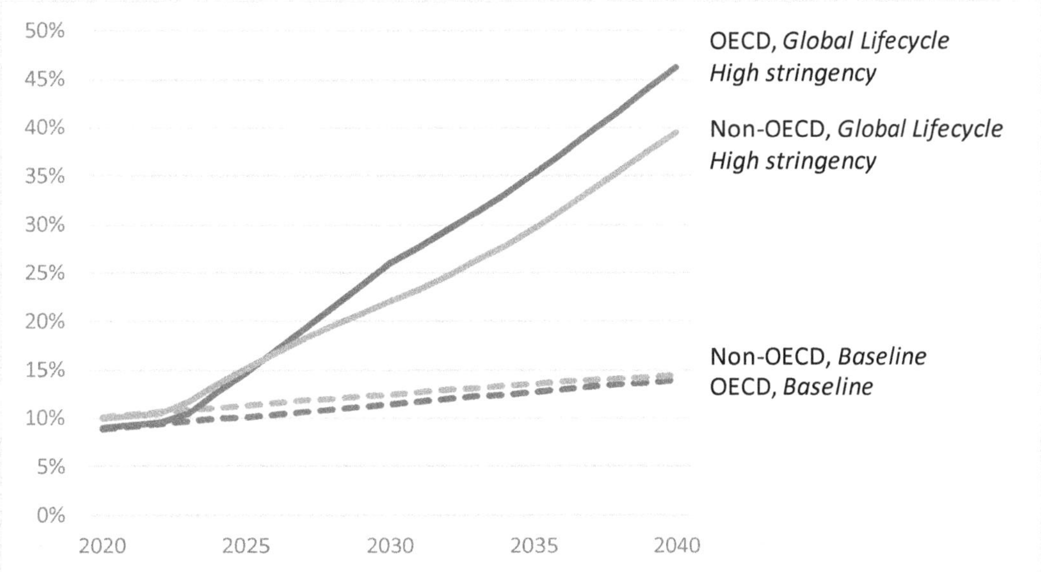

Note: The recycling rate expresses the percentage of total waste generated in a given year, that is recycled into secondary plastics.
Source: OECD ENV-Linkages model.

StatLink https://stat.link/zsxw72

In addition, reducing the volume of littered waste (i.e. waste that escapes collection, either because it is littered by individuals or due to fly-tipping) is an important action for reducing leakage to the environment. It is likely impossible to collect all littered waste via municipal collection, but the *Global Lifecycle High stringency* [*Global Ambition*] scenario assumes a significant increase in litter picking rates and street sweeping in all regions, beyond the improvements in this area already assumed in the *Baseline* scenario that stem from increased income levels (Figure 7.3). The required increases are especially high in Africa and India, where litter collection rates in 2040 are assumed to rise from 65% in the *Baseline* scenario to 75% in the *Global Lifecycle High stringency* [*Global Ambition*] scenario. Globally, the avoided leakage from improved litter removal is projected to be more than 1.2 million tonnes (Mt) by 2040.

Figure 7.3. Global Ambition requires strong improvements in the municipal collection of littered waste

Collected and uncollected litter in million tonnes (Mt)

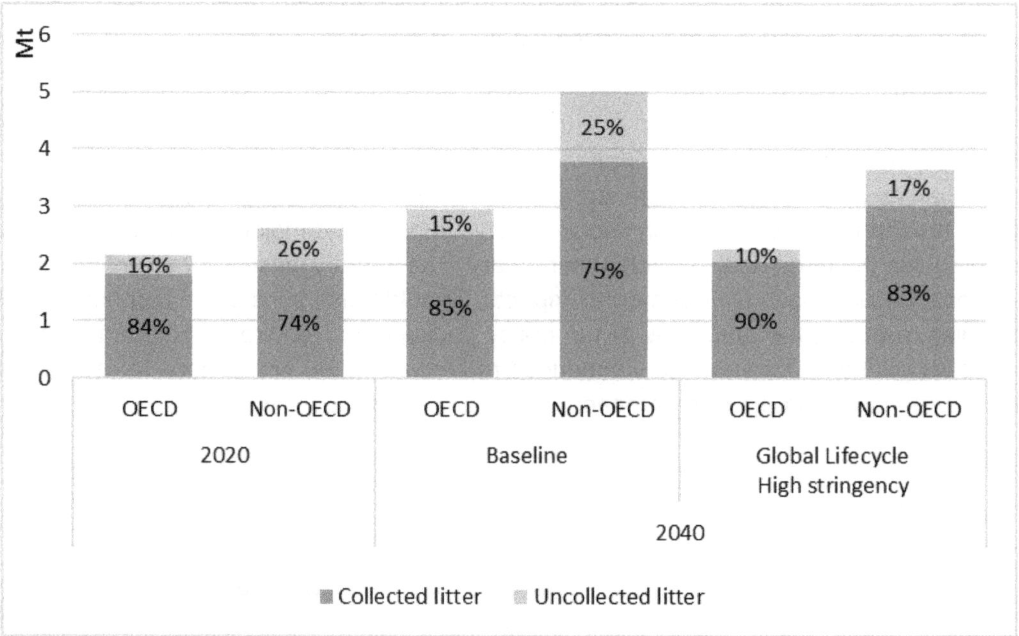

Source: OECD ENV-Linkages model.

StatLink https://stat.link/bj08g2

7.4. Further research is required to better inform action on microplastic leakage and the need for remedial action

Microplastic pollution is an emerging threat to ecosystem and human health. Due to data and information limitations, the *Global Lifecycle High stringency* [*Global Ambition*] scenario includes only a limited set of policies specifically targeting microplastic leakage, such as bans on the intentional addition of microplastics during the manufacture of cosmetic and personal care products. Reductions in microplastic leakage in this scenario would largely stem from reductions in overall plastics use or from expected improvements in end-of-pipe capture (e.g. wastewater treatment). Reductions in macroplastic leakage could also mitigate the generation of microplastics from the degradation of plastics polluting the environment.

Although not considered in the model, policies that can specifically mitigate the leakage of microplastics will also need to form an important part of the policy mix in order to ensure the effective mitigation of microplastic pollution. Further research is necessary to evaluate the cost-effectiveness of possible mitigation options and inform the choice of policy interventions. Despite existing knowledge gaps, significant progress can be achieved in the short term by focusing on mitigation options that generate co-benefits aligned with other environmental policy objectives, such as policies for climate change mitigation and improvements in air quality and water quality that also contribute to reducing microplastic leakage, such as reductions in road transport volumes. Other sources of microplastic leakage should also be investigated to broaden our understanding of the magnitude of the problem and the possible solutions.

Further research could also help to inform remedial interventions that may be required to reduce risks to the environment and human health. As discussed in Chapter 5, legacy plastic pollution and additional contributions that would still be expected between 2020 and 2040 would lead to an amplification of plastic pollution. Stocks of macroplastics in rivers and oceans, often taken as a proxy for plastic pollution, would rise from 152 Mt in 2020 to 226 Mt in 2040 in *Global Lifecycle High stringency* [*Global Ambition*] scenario (74 Mt less than in the *Baseline* scenario). In addition to the policy interventions envisioned in the *Global Lifecycle High stringency* [*Global Ambition*] scenario, remedial interventions would have an important role to play in mitigating risks to ecosystems and human well-being, especially in developing countries most affected by plastic pollution. Clean-up interventions, such as interventions targeted at hotspots and citizen clean-ups, may also help to gather data on environmental pollution and to inform policy efforts. At the same time, specific attention should be paid to the environmental impacts of clean-up interventions, especially in the case of novel technologies. Plastic clean-up technologies can play an important role in reducing litter in the environment; however, there are concerns that unregulated clean-up technologies may be inefficient and have unintended negative consequences on ecosystems, for example, through bycatch or removal of organic matter important for ecosystem functions (Falk-Andersson et al., 2023[4]).

7.5. Means of implementation and financing

While more ambitious policy action is needed in all countries to help move from a linear to a circular plastics economy and effectively end plastic pollution, it is important to recognise that a heavier burden is placed on many developing countries in order to achieve these objectives, including small island developing states. These countries often exhibit fast growth in plastics use (including in sectors that are pivotal for development, such as transport and infrastructure) and high levels of waste mismanagement. Concurrently, they can be particularly vulnerable to plastic pollution and the associated risks, especially when they rely heavily on sectors such as fisheries and tourism. This specific context underscores the critical role of developing countries in the global fight to end plastic pollution.

The benefits of the transition to plastic pollution-free economies is likely to benefit all countries, but the projected economic costs of the transition are uneven across world regions. As discussed in Chapter 6, the macroeconomic costs are larger for developing countries than for developed countries in all policy scenarios modelled, except the *Global Lifecycle Low stringency* scenario (where the costs are small and in relative terms roughly equal across countries) and in the *Advanced economies Lifecycle High stringency* scenario (where developing countries don't implement any new policies at all). In the *Global Lifecycle High stringency* [*Global Ambition*] scenario, eliminating macroplastic leakage would incur macroeconomic costs of approximately 0.5% of global GDP by 2040, compared to the *Baseline* scenario. However, Sub-Saharan Africa is expected to experience the largest macroeconomic impacts, reducing its GDP by 1.5% below the *Baseline* scenario, mainly due to the high additional waste management costs (Figure 7.4; see Chapter 6 for more details). In the *Baseline* scenario, waste management costs are relatively low in Sub-Saharan Africa, and the increase in collection activity and a transition towards more recycling comes with significant additional costs. Reduced costs associated with modelled measures to slow plastics use and waste generation (under the pillars to curb production and demand and to design for circularity) cannot fully compensate for the additional waste collection and treatment costs.

Figure 7.4. Costs to eliminate leakage are unevenly distributed across world regions

Distribution of economic costs (change in GDP) of implementing the policy scenario and policy-induced cumulative waste management costs by region, both in percentage changes compared to the *Baseline* in 2040, *Global Lifecycle High stringency* [*Global Ambition*] scenario

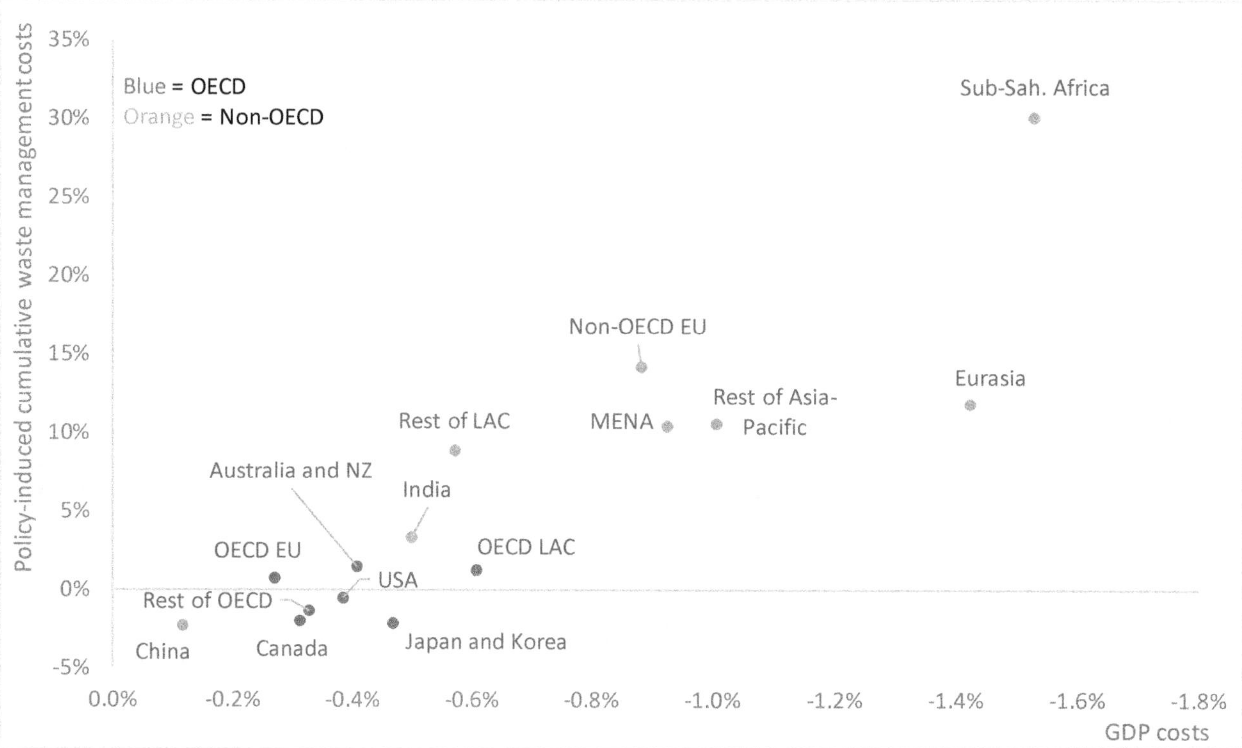

Source: OECD ENV-Linkages model.

StatLink https://stat.link/mxr0v7

7.5.1. Ensure that adequate financing of waste collection and treatment is available to all countries, in parallel to support for solutions that may contribute to waste prevention

The burden of policies and investments required falls more heavily on developing countries, especially those that currently have less advanced waste management systems. In the *Baseline* scenario, the largest increases in plastics use (and waste) are projected to occur in non-OECD economies already characterised by high rates of waste mismanagement and leakage to the environment. As a consequence, regions such as Sub-Saharan Africa, the Middle East and North Africa, are projected to represent an increasing share of global mismanaged waste over time, as the relatively rapid growth of plastics use and waste in these areas would outpace projected improvements waste management systems.

It is well known that continued increases in plastic leakage would amplify adverse impacts on biodiversity and ecosystems as well as on local communities in these countries, for instance due to increased risks of floods or negative impacts on ocean-based economies. Plastics do not biodegrade in natural conditions, however they may fragment into microplastics that are difficult to recover once in the environment and that may increase exposure pathways and risks for wildlife and humans. The remainder of mismanaged waste is expected to end up in dumpsites or to be burned informally, also with adverse consequences for local communities and human health.

A scaling-up of infrastructural investments is required to eliminate plastic leakage globally, but in particular to enhance waste management in developing countries that currently rely heavily on informal waste management practices and where waste collection rates remain low. Investment needs for waste management systems in non-OECD countries would amount to more than USD 1 trillion over a 20-year period in the *Global Lifecycle High stringency* [*Global Ambition*] scenario.[2]

Given the crucial contribution of developing countries to ending plastic pollution, this requires adequate development financing, including potentially a re-orientation and scale-up of Official Development Assistance (ODA). ODA aimed at curbing plastic pollution has been on the rise in recent years, reflecting the growing public consensus around the severity of the problem and the need to act (Box 7.2). However, ODA alone remains largely insufficient when compared to the cumulative investment needs across world regions to tackle plastic pollution. New approaches to fill the financing gap and mobilise more resources include i) supporting initiatives to scale up total resources available to curb plastic pollution in developing countries, including from the private sector; ii) enhancing global targeting of existing resources and their alignment to country needs and priorities, iii) adopting international good practices and fostering innovation and iv) promoting mutual learning and developing guidance for more effective development co-operation (Agnelli and Tortora, 2022[5]).

It is essential to establish reliable and sustainable revenue streams to pay for the operation of these improved and expanded waste management systems. For instance, the establishment of EPR schemes in developed countries has proven to be effective to help cover the costs of separated waste collection, sorting and recycling. In the case of developing countries, the design and implementation of EPR schemes should effectively involve the informal sector, in particular waste pickers.

Box 7.2. Recent trends in financial flows to support better plastics management

Financial commitments aimed at curbing plastic pollution have been on the rise in recent years, reflecting the growing public consensus around the severity of the problem and the need to act. The analysis of official development assistance (ODA) flows reveals that a total of USD 1 460 million (USD 269 million for plastics specifically and USD 1 191 million for solid waste management more generally) was mobilised in 2022 to support plastic and solid waste management (Agnelli and Tortora, 2022[5]). Although ODA for plastic and solid waste management has seen continued increases in the last decade (Figure 7.5), this remains insufficient when compared to the cumulative investment needs across world regions to tackle plastic pollution. However, ODA can play an important role to leverage other sources of financing, including private finance, to support interventions along the value chain of plastics.

Figure 7.5. Official Development Assistance to curb plastic pollution is growing

Official Development Assistance (ODA) for solid waste management and ODA for management of plastics specifically, 2010-2022, USD million (2022 constant prices)

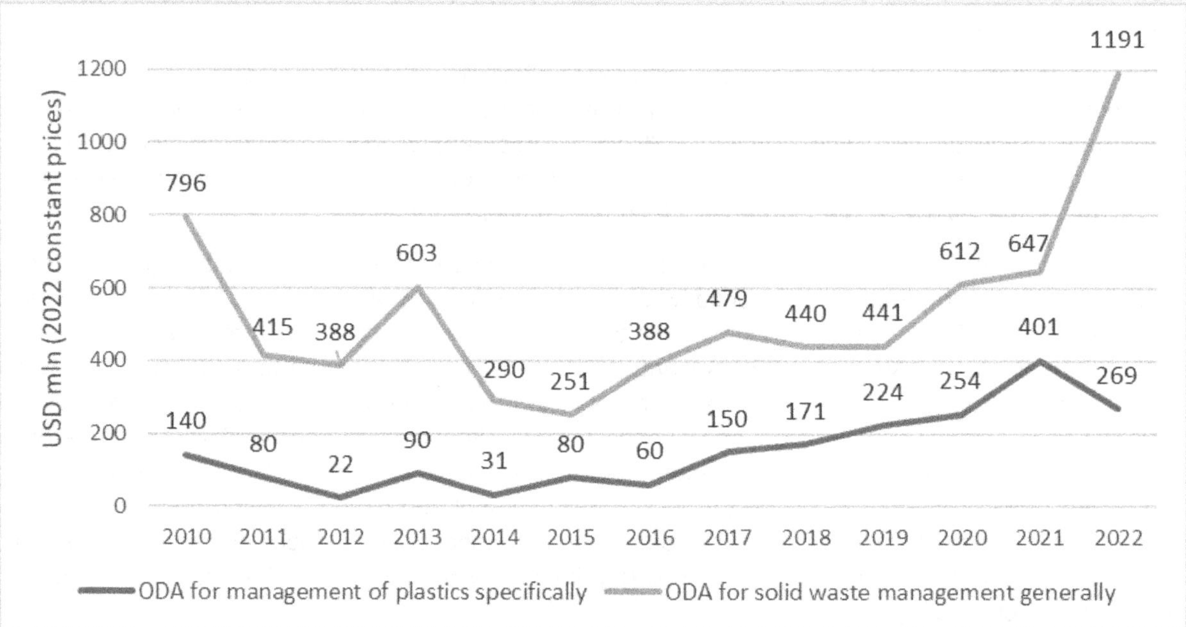

Source: (OECD, 2024[6]).

StatLink https://stat.link/ecpr9f

Flows of private finance to action to mitigate plastic pollution are also growing. Around USD 160 billion was invested into "plastics circularity solutions" globally between January 2018 and June 2023 (The Circulate Initiative, 2023[7]). However, the investment landscape is quite unevenly distributed, with nearly 90% of these financial flows having been directed to North America and Europe, presumably because policy environments are more stable and developed in terms of supporting circularity investments in these regions. Similarly, private finance is also unevenly distributed across different parts of the value chain, with down-stream recycling receiving most of the investments – around 85% (or USD 137 billion) – while upstream and midstream solutions, such as reuse models, receive much less.

Source: (Agnelli and Tortora, 2022[5]; The Circulate Initiative, 2023[7])

Beyond waste collection and management, directing investments towards the upstream and midstream stages of the plastics value chain is crucial to promote circular consumption patterns and alleviate burdens on waste management systems. Strategies may include supporting solutions to reduce avoidable and problematic plastics, to promote more reuse and repair, as well as to foster eco-design. Strong international co-operation will be essential for capacity building, technology transfer and governance strengthening, as well as to support the needed investments and innovation in developing countries, both via public (domestic and international) and private sources of financing.

7.5.2. Align financial flows with the objectives of the legally binding instrument on plastic pollution and explore options to utilise other sources of finance

Major redirections of plastics-related investments will be required around the world. Focusing on waste and recycling only, both OECD and non-OECD countries would need to invest more than USD 1 trillion over the 2020-2040 period to manage plastic waste volumes in the *Baseline* scenario, for a global total of USD 2.1 trillion. In the policy scenarios, these needs amplify as the sorting and recycling of waste is more expensive than e.g. using dumpsites, unless sufficient upstream and midstream action lowers total waste volumes enough to enable a reorientation of waste management activities rather than an expansion.

Beyond scaling up recycling and enabling the substitution of primary plastics with secondary plastics, redirections of investments will be required to support solutions further upstream, including to implement reuse systems for packaging and products. The alignment of financial flows from both public and private sources in line with the objectives and targets of the legally binding instrument under negotiation, will be critical to enabling a comprehensive transition across the plastics lifecycle.

7.6. Considerations for future research

A number of relevant economic aspects of plastic pollution could not be explicitly modelled in this analysis. Future research could complement the insights from the current report and investigate the following issues in more detail:

- A comparison of the costs and benefits of alternative policy options within policy pillars (e.g. regulation versus taxes to curb plastics demand) and in specific contexts. Governments may face political economy or other constraints regarding the use of specific instruments, or have preference for certain types of policy instruments. By investigating the economic consequences of different policy instruments that pursue the same targets (by pillar), further insights could be gained on the associated costs and benefits and potential trade-offs implied.
- An analysis of the sectoral consequences of the policies across scenarios, as well as of the drivers of changes in the economic structure of the economies in different regions. Certain sectors, such as motor vehicles and textiles, are more significantly affected by plastics policies than others. Given that the most affected sectors are implicated in global value chains and exposed to international competition to varying degrees, the domestic and international drivers of sectoral consequences can be further explored.
- An assessment of the costs and benefits of policies that target the leakage of microplastics. As discussed in Section 7.4, specific policy action is needed to tackle leakage of microplastics to the environment, and this in turn requires more research on the cost-effectiveness of different mitigation options.
- An assessment of the costs and benefits of policies that stimulate the use of plastics alternatives and substitutes. An important part of eliminating plastic pollution is to shift towards alternatives and substitutes. However, it is not always clear what the costs are, nor whether there are any trade-offs between environmental issues (and thus net environmental benefits) when replacing plastics with other materials.
- The integration of plastics policies into a wider framework of environmental policies to address the triple crisis of climate, pollution and biodiversity. The policy package in the *Global Lifecycle High stringency* [*Global Ambition*] scenario stabilises greenhouse gas (GHG) emissions at 2020 levels, but further reductions are foreseeable when integrating with climate mitigation policies. Similarly, integrating plastics policies with other environmental policies can lead to synergies and elucidate trade-offs where they exist.

- An assessment of the costs and benefits of removing plastics that have already leaked to the environment. It is generally assumed that remedial action is more expensive than avoiding plastic leakage, especially when plastics have entered rivers and oceans. But a full cost-benefit analysis of remedial action, including in different environmental media and employing different interventions (e.g. citizen clean-ups versus clean-up technologies), is lacking.
- An assessment of the social costs of plastic pollution and the distributional consequences of inaction for different household groups. Plastic pollution may affect disadvantaged households disproportionately, e.g. small-scale fisheries in small island developing states. Furthermore, the product cost increases associated with upstream policies may affect purchasing power of different household groups to differing degrees. Such effects may warrant flanking policies, which can only be effectively implemented when the consequences are quantified.
- The role of behavioural change in stimulating the elimination of plastic pollution. Households play a central role in reducing demand for plastics, both directly (e.g. packaging for online sales) and indirectly through plastics embedded in consumer products (e.g. synthetic fibres in clothing). Households can also play a role in improving recycling rates and incentivising industry to transition to a more circular use of plastics.
- A more differentiated analysis of the economic consequences of policies targeting specific polymers and applications in specific regions, including a focus on the most harmful plastics (i.e. those that are particularly likely to end up in the environment or contain chemicals of concern). The policy packages modelled in the current report are necessarily rather crude, allowing for a broad analysis. More in-depth analysis of particular plastics polymers and applications may shed light on opportunities for governments to avoid the most important sources of plastic pollution.
- An assessment of government support for primary plastics production and consumption, including fossil-fuel and other subsidies. The policies aimed at internalising the externalities of plastics production and consumption as investigated in this report can be undermined by implicit or explicit support to primary plastics production, in the same way that fossil fuel support undermines climate change mitigation objectives. An inventory of existing support provided to primary plastics, and further analysis of the consequences of reforming these, can contribute further to developing a cost-effective pathway to eliminate plastic pollution.

These issues for future research notwithstanding, the current report charts a clear path to the elimination of plastic pollution by 2040, achieving a near-total elimination of leakage of macroplastics to the environment and a stabilisation of GHG emissions at 2020 levels. An effective pathway combines globally co-ordinated policies to curb production and demand, promote design for circularity, enhance recycling and close leakage pathways. While these ambitions are formidable and the challenges to be overcome are significant, a balanced global approach that covers the entire lifecycle of plastics can deliver significant environmental benefits at lower economic costs compared to other, lower ambition scenarios presented in the report.

References

Agnelli, A. and P. Tortora (2022), "The role of development co-operation in tackling plastic pollution: Key trends, instruments, and opportunities to scale up action", *OECD Environment Working Papers*, No. 207, OECD Publishing, Paris, https://doi.org/10.1787/721355cb-en. [5]

Falk-Andersson, J. et al. (2023), "Cleaning Up without Messing Up: Maximizing the Benefits of Plastic Clean-Up Technologies through New Regulatory Approaches", *Environmental Science & Technology*, doi: 10.1021/acs.est.3c01885, pp. 13304-13312, https://doi.org/10.1021/acs.est.3c01885. [4]

Landrigan et al. (2023), "The Minderoo-Monaco Commission on Plastics and Human Health", *Ann.als of Global Health*, Vol. 89 (1)/23, https://doi.org/10.5334/aogh.4056. [2]

OECD (2024), *Sustainable Ocean for All Initiative: Data Platform on Development Finance for the Sustainable Ocean Economy*, https://oecd-main.shinyapps.io/ocean/ (accessed on 6 August 2024). [6]

OECD (2022), *Global Plastics Outlook: Policy Scenarios to 2060*, OECD Publishing, Paris, https://doi.org/10.1787/aa1edf33-en. [3]

Raubenheimer, K. and N. Urho (2024), *Global criteria to address problematic, unnecessary and avoidable plastic products*, https://doi.org/10.6027/temanord2024-508. [1]

The Circulate Initiative (2023), *Key findings from the global edition of the Plastics Circularity Investment Tracker*, https://www.thecirculateinitiative.org/_files/ugd/77554d_cf7f3eb1f4d1460baffbde23dc0f5db4.pdf?index=true. [7]

Notes

[1] Due to concerns with the feasibility and the environmental impacts of chemical recycling, the scenario analysis assumes that mechanical recycling technologies are the primary type of recycling technology adopted by countries.

[2] Importantly however, these investment needs currently only account for interventions downstream in the plastics lifecycle and notably do not include investments required to support the implementation of ambitious upstream and midstream policies such as reuse, eco-design and promoting material substitutes.

Annex A. Modelling framework

This Annex provides more details on the methodological framework employed to obtain the estimates and projections of plastics use, waste and environmental impacts presented in the report. These have been generated by building on the methodology employed in the OECD Global Plastics Outlook publications (2022[1]; 2022[2]).

The ENV-LINKAGES model

The OECD's in-house dynamic computable general equilibrium (CGE) model ENV-Linkages is used as the basis to project the economic activities that drive plastics use. ENV-Linkages is a multi-sectoral, multi-regional model that links economic activities to energy and environmental issues. A more comprehensive model description is given in Chateau, Dellink and Lanzi (2014[3]). The sectoral and regional aggregation of the model as used in the simulations are given in Table A A.1 and Table A A.2, respectively.

Table A A.1. Sectoral aggregation of ENV-Linkages

Agriculture, fisheries and forestry	Manufacturing
Paddy rice	Food products
Wheat and meslin	Textiles
Other grains	Wood products
Vegetables and fruits	Chemicals
Oil seeds	Basic pharmaceuticals
Sugar cane and sugar beet	Primary rubber and plastic products
Fibres plant	Secondary plastic products
Other crops	Pulp, paper and publishing products
Cattle and raw milk	Non-metallic minerals
Other animal products	Fabricated metal products
Fisheries	Electronics
Forestry	Electrical equipment
	Motor vehicles
Non-manufacturing Industries	Other transport equipment
Coal extraction	Other machinery and equipment
Crude oil extraction	Other manufacturing including recycling
Natural gas extraction	Iron and steel
Other mining	Non-ferrous metals
Petroleum and coal products	**Services**
Gas distribution	Land transport
Water collection and distribution	Air transport
Construction	Water transport
Electricity transmission and distribution	Insurance
Electricity generation (8 technologies)	Trade services
Electricity generation: Nuclear electricity; Hydro (and Geothermal); Solar; Wind; Coal-powered electricity; Gas-powered electricity; Oil-powered electricity; Other (combustible renewable, waste, etc.).	Other business services
	Real estate activities
	Accommodation and food service activities
	Public administration and defence
	Education
	Human health and social work

Table A A.2. Regional aggregation of ENV-Linkages

Macro regions	ENV-Linkages countries and regions	Most important comprising countries and territories
OECD	Canada	Canada
	USA	United States of America
	OECD Latin America (LAC)	Chile, Colombia, Costa Rica, Mexico
	OECD EU	Austria, Belgium, Czechia, Denmark, Estonia, Finland, France, Germany Greece, Hungary, Ireland, Italy, Latvia, Lithuania, Luxembourg, Netherlands, Poland, Portugal, Slovak Republic, Slovenia, Spain, Sweden
	Australia and New Zealand	Australia, New Zealand
	Japan and Korea	Japan, Korea
	Rest of OECD	Iceland, Israel, Norway, Switzerland, Türkiye, United Kingdom
Non-OECD	Rest of Latin America (LAC)	Non-OECD Latin American and Caribbean countries
	Non-OECD EU	Bulgaria, Croatia, Cyprus, Malta, Romania
	Eurasia	Non-OECD European and Caspian countries, including Russian Federation
	Middle East and North Africa (MENA)	Algeria, Bahrain, Egypt, Iraq, Islamic Republic of Iran, Kuwait, Lebanon, Libya, Morocco, Oman, Qatar, Saudi Arabia, Tunisia, United Arab Emirates, Syrian Arab Republic, Western Sahara, Yemen
	Sub-Saharan Africa	Sub-Saharan Africa
	China	People's Republic of China, Hong Kong (China)
	India	India
	Rest of Asia-Pacific	Other non-OECD Asian and Pacific countries

Production in ENV Linkages is assumed to operate under cost minimisation with perfect markets and constant returns-to-scale technology. The production technology is specified as nested Constant Elasticity of Substitution (CES) production functions in a branching hierarchy. This structure is replicated for each output, while the parameterisation of the CES functions may differ across sectors. The model adopts a putty/semi-putty technology specification, where substitution possibilities among factors are assumed to be higher with new vintage capital than with old vintage capital. In the short run this ensures inertia in the economic system, with limited possibilities to substitute away from more expensive inputs, but in the longer run this implies a relatively smooth adjustment of quantities to price changes. Capital accumulation is modelled as in the traditional Solow/Swan neo classical growth model, where economic growth is assumed to stem from the combination of labour, capital accumulation and technological progress.

Household consumption demand is the result of static maximisation behaviour which is formally implemented as an "Extended Linear Expenditure System". A representative consumer in each region – who takes prices as given – optimally allocates disposal income among the full set of consumption commodities and savings. Saving is considered as a standard good in the utility function and does not rely on forward looking behaviour by the consumer. The government in each region collects various kinds of taxes in order to finance government expenditures. Assuming fixed public savings (or deficits), the government budget is balanced through the adjustment of the income tax on consumer income. In each period, investment net-of-economic depreciation is equal to the sum of government savings, consumer savings and net capital flows from abroad.

International trade is based on a set of regional bilateral flows. The model adopts the Armington specification, assuming that domestic and imported products are not perfectly substitutable. Moreover, total imports are also imperfectly substitutable between regions of origin. Allocation of trade between partners then responds to relative prices at the equilibrium.

Market goods equilibria imply that, on the one side, the total production of any goods or services is equal to the demand addressed to domestic producers plus exports; and, on the other side, the total demand is allocated between the demands (both final and intermediary) by domestic producers and the import demand.

ENV Linkages is fully homogeneous in prices and only relative prices matter. All prices are expressed relative to the numéraire of the price system that is arbitrarily chosen as the index of OECD manufacturing exports prices. Each region runs a current account balance, which is fixed in terms of the numéraire.

As ENV-Linkages is recursive-dynamic and does not incorporate forward-looking behaviour, price-induced changes in innovation patterns are not represented in the model. The model does, however, entail technological progress through an annual adjustment of the various productivity parameters, including e.g. autonomous energy efficiency and labour productivity improvements. Furthermore, as production with new capital has a relatively large degree of flexibility in choice of inputs, existing technologies can diffuse to other firms. Thus, within the CGE framework, firms choose the least-cost combination of inputs, given the existing state of technology. The capital vintage structure also ensures that such flexibilities are larger in the long run than in the short run.

Estimates and projections for plastics use, plastic waste and end-of-life fates

The ENV-Linkages model has been extended to include plastics production and use, for both primary and secondary (recycled) plastics. The plastics production and use data is presented in million metric tonnes (Mt) and plastics use is split by region, polymer and application. Figure A A.1 presents estimates for plastics use by polymer and application in 2020. Waste estimates and end-of-life fates are derived based on average lifespans by application and country-specific end-of-life shares. Further information on the data sources used to derive the estimates for plastic flows, from production to disposal and mismanagement, is presented in (OECD, 2022[1]).

Figure A A.1. Plastics polymers and applications in the modelling framework

Polymer use shares by application, global, 2020

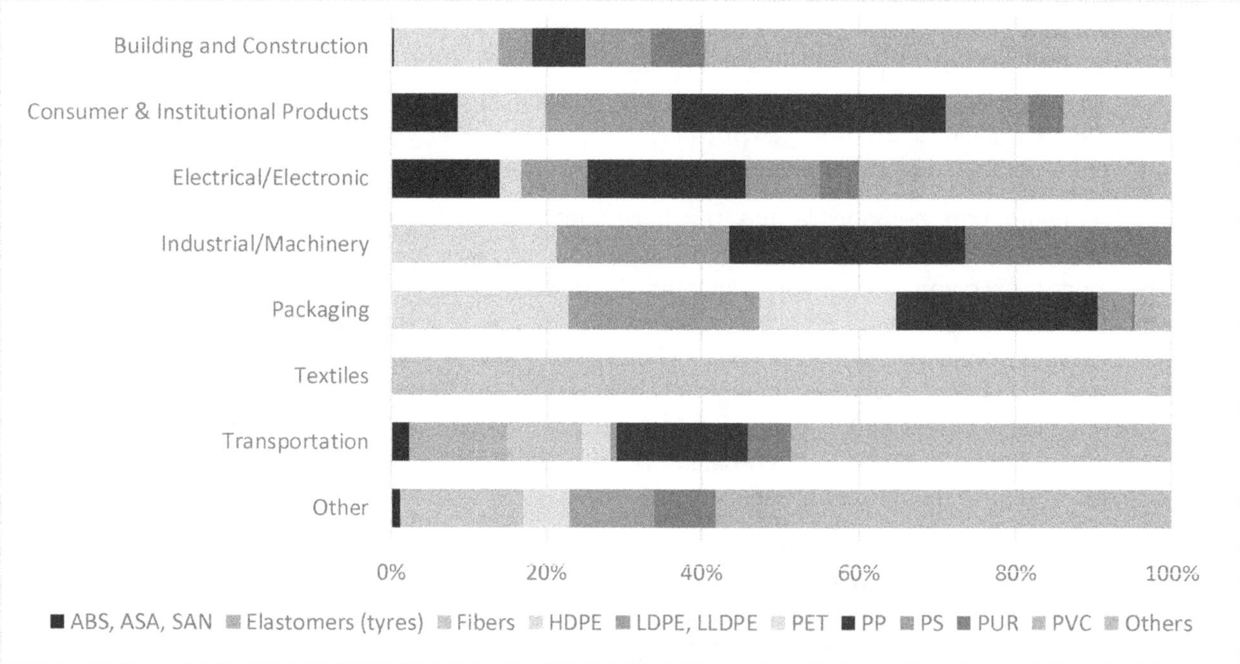

Source: OECD ENV-Linkages model. Estimates and projections for plastic leakage to the aquatic environment.

The projections on the leakage of waste plastics to aquatic environments are made by L. Lebreton (2024[4]), employing a methodology that estimates the amount of plastic waste entering aquatic environments (by region). As explained in more detail in (OECD, 2022[2]), the methodology employs results from a previous study by Borrelle et al. (2020[5]) which estimated leakage of mismanaged plastic waste into rivers, lakes, and the ocean at a global scale. The model computes the probability of releases of plastics (from mismanaged plastic waste produced in a certain region or country) to reach an aquatic environment (rivers, lakes, and oceans).

The model also assesses the mobility of plastics in aquatic environments as well as degradation. The whole-ocean plastic mass budget model presented in (Lebreton and Andrady, 2019[6]) is expanded to a simplified representation of the global aquatic environment. The model differentiates between annual inputs in freshwater and the ocean, allowing floating plastic waste to circulate from one compartment to the other over time. The model also differentiates inputs by polymer types using the OECD ENV-Linkages model estimates and waste projections presented in this report. The likely fate of emitted plastics is determined depending on their density. Additionally, the degradation rates vary across polymers based on laboratory results (Gerritse et al., 2020[7]). The general model framework is presented in Figure A A.2. The methodology is explained in more detail in (OECD, 2022[2]).

Figure A A.2. Mass balance budget model for plastic in global aquatic environments

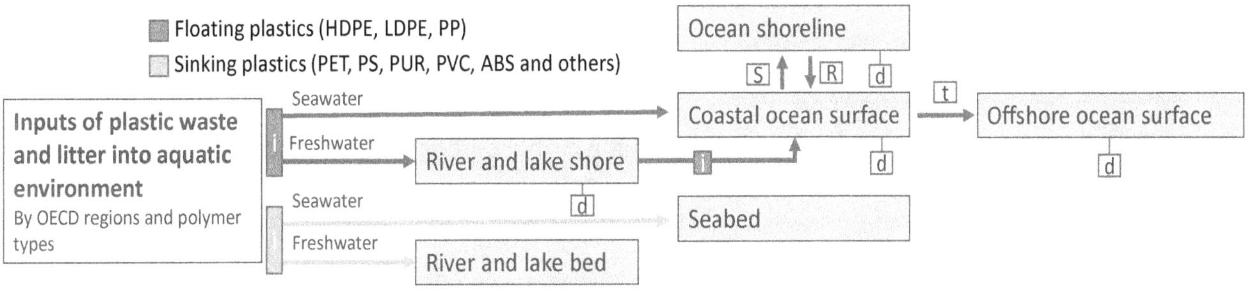

Note: Mass inputs by modelled region, characterised by polymer types, are accumulated from 1951 to 2060 into the plastic fate model. Plastics with a density higher than water sink and accumulate in riverbed, lakebed and seabed. Floating plastics (density lower than water) are transported between different aquatic compartments and are allowed to degrade into microplastics over time from contact with sunlight. The region-specific parameter 'i' is the ratio between plastics remaining in freshwater and the plastics entering the marine environment. The parameters 's' and 'r' represent the fraction of stranding and release from the global shoreline. The parameter 't' is the fraction of floating plastic circulating from the coastal to the offshore ocean. Finally, 'd' is the mass fraction degrading into microplastics annually and varies with polymer types.
Source: (OECD, 2022[2]).

Estimates and projections for plastics-related greenhouse gas emissions

The methodology and parameters employed to generate projections on the contribution of the lifecycle of plastics to GHG emissions, on a global level, are detailed in (OECD, 2022[2]). Plastics-related GHG emissions are calibrated based on emission factors for the year 2015 provided by Zheng and Suh (2019[8]), and calibrated over time as described in (OECD, 2022[2]). Only GHG emissions from production and conversion, recycling, landfilling and incineration are quantified. GHG emissions from other stages of the lifecycle of plastics, such as those generated from the open pit burning of plastic waste or from plastics in the environment, are not estimated due to a lack of underlying data.

References

Borrelle, S. et al. (2020), "Predicted growth in plastic waste exceeds efforts to mitigate plastic pollution", *Science*, Vol. 369/6510, pp. 1515-1518, https://doi.org/10.1126/science.aba3656. [5]

Château, J., R. Dellink and E. Lanzi (2014), "An Overview of the OECD ENV-Linkages Model: Version 3", *OECD Environment Working Papers*, No. 65, OECD Publishing, Paris, https://doi.org/10.1787/5jz2qck2b2vd-en. [3]

Gerritse, J. et al. (2020), "Fragmentation of plastic objects in a laboratory seawater microcosm", *Scientific Reports*, Vol. 10/1, p. 10945, https://doi.org/10.1038/s41598-020-67927-1. [7]

Lebreton, L. (2024), *Quantitative analysis of aquatic leakage for multiple scenarios based on ENV-Linkages*, unpublished. [4]

Lebreton, L. and A. Andrady (2019), "Future scenarios of global plastic waste generation and disposal", *Palgrave Communications*, Vol. 5/1, p. 6, https://doi.org/10.1057/s41599-018-0212-7. [6]

OECD (2022), *Global Plastics Outlook: Economic Drivers, Environmental Impacts and Policy Options*, OECD Publishing, Paris, https://doi.org/10.1787/de747aef-en. [1]

OECD (2022), *Global Plastics Outlook: Policy Scenarios to 2060*, OECD Publishing, Paris, https://doi.org/10.1787/aa1edf33-en. [2]

Zheng, J. and S. Suh (2019), "Strategies to reduce the global carbon footprint of plastics", *Nature Climate Change*, Vol. 9/5, pp. 374-378, https://doi.org/10.1038/s41558-019-0459-z. [8]

Annex B. Details on the policy scenarios

This Annex presents the details on the methodology employed to develop the policy scenario analysis focused on reducing plastic leakage to the environment by 2040. The report quantifies the environmental benefits and macroeconomic consequences of alternative policy scenarios, highlighting the impacts on GDP, as well as the financing needs across regions. The analysis takes a global approach but differentiates across 15 global regions, considering the characteristics of their economies and waste management systems.

Policy pillars

All scenarios are developed starting from a set of ten policy instruments, categorised in the following four policy pillars:

1. **Curb production and demand**: curb production and demand, by taking measures to avoid the production and use of unnecessary and problematic plastics, promote longer product lifespans, reuse products and shift demand to services. Controlling the production of virgin plastics, e.g. of specific polymers, could also be an effective strategy for reducing environmental impacts associated with the upstream segments of the plastics lifecycle, as well as curbing plastics use and slowing the flow of plastics through the economy.
2. **Design for circularity**: make production process for plastics more circular, for instance by avoiding the use of problematic materials and hazardous chemicals, facilitating reuse practices, or introducing product standards to improve repairability and substitution away from plastics (where environmentally beneficial).
3. **Enhance recycling**: close material loops by improving the separate collection, sorting and recycling of plastic waste.
4. **Close leakage pathways**: decrease losses of plastics into the environment, including via effective waste collection and disposal, as well as improved municipal litter collection and street sweeping.

Scenario descriptions

In the report, five core scenarios are modelled, in addition to a *Baseline* scenario.

Partial ambition scenarios

- The ***Global Downstream High stringency*** policy scenario reflects a possible outcome of treaty negotiations focused on targets and approaches for waste management (i.e. pillar 3 on enhancing recycling, and pillar 4 on closing leakage pathways). This includes stringent policies to improve waste collection, sorting, recycling as well as litter collection and municipal litter clean-up. Policy action to curb production and demand and to design for circularity is limited to current policies (i.e. no additional action is taken on pillars 1 and 2).

- The ***Advanced economies Lifecycle High stringency*** policy scenario models a situation where, in the absence of common, global targets, only select countries enhance policy stringency along the lifecycle of plastics. More specifically, a group of advanced economies (approximated as OECD and European Union countries) implement policies with a high level of policy stringency across all four policy pillars, while other countries do not go beyond the improvements already expected in the *Baseline* scenario.
- The ***Global Lifecycle Low stringency*** policy scenario reflects a possible outcome of the treaty negotiations with broad lifecycle coverage but low policy stringency. This scenario models additional, but more incremental policy action in all countries across all four pillars, but with limited policy stringency.

High ambition scenarios

- The ***Global Lifecycle Mixed stringency*** policy scenario combines the three individual scenarios outlined above. It reflects a treaty outcome characterised by moderate alignment across countries on the lifecycle scope of policies. Countries in this scenario agree to pursue all three aspects of the partial ambition scenarios above, but do not move beyond these. Advanced economies implement policies with high stringency throughout the plastics lifecycle (aligned with *Advanced economies Lifecycle High stringency*), while other countries implement high stringency for pillars 3 and 4 (aligned with *Global Downstream High stringency*) and limited stringency for pillars 1 and 2 (aligned with *Global Lifecycle Low stringency*).
- The ***Global Lifecycle High stringency*** [*Global Ambition*] policy scenario models a comprehensive and co-ordinated approach that entails a global ramp up of policy action across the lifecycle of plastics, aligned with the shared objective of ending plastic pollution by 2040. In the model, this is reflected as the (narrower) target to mitigate plastic waste mismanagement and end macroplastic leakage by 2040.[1] Compared to the *Global Lifecycle Mixed stringency* scenario, more stringent upstream and midstream policies would be implemented in non-OECD, non-EU countries, thus aligning their degree of policy ambition for all four policy pillars with the ambitions of the Advanced economies.

Specification of the policy instruments for the partial ambition scenarios

Pillar	Policy instrument	***Global Downstream High stringency***	***Advanced economies Lifecycle High stringency***	***Global Lifecycle Low stringency***
Curb production and demand	Packaging plastics tax	None	*OECD, EU*: USD 1 000/tonne by 2030, doubling by 2040. *Rest of the world*: none.	*EU*: USD 1 000/tonne by 2030, constant thereafter. *Rest of OECD*: USD 1 000/tonne by 2040. *Non-OECD*: USD 1 000/tonne by 2060.
	Non-packaging plastics tax	None	*OECD, EU*: USD 750/tonne by 2030, doubling by 2040. *Rest of the world*: none.	*OECD*: USD 750/tonne by 2040. *Non-OECD*: USD 750/tonne by 2060.
Design for circularity	Eco-design for durability & repair	None	*OECD, EU*: 15% lifespan increase by 2040; 10-20% decrease in demand for durables by 2030, constant thereafter; increase in demand for repair services such that *ex ante* total expenditures are unchanged. *Rest of the world*: 15% lifespan increase by 2040.	*Global*: 10% lifespan increase by 2040, 5-10% decrease in demand for durables by 2040, increase in demand for repair services such that *ex ante* total expenditures are unchanged.
	Ban selected single-use plastics	None	*OECD, EU*: phase-out of PP plastics for selected consumer products by 2030. *Rest of the world*: none.	None
	Substitute away from plastics	None	*OECD, EU*: reduction of plastics use in production by 17% by 2030 with compensating increase in use of other inputs, constant thereafter. *Rest of the world*: none.	Global: reduction of plastics use in production by 8.5% by 2030 with compensating increase in use of other inputs, constant thereafter.
Enhance recycling	Recycled content target	*Global*: 30% recycled content target by 2040.	*OECD, EU*: 30% recycled content target by 2040. *Rest of the world*: none.	*OECD*: 40% recycled content target. *Non-OECD*: 20% recycled content target.
	EPR for packaging, electronics, automotive and wearable apparel	None	*OECD, EU*: tax on plastics inputs USD 300/tonne by 2030, constant thereafter; 30% points increase in recycling by 2040; subsidy on waste sector such that the instrument is budget neutral. *Rest of the world*: none.	*OECD + EU*: 30% points increase in recycling, tax on plastics inputs – USD 300/tonne by 2030, constant thereafter, subsidy on waste sector such that the instrument is budget neutral. *Rest of non-OECD*; none.
	Enhance recycling through waste management	*EU, Japan & Korea*: 60% recycling rate target by 2030, 80% by 2060. *Rest of OECD, China*: 60% recycling rate target by 2040. *Rest of non-OECD*: 45% recycling rate target. by 2040.	*EU, Japan & Korea*: 60% recycling rate target by 2030, 80% by 2060. *Rest of OECD*: 60% recycling rate target by 2040. *Rest of non-OECD*: none.	*EU, Japan & Korea*: 60% recycling rate target by 2030, 70% by 2060. *Rest of OECD, China*: 60% recycling rate target by 2060. *Rest of non-OECD*: 40% recycling rate target by 2060.

Pillar	Policy instrument	***Global Downstream High stringency***	***Advanced economies Lifecycle High stringency***	***Global Lifecycle Low stringency***
Close leakage pathways	Improved plastic waste collection	*Global*: rate of reduction of mismanaged waste shares by 2040 aligned with *Global Lifecycle High stringency* scenario.	*OECD, EU*: full reduction of mismanaged waste shares. *Rest of non-OECD*: none.	*OECD*: full reduction of mismanaged waste shares. *Non-OECD*: halving of mismanaged waste shares.
	Improved litter collection	*High income countries:* collection rates increase 5%-points by 2040. *Middle income countries*: income-scaled increase (proportional between high income and low income rates). *Low income countries*: collection rates increase 10%-points by 2040.	*High income OECD, EU countries:* collection rates increase 5%-points by 2040. *Middle income OECD, EU countries*: income-scaled increase (proportional between high income and low income rates). *Rest of non-OECD*: none.	*High income countries:* collection rates increase 5%-points. *Middle income countries:* income-scaled increase (proportional between high income and low income rates). *Low income countries*: none.

Note: The stringency of instruments that are specified with a target date are linearly interpolated between 2023 and the target date.

Specification of the policy instruments for the high ambition scenarios

Pillar	Policy instrument	***Global Lifecycle Mixed stringency***	***Global Lifecycle High stringency*** [*Global Ambition*]
Curb production and demand	Packaging plastics tax	*OECD, EU*: USD 1 000/tonne by 2030, doubling by 2040. *Rest of the world*: USD 1 000/tonne by 2060.	*Global*: USD 1 000/tonne by 2030, doubling by 2040.
	Non-packaging plastics tax	*OECD, EU*: USD 750/tonne by 2030, doubling by 2040. *Rest of the world*: USD 750/tonne by 2060.	*Global*: USD 750/tonne by 2030, doubling by 2040.
Design for circularity	Eco-design for durability & repair	*Global*: 15% lifespan increase by 2030, constant thereafter; *OECD, EU*: 10-20% decrease in demand for durables by 2030, constant thereafter; increase in demand for repair services such that *ex ante* total expenditures are unchanged. *Rest of the world*: 5-10% decrease in demand for durables by 2040, increase in demand for repair services such that *ex ante* total expenditures are unchanged.	*Global*: 15% lifespan increase by 2030, constant thereafter; 10-20% decrease in demand for durables by 2030, constant thereafter; increase in demand for repair services such that *ex ante* total expenditures are unchanged.
	Ban selected single-use plastics	*OECD, EU*: phase-out of PP for selected consumer products by 2030. *Rest of the world*: None.	*Global*: phase-out of PP for selected consumer products by 2030.
	Substitute away from plastics	*OECD, EU*: reduction of plastics use in production by 17% by 2030 with compensating increase in use of other inputs, constant thereafter. *Rest of the world*: reduction of plastics use in production by 8.5% by 2030 with compensating increase in use of other inputs.	*Global*: reduction of plastics use in production by 17% by 2030 with compensating increase in use of other inputs, constant thereafter.

Pillar	Policy instrument	***Global Lifecycle Mixed stringency***	***Global Lifecycle High stringency*** [*Global Ambition*]
Enhance recycling	Recycled content target	*Global*: 30% recycled content target by 2040.	*Global*: 30% recycled content target by 2040.
	EPR for packaging, electronics, automotive and wearable apparel	*OECD, EU*: tax on plastics inputs USD 300/tonne by 2030, constant thereafter; 30% points increase in recycling by 2040; subsidy on waste sector such that the instrument is budget neutral. *Rest of the world*: none.	*Global*: tax on plastics inputs USD 300/tonne by 2030, constant thereafter; 30% points increase in recycling by 2040; subsidy on waste sector such that the instrument is budget neutral.
	Enhance recycling through waste management	*EU, Japan & Korea*: 60% recycling rate target by 2030, 80% by 2060. *Rest of OECD, China*: 60% recycling rate target by 2040. *Rest of non-OECD*: 45% recycling rate target.	*EU, Japan & Korea*: 60% recycling rate target by 2030, 80% by 2060. *Rest of OECD, China*: 60% recycling rate target by 2040. *Rest of non-OECD*: 45% recycling rate target. by 2040.
Close leakage pathways	Improved plastic waste collection	*Global*: rate of reduction of mismanaged waste shares by 2040 aligned with *Global Lifecycle High stringency* scenario	Global: full reduction of mismanaged waste shares by 2040
	Improved litter collection	*High income countries:* collection rates increase 5%-points by 2040. *Middle income countries*: income-scaled increase (proportional between high income and low income rates). *Low income countries*: collection rates increase 10%-points by 2040.	*High income countries:* collection rates increase 5%-points by 2040. *Middle income countries*: income-scaled increase (proportional between high income and low income rates). *Low income countries*: collection rates increase 10%-points by 2040.

Note: The stringency of instruments that are specified with a target date are linearly interpolated between 2023 and the target date

Note

[1] A variant of the *Global Lifecycle High stringency* [*Global Ambition*] scenario is the *Global Lifecycle Delayed stringency* scenario. The latter models the implementation of the policy package of the *Global Lifecycle High stringency* scenario over an extended timeframe, towards a 2060 target for the elimination of leakage.

www.ingramcontent.com/pod-product-compliance
Lightning Source LLC
Chambersburg PA
CBHW061221240926
51846CB00006B/1300